BOOKS BY MALCOLM FORBES

What Happened to Their Kids?
More Than I Dreamed
They Went That-a-way . . .
The Further Sayings of Chairman Malcolm
Around the World on Hot Air and Two Wheels
The Sayings of Chairman Malcolm
Fact and Comment
*The Forbes Scrapbook of Thoughts
on the Business of Life*

MALCOLM FORBES

with JEFF BLOCH

WHAT HAPPENED TO THEIR KIDS?

Children of the Rich and Famous

SIMON AND SCHUSTER

NEW YORK · LONDON · TORONTO
SYDNEY · TOKYO · SINGAPORE

SIMON AND SCHUSTER
Simon & Schuster Building
Rockefeller Center
1230 Avenue of the Americas
New York, New York 10020

Copyright © 1990 by Malcolm Forbes
All rights reserved
including the right of reproduction
in whole or in part in any form.
SIMON AND SCHUSTER and colophon are
registered trademarks of Simon & Schuster Inc.
Designed by Edith Fowler
Manufactured in the United States of America

10 9 8 7 6 5 4 3 2 1

Library of Congress Cataloging in Publication Data
Forbes, Malcolm S.
    What happened to their kids? : children of the
rich and famous
    Malcolm Forbes with Jeff Bloch.
        p. cm.
    1. Celebrities—Biography. 2. Children—
Biography. 3. Children of the rich—Biography.
I. Bloch, Jeff. II. Title.
CT105.F64 1990
920.02—dc20   89-26166
                                        CIP
ISBN 0-671-66415-8

CONTENTS

INTRODUCTION

A PRIME MOTIVATOR driving Successful Ones is to do better by, for, with their children than perhaps these achievers' parents might have been able to do for them.

Do they succeed in this most difficult of all life's goals?

Sadly, the answer too often is no.

Many rich and famous can't cope with their own lives, never mind their children's. Though widely envied, their success has sometimes been their own undoing. Celebrity proves too tough for them to handle.

This is a book about some kids who were able to overcome the illusionary advantages of a parent's fame, pelf, power. They've been able to live relatively "normal" lives.

But it's also a book about many offspring who couldn't quite make it.

And it's about others who were done in by it.

Here on these pages are 123 answers to the question "What Happened to Their Kids?"

Malcolm Forbes

A

CHILDREN of JOHN QUINCY ADAMS

WHAT THE KENNEDYS and the Rockefellers are to twentieth-century America, the Adams family was to the nation in its first hundred years. It produced, in Founding Father John Adams and his son John Quincy Adams, two U.S. presidents and created a daunting family dynasty. And John Quincy Adams was adamant that his three sons not forget it. "My sons have not only their own honor but that of two preceding generations to sustain," he said.

The bulk of that burden fell on John Quincy's oldest son, hopefully named George Washington Adams, who was born in 1801 in Berlin while his father was U.S. minister there. George obliged his father by graduating in 1823 from Harvard—where he had edged out Ralph Waldo Emerson for the prestigious Boylston Prize for declamation—and then studying law with Daniel Webster. He was elected to the Massachusetts legislature at the age of twenty-five. "George is a treasure of diamonds," John Adams wrote of his favorite grandson. "He has a genius equal to anything; but like all other genius requires the most delicate management to keep it from running into eccentricities."

In fact, George was more interested in music and poetry than in the law. An extremely sensitive youth, he once became so depressed reading Dante that he had to step outside for air. His father's insistence that he study law and prepare to enter politics only heightened his nervous condition. So affected by his father was George that he suddenly ended a promising relationship with a girl during his freshman year at Harvard after he dreamed he kissed her, only to see John Quincy appear and scold, "Remember, George, who you are and what you are doing."

George was just beginning his law career in Boston when his father was elected to the White House in 1824. The elder Adams tried to help his son get started by assigning him all of his personal business matters in Boston, but George simply didn't have the discipline for it. He slept late, took naps, and worked on his poetry while his father's accounts fell into disarray.

President Adams ended up paying his son's debts, insisting he shape up. As he did with all his sons, he wrote detailed weekly letters to George prescribing for him a daily schedule of his work and leisure time; the president instructed his son to read regularly, keep a diary, and chew tobacco to "tone the stomach." All of this served only to make George more aware of his shortcomings. After his mother visited him in 1827 she complained that George was "constantly acting like one divested of understanding." But George was apparently too afraid to behave like that in front of his father. When the president visited a few months later, he found a "dutiful and affectionate" son who "wants nothing but a firm purpose to be all that I could wish." He wrote to George urging him to "perseverance in the cause of virtue" and reminding him "of the blood from which you came."

After Adams lost his reelection campaign in 1828, he summoned George to Washington to help the family move back to Massachusetts. George, who had a drinking problem by then, had dropped out of the legislature and was horrified at having to face his father. He began acting paranoid and seemed to think someone was hiding in his Boston rooms.

Nevertheless, he set out for Washington, going first to Providence, where, on April 29, 1829, he boarded a steamboat bound for New York. That evening he complained of a severe headache and said he thought the boat's engines were repeatedly droning, "Let it be, let it be." He got up in the night with a candle and roamed the vessel, gazing at the sleeping passengers. As the boat steamed through Long Island Sound, George asked to be put ashore because he thought the other passengers were laughing at him. Some minutes later, his hat was found on the upper deck near the stern; his coat was nearby. It was not until June that his body washed ashore, at City Island. It never was determined whether the president's twenty-seven-year-old son committed suicide or was merely so disoriented that he fell overboard.

Adams was distraught over his son's death and over his wife's accusation that his political career had caused it. But he had two other sons who showed promise. John Adams II, born in 1803, survived his father's demands only somewhat better. Although he ranked only forty-fifth out of his class of eighty-five students at Harvard, and the president wouldn't let him come home for Christmas one year as a result, John graduated, went on to study law and became his father's private secretary in the White House. After Adams left Washington, John II stayed behind to run a failing mill on Rock Creek that the president had acquired. The mill continued to do badly, and John, overwhelmed by his duties, began drinking heavily. His health failed and he died in 1834 at the age of thirty-one.

Finally the mantle passed to Adams's youngest son, Charles Francis. Born in 1807 and raised in the Russian court at St. Petersburg, where his father was then the American minister, Charles also went to Harvard, and he was admitted to the bar when he was twenty-two. Of the three, he was the most like his father. After John II died, Charles stated, "I cannot regret the loss of either of my brothers as a calamity either to their families or to themselves."

Charles Francis went a long way toward extending the Adams political dynasty to a third generation. He was elected to Congress in 1858 from the same district his father had represented for seventeen years after leaving the White House. Later, Charles became minister to the Court of St. James's under President Lincoln and was instrumental in preventing England from officially siding with the Confederacy. But when his name was submitted as a candidate at the 1872 Republican presidential convention, Charles lost. The Adams dynasty has never recovered.

SON of AGRIPPINA

EVERYBODY KNOWS what became of Nero: he fiddled while Rome burned. But how his mother helped him get there—and how he repaid her—is an even better story.

Nero's mother was Agrippina the Younger, great-granddaughter of Caesar Augustus and sister of Caligula. Taking after that murderous brother, Agrippina was ruthless in her pursuit of the emperor's throne. It is said that Agrippina once consulted an astrologer about Nero's future and was told that Nero would become emperor and kill his mother. "Let him kill as long as he rules," Agrippina is said to have replied. Twice Agrippina was married and was widowed well; she gained a son, Nero, by her first husband and a fortune by the second, whom some say she poisoned. But Caligula banished Agrippina, and Nero grew up poor outside of Rome until his mother was allowed to return to the city and to her privileges under the next emperor, Claudius, who was also Agrippina's uncle. Claudius was crippled and unattractive and he stuttered. But he was emperor, and in A.D. 49 Agrippina married him. She was thirty-two, he was fifty-seven.

She persuaded Claudius to adopt Nero as his son, putting her boy in line for the throne behind Claudius's own son. Agrippina also had sixteen-year-old Nero marry Claudius's thirteen-year-old daughter, Octavia. At the same time Agrippina increased her power outside her family. To a large extent she ruled Rome from behind the throne, though eventually she came to sit next to her husband on the dais. She ordered hundreds of wealthy citizens executed so she could confiscate their estates and replenish the emperor's coffers. When Claudius finally caught on that his wife had usurped his power, Agrippina fed him poisonous mushrooms and he died suddenly in A.D. 54.

Claudius's death was not announced until Agrippina made sure her seventeen-year-old son had seized the throne. But his control was nominal, as it was his mother who still made decisions. The password she gave the guards was "Optima Mater"—Best of Mothers. She hid behind curtains to listen while her son met with foreign diplomats. And she had coins engraved with both their images. Nero, meanwhile, was enjoying the privileges of his position. He slept with many men and women, threw lavish banquets, and prowled Rome at night harassing women, abusing boys, and occasionally killing passersby.

Eventually Nero began to take more responsibility for his empire and his mother retired to her villa. But she returned in A.D. 59, when her son announced he wanted to divorce his wife. Agrippina refused to allow it, and some say she even offered herself to relieve her son's boredom with Octavia. Agrippina, deciding her son was ungrateful, threatened to help raise Claudius's son to power. Nero responded by killing his stepbrother.

Prodded by his mistress, who teased Nero that he couldn't stand up to his meddlesome mother, Nero decided also to murder Agrippina. The twenty-two-year-old emperor arranged to send her into the Bay of Naples aboard a ship that was designed to fall apart at sea. The boat did indeed collapse, but Agrippina managed to swim safely to shore. Nero then sent his men to kill Agrippina at her villa. When they arrived, the forty-three-year-old woman bared herself and said, "Plunge your sword into my womb." They did, and later when Nero saw her bloodied body he said, "I did not know I had so beautiful a mother."

Nero finally divorced his wife in A.D. 62 and married his mistress. But she died after Rome burned in 64, and Nero took as his third wife a boy whom he had had castrated. Four years later Nero was overthrown and committed suicide, leaving no children. Said the ancient historian Suetonius, "The world would have been a happier place had Nero's father not married that sort of wife." It is unclear whether the insult was meant for Agrippina or her thankless son.

SON of POPE ALEXANDER VI

IN ITALY OF the fifteenth century, dubbed the "Golden Age of Bastards," Pope Alexander VI had fathered at least six and possibly eight children by four different women before he took over the Vatican. It didn't hurt his career at all. On the contrary, "other popes, to conceal their infamy were wont to term their offspring nephews, but Alexander took delight in letting all the world know that they were his children," said one writer at the time.

Alexander—born Rodrigo Borjas in Spain and changed to Borgia when he began working in the church in Italy—most of all was proud of the second son of his third mistress. Cesare—tall, handsome, blond—was just eighteen when Alexander named him to the powerful position of cardinal. Cesare wasn't religious in the least, but he had "an air of one who felt that he inherited the world," said one historian, and he proved admirably capable of carrying out what his father needed done.

Together, the pope and his son set out to rebuild the church, which was weak and disorganized when Alexander inherited it in 1492. Whether they succeeded or not depends on what history book you read. On the one hand, the Borgias—for a time—restored order in Rome, balanced the budget, reasserted the church's power over many of the papal city-states, and repelled invasions by stronger European powers. On the other hand, according to one contemporary, "Cesare murdered his brother, slept with his sister, spent the treasure of the church, and was the terror of his father."

Cesare clearly was his father's son. Alexander made it a practice to appropriate the estates of dead church officials to aid the Vatican treasury, and many suspected he poisoned some who didn't die soon enough. When Cesare marched against the disloyal papal states—aided by Leonardo da Vinci as his chief engineer and brandishing a sword inscribed, "Either Caesar or nobody"—he reputedly slew the firstborn sons of the leading families to prevent future uprisings.

On one occasion, Cesare was said to have had several prisoners released into a courtyard, where he proceeded to take target practice on them with his bow and arrows. Cesare also had his sister's husband killed after he had attempted to kill Cesare (though in fact, the brother-in-law had only acted on the mistaken assumption that Cesare had tried to kill him earlier). Most famous of all is the rumor of a dinner party in the pope's private apartment in 1501 at which Alexander and Cesare and his beautiful sister, Lucrezia, were said to have scattered chestnuts over the floor while fifty nude prostitutes crawled around to retrieve them. The pope later awarded prizes to his guests who had sex with the most courtesans.

For all the sordid tales, Alexander, largely through his son, had by 1503 consolidated his power to the point that Cesare was preparing to take on the great powers of France and Spain. Then on August 12, both men fell violently ill after a big celebration. The half-hopeful rumor was that they had meant to poison another cardinal but drank the fatal wine themselves by mistake. Alexander died six days later, officially of malaria. Cesare, who had seemed poised to inherit the church from his father, remained deliriously ill and bedridden for another week. He did, however, summon enough strength to order his soldiers to plunder his father's treasury before the pope's death was announced.

During Cesare's illness, Pope Julius II took over. Cesare had thrived on his father's power, but stripped of that alliance, he was hopelessly vulnerable. Cesare had told his friend Machiavelli that he had planned for every possible power struggle upon his father's death—except the possibility that he, too, would be ill. Machiavelli concurred and later wrote, "If when Alexander died, Cesare had been well himself, everything would have been easy for him." But with his father dead, so was Cesare's good fortune. He was arrested and eventually exiled to Spain, his father's homeland. After two years in prison, in 1506, Cesare escaped with the help of the king of Navarre, who was Lucrezia's new husband and ruled what is now part of northern Spain.

A few months later, Cesare jumped at the chance to repay his rescuer when one of the king's counts started a rebellion. Eager for action, Cesare brazenly rode ahead of his troops in pursuit of the enemy's reinforcements. He traveled so fast that he was quite alone when he was ambushed by the count's men in the town of Viana. As he raised his sword against too many men, a lance pierced his side. The thirty-one-year-old son of a pope was then stabbed twenty-five times and stripped naked before the soldiers rode off leaving his body behind.

GRANDSON of
KING ALFONSO XIII OF SPAIN

GIVEN THE MANY more stable crowns that have fallen in Europe in the last century, it's amazing that the only one to be restored has been in Spain, a country that has seen eight constitutions, two republics, and three civil wars in the past 170 years and where every monarch for 150 years spent time in exile. As with most royal legacies, a number of flukes were required for Juan Carlos to gain his throne—and a hell of a nerve for him to keep it.

Spain's troubled line of Bourbon kings ended in 1931, when Alfonso XIII abdicated the crown he had held since before he was born (his father had died six months earlier). Alfonso's reign had deteriorated for a number of reasons, but one was that most of his sons were deemed unfit to inherit the throne. The king's first and fourth sons had hemophilia, passed down by his wife, a granddaughter of England's Queen Victoria. His second son, Don Jaime, went deaf at the age of three. Only his third son, Don Juan, born in 1913, was healthy, and he was serving in the British Navy when Alfonso abdicated. With the Spanish Civil War and the rise of Generalissimo Francisco Franco, Don Juan's chances of ever becoming king seemed slim.

Not until fellow Fascist Benito Mussolini advised Franco that Don Juan's son, Juan Carlos, born in Rome in 1938, should be brought back to Spain for his education that the possibility of regaining the throne seemed real for Don Juan. Although Franco was not on friendly terms with Don Juan, who in 1945 publicly called for the general to be overthrown, the two men met, and Don Juan, hoping that sending his son to Spain would put his family back in line for power, acquiesced to the plan.

It worked better than Don Juan might have wanted. Franco had no sons, and Juan Carlos became the substitute. The boy received a tour of training in all the Spanish military academies and soon began showing up in the background at Franco's public appearances. Juan Carlos, it seemed, was learning how to continue Franco's fascism instead of how to restore the Bourbon crown. It led to a split between Don Juan and his son, who during one argument in 1968 told his father, "You've played your cards and I've played mine. If you win, congratulations—but I don't think you will."

In 1969 Franco named Juan Carlos his successor, though it was not without some reservations. When Juan Carlos asked Franco for advice, the leader would reply, "Why should I tell you anything? You are not going to govern the way I did." One story has it that Franco first offered the throne to Otto von Habsburg, heir to the defunct Austrio-Hungarian Empire, who refused it. There also was speculation that Franco might change his mind in 1972 after his granddaughter married Juan Carlos's cousin, Alfonso, the son of Don Juan's older brother.

But Franco stood by his choice. Don Juan issued a statement that said, "I am a spectator and I assume no responsibility in this restoration." Later he said, "I love my son. I see him on television and I cry. But he thinks like a Fascist."

Franco died on November 20, 1975, and two days later Juan Carlos was crowned king of Spain. Don Juan did not attend the coronation. With Franco gone, the king's future seemed bleak. The

liberals didn't like him because he was Franco's follower. But neither were Franco's military leaders enamored of their new boss,
whom they thought weak. People began calling the new king
Juan Carlos el Breve—the Brief.

To the surprise of nearly everyone, Juan Carlos remains on the
throne today. Though he had accepted the crown as a follower of
Franco, Juan Carlos soon pushed out many of Franco's men,
reached out to the outlawed left-wing opposition, and brought in
moderates to rule the country. In 1979 Spain conducted its first
free elections in more than forty years, prompting Don Juan finally
to renounce his rights to the throne and say to his son, chokingly,
"Long live the king."

In 1981 the king no one thought could survive was credited with
almost single-handedly thwarting a serious coup attempt. Five
years later the king's son, eighteen-year-old Prince Felipe, was
sworn in as the heir to his well-liked father. Don Juan continues
to live outside his native country, in Estoril, Portugal. He never
got to be king, but his wish for a constitutional democracy in Spain
has been granted by his son.

CHILDREN of
ANTONY and CLEOPATRA

THE DEATHS OF Antony and Cleopatra didn't just break up one of
history's great romances. They also broke up a family. The queen
of Egypt and the would-be ruler of the Roman Empire left three
children: ten-year-old twins Alexander Helios and Cleopatra Selene,
and four-year-old Ptolemy Philadelphus. In addition, Antony had
five other children by his three Roman wives and Cleopatra had a
seventeen-year-old son by Julius Caesar. At a time when rulers
and their heirs were slain with regularity, the deaths of Antony

and Cleopatra may have unified the Roman Empire but left a lot of nervous children.

The children were especially at risk because Antony and Cleopatra had made them pawns in their political battles with Rome's other contending leader, Octavian, later called Caesar Augustus. Cleopatra called her son by Julius Caesar, Caesarion—"Little Caesar"—to press his claim to the title of his assassinated father. In a grand ceremony that shocked Rome in 34 B.C., Antony gave his three little children by Cleopatra title to much of the Roman Empire in Africa and Asia as a way of asserting his own control over the territories. Two-year-old Ptolemy was crowned king of northern Syria.

Ironically, their children were considered illegitimate in the eyes of Rome. Just a few weeks before Cleopatra gave birth to their twins, Antony had married his third Roman wife, Octavia, who was Octavian's sister. Antony and Cleopatra were married in Egypt in 36 B.C., but Antony didn't divorce Octavia in Rome until four years later.

Still, after Antony fell on his sword and Cleopatra dallied with that elusive asp in 30 B.C., the triumphant Octavian was reputed to have said, "A multitude of Caesars is no good thing." He sent troops after Caesarion, who had fled for Arabia, and had him killed. Soldiers also dragged Antyllus, Antony's older son by his second wife, out of the temple that Cleopatra had built for Julius Caesar and beheaded him.

The younger children were more fortunate. Octavian sent the twins and young Ptolemy back to Rome, where they were paraded next to the statue of Cleopatra. The three children were raised by Antony's ex-wife, Octavia. No further record exists of the two boys, but Cleopatra Selene later married a prince who became King Juba of Numidia and Mauretania, which ruled northern Africa west of Libya. Her son, Ptolemy, ruled as Juba II until he was killed by Caligula.

Meanwhile, Iullus, the younger brother of the slain Antyllus, survived Octavian's wrath. But in 2 B.C. he was caught as the lover of the libidinous Julia, daughter of Octavian (then Caesar Augustus), and was either executed or forced to commit suicide. Antony also had two daughters by Octavia. Antonia the Elder was the grandmother of Nero. Antonia the Younger was the grandmother of Caligula. If only Octavian had been more thorough.

CHILDREN of MRS. WILLIAM ASTOR

THERE HAVE BEEN many Mrs. Astors, but only one for whom the title was barely shy of royalty. *The* Mrs. Astor, actually Caroline Webster Schermerhorn Astor, wife of J. J. Astor's grandson, William Backhouse Astor, Jr., was the self-crowned queen of New York Society from 1872 until nearly the turn of the century. With the help of the Cromwellian Ward McAllister—her social aide-de-camp—Mrs. Astor hosted the most sought-after weekly dinner parties of each season. Her annual January ball was the birthplace of the original Four Hundred, a measure of social exclusivity derived from the number that could fit into her ballroom. Laden with so many diamonds that one gentleman called her "a walking chandelier," the heavyset, plain-looking Mrs. Astor, decked out in a black wig and a black gown, would preside over every occasion in such a stiff, even rude, manner that the affairs were much more like command performances than parties, which is just what she intended.

And she did it all—well, partly—for her four daughters. Herself born of older money than her Astor in-laws, Mrs. Astor believed that the only way to ensure that her daughters found suitable husbands was for her to select for them a suitable society. So she took it upon herself, with Mr. McAllister, to anoint the select few for the debut of her oldest daughter, Emily, in 1872. The rule was that your money had to be four generations old to be respectable, never mind that the Astors' fortune went back only three.

But the bigger irony is that none of her children married into any of the Four Hundred families. And Emily, two years after her mother began her crusade on her behalf, chose a husband that the Astors considered so far beneath them that their public distaste led the groom's father to challenge William to a duel. (It was settled off the field.)

It was, however, Mrs. Astor's third daughter, Charlotte, who pulled the biggest faux pas. She started out respectably by marrying James Coleman Drayton of Philadelphia, though he was not on her mother's precious list. But then, in 1891, the mother of four, Charlotte fell in love with Hallett Alsop Borrowe, the son of an insurance tycoon. The next year, after telling her bank to give Drayton $12,000 a year for her children, Charlotte sailed to England for a secret rendezvous with her lover. Drayton soon followed and, though it was later revealed he had accepted $5,000 from the Astors to keep quiet, he challenged Borrowe to a duel in Paris.

The whole affair exploded in the press after one of Drayton's seconds sold the *New York Sun* a series of letters that had been written to arrange the duel. William Astor, who had long been estranged from his domineering wife, went to be with his daughter in Paris, where he died of a heart attack. After a nasty custody fight, Charlotte was able to divorce Drayton with her honor intact, at least legally.

Presumably all this was enough to mortify Mrs. Astor. But never given to public emotion, she did not acknowledge that attendance at her annual January ball declined somewhat during the affair. Neither did she grant recognition to the fact that when she summoned her usual guests to a reception for Charlotte in Newport in 1894, many did not attend. Charlotte later returned to Europe and married a rich Scotsman. She died in 1920 at the age of sixty-two.

Mrs. Astor's reign had ended some years earlier, in 1906, when she fell on the stairs of her mansion. She died shortly thereafter at the age of seventy-seven. Besides her daughters, of course, Mrs. Astor was survived by her only son, John Jacob Astor IV. He would suffer the wrath of Mrs. Astor's Society after he divorced his first wife and married an eighteen-year-old girl in 1911. Partly to escape such societal outrage, John IV took his young bride on a second honeymoon to Egypt and Europe. On the return voyage, he went down with the *Titanic*.

DAUGHTER of CAESAR AUGUSTUS

THE ROMAN EMPIRE reached its zenith under the long and steady reign of Caesar Augustus. Octavian, as was his name before he was given the title Augustus, "the Revered," restored order to the far-flung empire after he defeated Mark Antony and Cleopatra in 31 B.C. And for more than forty years afterward, Augustus promoted economic and bureaucratic reforms that allowed the Roman world influence to soar.

When he got older, Augustus also decided to restore the empire's moral order, especially that of Rome. Long given to wine, women, and song, the city also faced a decline of newborn citizens, and Augustus instituted a series of "Julian laws," as they were called, designed to encourage marriage and sound family life. All men under sixty were required to marry, as were women under fifty, and celibates were taxed. Also under the new laws, a father, husband, or lover had the right to kill a woman caught committing adultery. As an alternative, the adulterous woman could be banished for life, lose one-third of her wealth, half her dowry, and could never marry again. A man, of course, could not be accused of adultery.

Augustus had plenty of trouble enforcing these morality laws among his citizens. And in his own home, he failed completely. For all his insistence that Romans produce lots of children, Augustus, who married three times, had just one child, a daughter. After divorcing her mother the day she was born, Augustus raised Julia strictly; she was required to spend her free time weaving and spinning, which even then was considered old-fashioned. Concerned that he had no male heir, Augustus arranged for Julia to marry when she was fourteen, and he selected his sister's son, Julia's cousin, as the groom. Marcellus reluctantly had to divorce his wife to marry Julia; he died two years later.

Augustus then forced his close friend and counsel, forty-two-year-old Marcus Agrippa, to divorce his wife and marry Julia when she was eighteen. It was during this mismatch that Julia started to throw wild parties and became the center of the young "in" crowd in Rome. She was rumored to carry on so many affairs that when all of her five children actually turned out to resemble Agrippa, people were surprised. "I never take on a passenger unless the vessel is already full," Julia is said to have explained.

After Agrippa died in 12 B.C., Julia breached her father's morality laws even more openly, much to the shock and pleasure of the citizens of Rome, who never had liked the laws. Augustus then got Julia a third husband. This time it was Tiberius, Augustus's stepson, who was forced to divorce his pregnant wife in 9 B.C. Neither Tiberius nor Julia was happy about the arrangement, and Tiberius soon left her and retired outside of Rome (later he was recalled to succeed Augustus as Caesar). Julia continued her wild ways, which included drunken orgies in the Forum at night.

According to the law, which he himself had decreed, Augustus should have taken Julia to court. Finally, in 2 B.C., he did, and ordered her banished to the desolate island of Pandateria, off the coast south of Rome. There he prohibited her from having wine and men, though after a while he permitted certain men he approved of to visit his daughter. Several of Julia's lovers also were banished, and one, a son of Antony, killed himself. Some historians say that more than morality was involved in the punishments, that Julia and her playmates actually were engaged in a plot to kill Augustus.

Julia was not the last of Augustus's descendants to plague the great ruler. In A.D. 8, Augustus banished her daughter, also named Julia, for the same sort of philandering. "He's a lucky man who remains a bachelor and dies without having had children!" cried the author of laws requiring both marriage and children. He once referred to the two Julias and one of his misbehaving grandsons as his "three abscesses." Actually, Augustus's greatest abscess showed up a few generations later, since another of Julia's daughters was the grandmother of Nero. Julia herself never was recalled by her father. She died in exile in A.D. 14, just a few weeks after the death of her father.

B

SONS of JOHANN SEBASTIAN BACH

IT IS HARDLY surprising that one of the world's greatest musical geniuses came from the Bach family. Johann Sebastian Bach actually belonged to the sixth generation of a veritable musical dynasty that reigned over much of Germany from the sixteenth to the nineteenth century. Music was the family business, and like any other it was passed on from father to son. Family members taught each other to play and write music, and even their valuable posts in churches and cities often were handed down.

Johann Sebastian Bach had many, many chances to pass on his talent. Between two wives he fathered a total of nineteen children, though only ten of them reached the age of five. Four of his sons attained some prominence as musicians or composers. Carl, his second and perhaps most famous son, served the court of Frederick the Great for thirty years and left his own admirable musical legacy. Johann Christian, Bach's youngest son, staged commercially successful concerts and operas in London, where he met an eight-year-old named Wolfgang Amadeus Mozart and is credited with greatly influencing that budding composer.

But Bach's favorite child was his oldest, Wilhelm. Bach began training his son when he was very young, and composed some of his organ sonatas so Wilhelm could have something to practice. By the end of his teens, Wilhelm was Bach's musical assistant, conducting rehearsals and copying the master's music. With his father's help, Wilhelm became an organist in Dresden in 1733; he was twenty-two at the time.

By 1746, Wilhelm was regarded as the best organist in Germany, a grand achievement, and he was named music director of the prominent Liebfrauenkirche in Halle. Though he was musically successful, Wilhelm personally didn't get along with his superiors in the strictly religious Lutheran city, and after many strained years he abruptly walked away from his job in 1764. He continued teaching and performing, but he never attained a fulltime position again.

By the time he moved to Berlin in 1774, Wilhelm was a poor and bitter man. Having inherited half of Johann Sebastian's manuscripts when his father died of a stroke in 1750 (younger brother Carl got the other half), Wilhelm began selling them off to support his family, though he allowed his widowed stepmother to die impoverished in 1760. Wilhelm grew more and more careless with his father's profound musical legacy. He sold Bach's compositions and autographs, claimed some of the music as his own, and, more profitably, signed his father's name to some of his own works. When Wilhelm died of heart disease at the age of seventy-three, his wife and daughter were left penniless. A benefit performance of Handel's *Messiah* was held for them the next year.

As for what was lost by Wilhelm's desperate sales, music historians can only speculate. "Careless custody must have robbed the world of numerous masterpieces," wrote biographer Malcolm Boyd. "Our understanding of Bach's music today would be very different if [his music] had all gone to Carl Philipp Emanuel, who took good care of his share."

CHILDREN of JOSEPHINE BAKER

GIVEN THAT Josephine Baker grew up poor in St. Louis, it was understandable that once she became the star of the Folies Bergère in Paris she would be a big spender. Onstage her skimpy costumes consisted of nothing more than a string of bananas or a single pink flamingo feather, but offstage Baker acquired closetfuls of lavish gowns and jewels as if to mock the American racism from which she and many other black performers fled to Paris in the 1920s. Baker even bought herself a fifty-room, fifteenth-century château in the Dordogne valley. She poured earnings from her show-business career into Les Milandes, converting it into an amusement park—complete with hotels, restaurants, paddleboats, and a wax museum of her life—that attracted thousands of tourists in the 1950s.

It was also at Les Milandes that Baker began building her most cherished collection—children. "I suffered a lot because I couldn't have children of my own," Baker said. "I felt inferior because of that." So Baker decided to adopt children of different races and nationalities to demonstrate to the world that they could live together in peace. "If children can, grown-ups can, too," Baker said. She started in 1954 when she visited an orphanage in Japan and left with two Korean babies who had been fathered by American occupation troops. She traveled around the world searching rural villages for abandoned children or, in some cases, children whose parents had too many other mouths to feed and were willing to take money to give up their youngest. Though she promised her fourth husband that she would stop at four children, Baker, in the next eleven years, adopted a total of twelve babies from nine different countries, including Korea, Colombia, Finland, and the Ivory Coast.

When she was home, Baker took great interest in her Rainbow Tribe, as she called her children. She would cook for them, mother

them and even attend their school meetings. But at least half the year, she was on tour singing to support her family, which also included her mother, brother and sister, and the many governesses who took care of the children. She would return to the château laden with so many gifts that the children called her Maman Cadeau, Mother Gift. As the children got older, visitors said they were undisciplined and spoiled. But Baker wrote proudly, "My children have proved that there were no more continents, no more obstacles, no more problems which could prevent understandings and respect between humans. . . . The Milandes is the earthly paradise."

Not to the bankers. In 1963, Les Milandes was $400,000 in debt. Baker's fanciful amusement park was looking tarnished, while some of its workers took advantage of her free-spending ways. Baker sold her jewels, but that wasn't enough. Then she had the idea to turn Les Milandes into the "International Brotherhood College." But when that didn't catch on, Brigitte Bardot hosted a fund-raiser for her on French television. "I'd never had children," Baker said. "I didn't know it costs so much. Food is important, atmosphere is important for the development of the brain."

Baker drove herself so hard to support her massive enterprise, including the children, that in 1964 she had a heart attack. The next year she wooed a Middle Eastern king who gave her $6,000, and thereby blocked an auction of her personal possessions. But despite Baker's efforts, Les Milandes was ordered to be sold at auction in 1969. The property went for a paltry $320,000, while Baker's own items netted another $52,000. When it came time to leave her château, Baker refused. She sent the children to live with a friend in Paris, then holed herself up in the kitchen and slept on an army cot. When the hotel owner who had bought the property sent his men to evict her, Baker was waiting with television crews. She was dragged kicking from the kitchen and left outside in the rain, where she sat in a housecoat crying for seven hours until she was taken to a hospital.

She was able to purchase a four-bedroom, two-bath villa near Monaco, but it was too cramped for twelve children and a diva like Baker. The children argued with her and misbehaved. One night at dinner a friend of Baker's read a letter from her doctor. "Dear Boys and Girls," it said. "You are being very mean to your mother. You are killing her. If you don't start being nice soon, she will die." After Baker had run out of the room, one of the older sons said, "It's an act. She's nutty. Leave her alone."

In 1973, a few weeks after a smash comeback at Carnegie Hall, Baker suffered another heart attack and a stroke that left part of her face temporarily paralyzed. Within a week she was rehearsing for her planned concert tour, ignoring her doctor's orders that she rest. "I can't. I have twelve children to raise," Baker said. But the star who had teased them for years at the Folies was less able to carry it off in her late sixties. "I'm an old lady now. It's embarrassing to have to do this," Baker said of her sheerly costumed act. Because of the stroke, Baker suffered memory lapses that disrupted some of her performances. Also, she sometimes couldn't remember the names of her younger children.

On April 8, 1975, the sixty-eight-year-old performer staged another comeback in Paris and got rave reviews. Two nights later, after a celebration party at which she danced on a table, Baker suffered another stroke. She died on April 12. Her friend Princess Grace of Monaco arranged for the Red Cross to provide proper clothes for the children for the funeral. The younger children moved in with Baker's last husband, who had divorced her and was living in Buenos Aires. Among the older children, as of a few years ago there was a waiter, a florist, a baker, an insurance salesman, a secretary and a hotel manager. None of the Rainbow Tribe went into show business.

CHILDREN of P. T. BARNUM

WHEN IT BECAME CLEAR that master promoter and circus mogul Phineas Taylor Barnum would leave no male heir, he wrote his will to ensure that his name would live on. To his oldest grandson, Clinton Seeley, Barnum's will provided $25,000 and 3 percent of the circus's profits "On this express condition: that he shall in a legal and proper way change his name, or cause his name to be changed to that of Clinton Barnum Seeley, and that he shall habitually use the name of Barnum, either as Clinton Barnum Seeley, or C. Barnum Seeley, or Barnum Seeley in his name, so that the name Barnum shall always be known as his name."

Clinton complied. But it was Barnum's more immediate family that garnered public attention. Six years after Barnum died at the age of eighty in 1891, a New York newspaper published a long exposé of the schemer's life. It seems Barnum did have a male heir, albeit an illegitimate one by a French actress who had performed in Barnum's museum. Barnum apparently supported the child, born in the early 1850s, through medical school and the boy eventually became a doctor in Richmond, Virginia. In the 1870s Barnum paid the young man $60,000 with the stipulation that he not try to get anything out of Barnum's will.

So it was that when Barnum scolded the second of his three legitimate daughters for her philandering, she shot back, "How could I help it? Am I not P. T. Barnum's daughter?" Helen was the most troublesome of Barnum's daughters, but all were somewhat spoiled. Barnum, whose fortune was entirely self-made, ruefully admitted, "They had been brought up in luxury, accustomed to call on servants to attend to every want, and almost unlimited in the expenditure of money." His oldest daughter, Caroline, married a rich saddle-maker in Barnum's hometown of Bridgeport, Connecticut, and his youngest daughter, Pauline, mother of Clinton, left three children and a stockbroker husband when she died of diphtheria at thirty-one.

Helen married Samuel Hurd in 1857 when she was seventeen. Barnum adored his son-in-law and took him into his circus business. But Helen, after producing three daughters, had an affair with a tailor's clerk and later ran away to Chicago with another lover, a doctor. The scandal made the papers. When she finally divorced Hurd several years later, Barnum wrote her out of his will, keeping Hurd in the family business, although after a stormy fight, he grudgingly gave her a tract of land near Denver. The land turned out to be rich in mineral deposits and Helen's doctor friend, whom she married in 1871, became president of a Denver medical school.

Meanwhile, Clinton, though he did change his name, did not keep the implied part of his bargain, which was to maintain the great showman's dazzling reputation. Living a quiet life, Clinton Barnum Seeley was best known as a member of Bridgeport's park board, which he served for thirty-one years before he died in 1958. "The rest of the Barnum descendants," said one offspring, also "led quiet humdrum lives, far from the bright lights, the tinsel, the sawdust, and all seemed rather ashamed of their circus money."

CHILDREN of THE BARRYMORES

ABSENT A LEGITIMATE THRONE, Americans often look to the theater for their royalty. And in the first half of the twentieth century they bowed to the Barrymores. "The royal family of the theater," siblings Lionel, John, and "First Lady" Ethel became the most successful generation in a theatrical family that dated back three-hundred years. First on Broadway and then in Hollywood, the Barrymores seemed to bless every production they were in, most notably John's *Hamlet* and *Richard III*, which was called the "most inspired performance which this generation has seen."

But later, after their father, Maurice, died of syphilis, Lionel broke his hip and became confined to a wheelchair and his two daughters died young, and John became an alcoholic, people spoke of "the Barrymore curse." It seemed mostly to afflict John. Ethel's three children basically grew up and enjoyed their money. John and two of his three children did not. John's heavy drinking eventually began to drain his performances, and his offscreen romantic scandals severely tarnished his Hollywood star. He had four failed marriages, producing three children he hardly ever saw.

His firstborn was by his second wife, temperamental poet Michael Strange. John said of his infant daughter, Diana, born in 1920, "I'm glad Trepie is a girl. If she were a boy, she'd inherit all my habits, and I wouldn't know how to combat them. I'd have such sympathy for them." Diana later said, "Two parents like mine would discourage anybody." After her parents divorced when she was four, Diana didn't see her father again until she was ten. Her mother wouldn't even admit that the movie star John Barrymore was Diana's father. In 1939, Diana set out to take her place in the Barrymore legend. She immediately was given a screen test, film roles, and a big studio buildup. And since the studios treated her like a star, she acted like one. Even her father, on one of the rare occasions they met for dinner, didn't like his daughter's debutante behavior. "Stop trying to be a Barrymore," he told her. "Be yourself."

John died in 1942 at the age of sixty, done in by cirrhosis of the liver, kidney failure, and bronchial pneumonia. (Lionel died in 1954 at seventy-six, and Ethel died in 1959 at seventy-nine.) Off-screen, Diana seemed to take her father's place almost at once. She ran through her inheritance and three bad marriages, carousing with many, many men and drinking heavily along the way. Her film career never did take off. "No doubt," sniffed the *New York Times* in one review, "even the offspring of royal families must be allowed their little indiscretions, but why display them?"

By 1955, Diana was living in a tawdry Times Square hotel and the following year she entered a hospital for treatment of alcoholism. In 1957 she wrote a best-selling autobiography, *Too Much Too Soon.* "I regret now that I let myself be persuaded to identify myself with my father," Diana said. "The question will always be in the back of my mind, 'How far could I have gone without the name?'" That remained unanswered on January 24, 1960, when Diana was found dead of an overdose of alcohol and pills in her New York apartment.

John Barrymore, Jr., remembered seeing his father only once, on Christmas Eve in 1939 when he was seven years old. His mother, retired film star Dolores Costello, who divorced John Sr. in 1935, didn't want her two children to follow in their father's footsteps. While John Barrymore's second daughter, Dolores, became a housewife, John Jr. ran away from home and soon had his screen test. But unlike his half-sister, Diana, John Jr. tried to develop his career more slowly. In 1951, the nineteen-year-old backed out of a summer-theater production of *The Hasty Heart*, explaining, "I'm not ready yet." That drew the significant wrath of his Aunt Ethel, who declared, "Never in 300 years has a Barrymore walked out of a contract. After all, we're professionals. We don't do things like that."

John Jr. did, and worse. The following year he was married and a week later was arrested for drunkenness during a public fight with his bride. He appeared in many television productions in the 1950s, but got in trouble with the actors' union for regularly showing up late on the set, arguing with directors, and changing his lines. In 1956, he changed his name from John Barrymore, Jr., to John Drew Barrymore, then passed "John Jr." on to his own infant son. After divorcing his first wife and suffering professional troubles and several arrests for reckless driving and drunkenness, John moved to Italy, where he had a fairly successful film career in the early 1960s.

Several legal scrapes, one daughter, and a failed marriage later, John moved back to California. In the late 1960s and early 1970s he did little acting but was arrested several times for possession of marijuana. He ended up living alone in the California desert, where he meditated and lived on watercress and hickory nuts and was dubbed "the Beatnik Barrymore." He emerged in 1974 with long gray hair and a shaggy beard and said, "I have found God and myself. It is pure bliss." John has stayed out of the news since then. His son, an actor who changed his name back to John Barrymore III, has said of his father, "He's more like my son than my father. I always have to be looking out for him."

But the Barrymore line doesn't end there. John is also the estranged father of Drew Barrymore, one of the child stars of *E.T.: The Extra-Terrestrial*, and other major films. In 1989, the thirteen-year-old wrote a cover story for *People* magazine, in which she described her bouts of alcoholism and drug addiction.

CHILDREN of NIELS BOHR

SINCE THEY BEGAN awarding Nobel Prizes in 1901, you can almost count on one hand the number awarded to the children of past recipients. Of those, the one where the odds perhaps most favored a repeat performance occurred in the Bohr family. The son of an internationally recognized Danish physiologist and brother of a distinguished mathematician, Niels Bohr won the Nobel Prize for Physics in 1922 for his quantum theory that defined the structure and behavior of atoms, and laid the foundation for the development of the atomic bomb.

Despite the mind-boggling sophistication of his theories, Bohr didn't leave his work at the office. He would guide his five sons through a barrage of math and logic problems at the dinner table, using (to his wife's dismay), forks, glasses and napkin rings to demonstrate simple laws of physics. Even Sunday rowing outings were not entirely recreational. Remembered his son, Hans, "We always had to go up the tower of the Church of Our Saviour, both to enjoy the view from the spiral staircase on the outside of the spire, and also to study the mechanism of the big clock." Revered by his fellow scientists for his thoughtfulness and humanity, "Father," Hans said, "was kindness itself."

Christian, the oldest, drowned at the age of seventeen in 1934. Hans, the second son, did not follow his father into the physics lab. He became an orthopedist. His younger brother Erik became a chemical engineer, and Ernest a lawyer. It was Bohr's youngest son, Aage, who entered the family business.

When Bohr and his family fled Nazi-occupied Denmark in 1943, the twenty-one-year-old Aage, already a budding physicist, accompanied his father to England and later to Los Alamos, New Mexico, to help him work on the Manhattan Project. Aage, who had been born the year Niels won the Nobel Prize, was his father's secretary. Since there was no one "to whom we could entrust such documents," Aage said, "therefore I typed them." Meanwhile Niels, often called the most important scientist of the twentieth century after Einstein, "darned socks and sewed buttons on for us, a job which he carried out with his usual thoroughness and manual skill."

Niels and his son returned to Denmark after the war, and Aage took over the prestigious Niels Bohr Institute of Theoretical Physics after his father died in 1962 at the age of seventy-seven. In 1975— fifty-two years after his father—Aage (pronounced "O-ah," like Noah) was awarded the Nobel Prize for Physics with two other scientists for their work on the atomic nucleus, an important step in nuclear fusion.

DAUGHTER of PAT BOONE

SOMETIMES THE PENDULUM seems to swing both ways at once. While hip-swiveling Elvis Presley was shocking his way to stardom in the mid-1950s, one of his biggest rivals was a squeaky-clean apple-pie-of-a-kid. Pat Boone's croons not only made the smiling Tennessee teenager a teen idol, parents liked him too. In very short order, Boone went from being a twenty-year-old winner of the Ted Mack Amateur Hour to a million-record seller who also starred in movies and his own television show.

During that same period, Boone, who had eloped at nineteen, graduated from Columbia University and had four daughters in three and a half years. One of those daughters, of course, grew up to be the Debby Boone who herself topped the charts with one of the biggest records of 1977, "You Light Up My Life." But for Pat Boone's oldest girl, growing up was much more difficult.

"My parents had made a decision early in their lives," said Cherry Boone O'Neill in her 1982 autobiography, *Starving for Attention.* "It was better to be too strict than too lenient, and strict they were. After all, raising children in the modern world was challenging enough, but raising four pretty little girls to be un-spoiled Christian young women while living in a show-business environment was like a family version of 'Mission Impossible.' "

Cherry said her parents had specific rules about hair length, makeup, clothes, and, especially, dating. When the rules were broken, Pat Boone spanked his daughters, according to Cherry and Debby. Such punishment continued until they were eighteen. Pub-licly, the Boones seemed a model family. When they appeared on Merv Griffin's television show he asked, "Now come on, Boones, level with me. With your parents' strict guidelines don't you hon-estly feel you're missing out on some things?" "Yes, sir," an-swered Cherry. "Trouble. Lots of trouble."

In fact, Cherry's trouble began in the eighth grade at about the time she and her sisters began performing with their father. Cherry thought she looked fat on television, so the fourteen-year-old began dieting. She swiped some of her mother's diet pills and began exercising heavily. During her high school years, she said, she exercised four hours a day, yet ate very little and forced her-self to throw up what she did eat. "Being thin was the one identity I had established for myself," Cherry said in one interview. "I liked the feeling of control I had when I refused food."

By her senior year, Cherry's five-foot-seven-inch frame weighed just ninety-two pounds. Her parents had her examined by many doctors, but tests for various viruses always came up negative. It wasn't until later that she finally was diagnosed as anorexic. She was still suffering from the disorder when she married in 1975 at the age of twenty-one. Two years later, weighing a dangerously low eighty pounds, Cherry was put in the hospital. She stopped per-forming with her family and she and her husband moved to

Seattle, where she was treated for two years by a Christian psychiatrist. She recovered almost completely, though she had to have twenty-two teeth capped after they had eroded.

In 1981 Cherry gave birth to a baby girl. Also that year she and her husband converted to Catholicism. Cherry said growing up in her strict family made her feel insecure and guilty that she wasn't measuring up. But she said she doesn't blame her parents. They were, she said recently, "the best parents they knew how to be."

SON of GUTZON BORGLUM

"OUR AGE will some day be called the Colossal Age, yet there is not a monument in this country as big as a snuff box." So determined was Gutzon Borglum to rectify the situation that he created the most colossal monument of any age—four presidential visages covering one and a half acres of the side of Mount Rushmore. The son of Dutch immigrant Mormons, Borglum later studied sculpture with Auguste Rodin in Paris and was one of the most renowned American sculptors in the early twentieth century. His bust of Lincoln still stands in the rotunda of the U.S. Capitol, and he carved several figures for the Cathedral of St. John the Divine in New York.

The size of Borglum's sculptures was matched only by his ego. After he got angry and quit his first massive monument—a Confederate memorial on the face of Stone Mountain in Georgia—he smashed his 12-by-24-foot model to try to prevent anyone else from proceeding. His insistence on rewriting a five hundred-word history of the nation that had been penned by President Coolidge killed plans to carve the essay next to Borglum's faces on Mount Rushmore. "My life," Borglum said on his seventy-first birthday, "has been a one-man war from beginning to date."

To a large degree, while Borglum was fighting his wars, Mount Rushmore was being sculpted by his son, Lincoln. Borglum had begun blasting away the face of the South Dakota mountain in 1927. But because of the Depression, work progressed slowly. Lincoln, whose father had prevailed on him to put off his plans to study engineering so he could assist him, joined the project full time in 1933 when only Washington's face had been completed.

In 1938, when Borglum was seventy-one, Lincoln became the project's superintendent. Borglum was not in good health and often had to spend time in Washington stubbornly demanding more money. On his way to Washington in 1941 for another appeal, Borglum stopped in Chicago to give a speech, and to see a doctor about a prostate problem. He had surgery on February 17 and developed some blood clots, one of which caused a heart attack that killed him on March 6.

So, at the age of twenty-nine, Lincoln was put in charge of the monument, which after years of controversy had gained national support. His father's dream called for the four presidents to be sculpted to their waists, but when World War II killed all further funding for the monument, Lincoln was left with just enough money to finish off their hair and Roosevelt's collar. On October 31, 1941, Mount Rushmore was left permanently unfinished.

Lincoln went on to become a sculptor and a photographer. Some of his pictures appeared on the cover of the *Saturday Evening Post*. He promoted his father's work until he died in 1986, but he never attempted his own massive monument, as he said his father had expected he would. "Gutzon did not anticipate a time when large sculptures, memorials and monuments would be in so little demand as they are now," Lincoln wrote in a 1976 biography of his father. Borglum had set his son up to take over his business only to have Lincoln find out there was no business left.

GREAT-GRANDDAUGHTER of
WILLIAM BOYCE

IN 1910 William Dickson Boyce, a self-made millionaire publisher from Chicago, founded the Boy Scouts of America. More than half a century later, one of his great-granddaughters proved to be no Girl Scout. Diana Oughton grew up a child of privilege. On her father's side, the Oughtons had been one of the original leading families of Dwight, Illinois, a farm town of 3,100 people sixty miles southwest of Chicago. There Diana was raised on an estate with a deer park and a pond. She rode horses and hunted pheasant with her father, who was vice president of the family's bank, a Republican state legislator, and the owner of thousands of acres of farmland.

Everyone said, sincerely, that Diana was a model child. The oldest of four girls and a member of the 4-H Club, the tall attractive blonde would have been a debutante had she grown up in a large city. In 1956, intending to broaden her outlook, her parents sent her to the Madeira School, a girls' boarding school in Greenway, Virginia. Later, at Bryn Mawr, she majored in German and spent her junior year in Munich.

When she returned to the United States, Diana rejected a marriage proposal from a Princeton football player, and began tutoring ghetto children. Then, after she graduated in 1963, she joined a Peace Corps–type program and moved to Guatemala to teach impoverished Indians. Diana, who had grown up in a Tudor-style mansion, took her mission seriously and, unlike some of the other American volunteers with wealthy backgrounds, actually lived solely on her salary of fifteen dollars per month.

In 1966, Diana ended up at the University of Michigan, where a few years earlier Tom Hayden and others had started Students for a Democratic Society (SDS). Diana was teaching in an experimental school in Ann Arbor where she fell in love with Bill

Ayers, an SDS member and the son of the chairman of Chicago's Commonwealth Edison. Diana and Bill moved into a commune and she rebuffed her parents' attempts to give her money.

By 1968 the experimental school had failed (the curriculum was so loose that none of the children had learned to read) and Bill and Diana became more involved in SDS, which had become the vanguard of student protests around the country. Bill Ayers emerged as a leader in the group's most radical faction, the Weathermen, and Diana was one of his most ardent followers. She was part of a task force that went to Cuba to meet with North Vietnamese officials.

In Flint, Michigan, the Weathermen organized themselves into a collective, where they underwent military training, lived in filth, and forbade monogamy in order to break down individual relationships and unite the group. They joined with Weathermen from other cities to create small, sometimes violent, disruptions, mostly on campuses. Their efforts were to culminate in Four Days of Rage in Chicago in October 1969, when the three hundred who showed up for a disorderly march downtown were beaten by police.

Diana was arrested, and her father, nearly blind, was driven to Chicago to pay the $500 to bail her out. It was one of the few contacts between Diana and her family. Several months before, she had written to her parents, "It gets harder, and I get more reluctant to justify myself over and over again to you . . . I feel like a moral person, that my life is my values, that most people my age or even younger have already begun to sell out to materialism, status, hypocrisy, stepping on other people, etc. Politically, I'm not surprised you don't understand."

Diana spent a fairly peaceful Christmas with her family in Dwight in 1969, though the pale, drawn woman with shorn hair and wire-rimmed glasses looked a far cry from the former perky 4-H member. When she returned to Michigan, the Weathermen were deciding to step up the revolution. They made plans to go underground and plant bombs. Diana talked to her parents the next February. "You know, Diana, you're killing us both," said her mother. "I'm sorry, Mummy," she answered.

In early March Diana and some others went to New York City

to learn how to make bombs. Just before noon on Friday, March 6, 1970, an explosion shot out of a red-brick townhouse on West 11th Street in Greenwich Village, just off Fifth Avenue. Soon after, two more explosions collapsed the front of the building, shattered windows across the street, and blew a hole into the adjoining basement of a house belonging to Dustin Hoffman, who soon after was seen leaving, carrying paintings and a Tiffany lampshade. Two women, one nude, the other wearing jeans, were rescued from the rubble by neighbors. But after one neighbor let the women clean up in her home and gave them clothes, they disappeared.

Police first thought the explosion had been caused by a gas leak. But crushed inside the collapsed townhouse they found a body that they identified as Ted Gold, an SDS leader. They also determined the building was owned by the father of an SDS member. Investigators continued to search through the rubble, but it was not until Tuesday, March 10, that they found the badly mutilated torso of a woman near a workbench in the basement. They also found four foot-wide pipes loaded with dynamite as well as a total of fifty-seven sticks of explosives, thirty blasting caps, and several alarm clocks. They found a man's body in the basement four days later.

The female torso was still unidentified on March 15 when the investigators' exhaustive sifting uncovered the torn-off tip of a little finger. Finally, on Tuesday, March 17, eleven days after the explosions, the FBI determined that the fingerprint belonged to Diana Oughton. She and Terry Robbins, the man whose body was also found in the basement, had been manufacturing bombs when they made a fatal mistake.

Diana was buried in the Oughton family plot next to her grandparents.

SON of CHARLES BOYER

THAT FRENCH-BORN movie star Charles Boyer was only acting the part of being one of Hollywood's greatest "lou-vaires" was apparent every time he left the set. The dark-eyed, debonair actor who seduced Garbo and Dietrich and many others on the silver screen quietly went home to the same wife for forty-four years. The ladykiller in *Algiers* and *Gaslight*, Boyer enjoyed reading at home and was considered aloof at parties.

The only time Boyer really seemed to let down his guard was around his son, Michael. Boyer was married nine years before his wife finally became pregnant, and when Michael arrived in 1943 the forty-four-year-old actor played and gurgled with him so often that his wife was embarrassed. Boyer called home daily from the movie set. He worried that Michael would get sick, and when he didn't, Boyer worried that the baby wasn't going through the normal baby illnesses. Boyer, who had worn a toupee in his movies, had a permanent hair transplant so his son wouldn't think his father was old.

Clearly, unlike many Hollywood children, Michael Boyer received plenty of attention from his parents. He traveled with them between their homes in Beverly Hills, New York, and Paris. When his parents took up painting at their villa off the coast of Italy, so did Michael. And when Michael turned twenty and decided he wanted to be a television producer, his father helped him get started. Boyer, who was one of the founding partners of Four Star Television Productions in the 1950s, arranged for his son to be hired as an associate producer on the company's detective series, "The Rogues," which featured rotating stars, including Boyer. Michael's job was to be the dialogue director. Soon after Michael joined the company, Four Star went public and Boyer cashed out. Soon after that, "The Rogues" was canceled and Michael lost his job.

Michael, a tall, stocky young man who wore designer clothes and cut much more of a playboy image than his father, told his parents he didn't want their help this time. Still, for his twenty-first birthday they bought him a two-bedroom luxury apartment in West Los Angeles. The next year Michael also became interested in the record business, so his father recorded a single, "Where Does Love Go?" and Michael produced it. On September 20, 1965, while Boyer was shooting a movie in Paris, he said in an interview that he wanted to help his son find a career. "Michael is searching," Boyer said. "I'm trying to help him find himself."

Three days later Boyer was called home to Beverly Hills because his son was dead. Michael had apparently shot himself in the temple after his girlfriend of six weeks, who had previously agreed to marry him, told him she wanted to break up. The woman said that Michael, who had a gun collection, had been playing Russian roulette earlier that evening. "He told me that he was a loser and had always been a loser, and that if he lost me he would kill himself," she said. "Then he went into the den." After finding one bullet shell in the revolver and five more neatly lined up on a table, police said Michael had committed suicide.

Boyer said soon after, "I don't expect anyone to believe me, but it was a tragic accident." Still, Boyer and his wife couldn't help feeling guilty that they hadn't done enough for their son. They sold their homes where Michael had grown up and retired to Geneva, from which Boyer emerged infrequently to appear in movies such as *Casino Royale* and *Barefoot in the Park*. Boyer's wife died of liver cancer on August 24, 1978. Boyer remained at their home in Paradise Valley, Arizona, while his wife's funeral took place in California. On August 26, he took an overdose of Seconal and died two days before his eightieth birthday.

CHILDREN of MARLON BRANDO

MARLON BRANDO may be one of America's greatest actors but he is also one of its sloppiest, known almost as well for his string of film flops as for his stunning triumphs like *A Streetcar Named Desire, On the Waterfront,* and *The Godfather.* After he appeared in one particularly awful movie, *Morituri,* in 1965, Brando—the consummate Method actor whose mumbled style deeply influenced James Dean and many afterward—explained why he did it. "Every so often I look at my financial condition and I find I need money," Brando said simply. "So I do a good-paying picture. You see, I have three households to support and I pay alimony to two women."

Indeed, Brando's domestic life has been almost as volatile as his acting career. With a reputation as a ladies' man in Hollywood, Brando, born in 1924, wasn't the marrying kind. Some say the only reason he legalized his stormy relationship with actress Anna Kashfi in October 1957 was because she was pregnant. Kashfi threatened divorce by New Year's, but they stayed together until their son, Christian, was born in May 1958. By then, however, Brando already was engaged in other affairs, and he and Kashfi divorced in 1959.

Kashfi received custody of Christian, but the matter was far from over. When Brando tried to visit his son, he and his ex-wife would end up fighting, sometimes violently, according to their testimony against each other in repeated court hearings. Kashfi charged that Brando beat her, Brando said she threw a tricycle at him.

The accusations and the courtroom scenes escalated for years. The fourteenth custody hearing came in 1965 after Kashfi had attempted suicide by swallowing pills, then had left the hospital, broken into Brando's home and taken Christian with her. Brando testified: "On one occasion she attempted to stab me; this occurred in front of the boy." A psychologist testified that Christian was "a very tense, fearful, terrorized youngster who is very hypersensitive and is unable to maintain attention or relate well to adults." Christian was sent to live with Brando's sister in Illinois for a while.

The final custody battle came in 1972 after Kashfi took Christian to Mexico with another man and then said the man had disappeared with the thirteen-year-old boy. Christian was later found wheezing in a tent in a Mexican village, suffering from bronchitis. The man said Kashfi had offered him $10,000 to hide out with the boy. After that, Christian lived with his father and didn't see his mother for seven years.

Brando, meanwhile, created two more families. In 1960 he married Movita, an actress with whom he had had a sometime relationship since they met on the set of his 1952 film *Viva Zapata!* As with Kashfi, Movita already was pregnant when Brando married her. He left soon after Miko was born, though the marriage lasted officially until 1968. Before then, in 1966, Movita sued Brando, claiming he had fathered her second child, Rebecca, and demanding increased child support. Today, stories still variously do or don't include Rebecca among Brando's children.

Brando met the third mother of his children in 1962 when he was in Tahiti to film *Mutiny on the Bounty.* She was Tarita, a nineteen-year-old waitress he selected to play his island mistress in the movie. Partly to be with Tarita, whom he never married, and partly to escape his two wives, Brando bought an island near Tahiti called, Teti'aroa. He built a hotel and talked of harvesting seaweed to feed the Third World. Tarita bore him two children: a son, Simon Tehotu, in 1962, and a daughter, Tarita Cheyenne, in 1970. They grew up mostly with their mother.

In recent years, Brando's oldest child, Christian, has been described variously as an actor, a welding teacher, and, for seven years in Beverly Hills, a tree surgeon. In 1987 he was making a movie in Italy and sounding much like his father. "The only reason I'm here making my first film is that they made me an offer I couldn't refuse," Christian told the *San Francisco Chronicle.* "My pop and I are real close. We've had our squabbles, but there was never anything bad. And I was never sheltered. I've worked for myself ever since I was 16; been up to Alaska, worked in bars. But I never dropped out. I was never a bum. Wild, sure."

But the Brando child who has come closest to fame is Miko. A bodyguard for Michael Jackson, Miko was the first person to reach the singer when his hair caught fire during the filming of a Pepsi commercial in 1984. "I tore out," Miko said, "hugged him and ran my hands through his hair." He burned his own fingers. Almost twenty years after Brando explained why he made bad movies, Miko said his father's attitude hadn't changed. "He thinks acting is pretty stupid, but it pays him well," Miko said in 1984. "He's not the film star type, but he has a lot of people to support."

SON of
ADMIRAL RICHARD EVELYN BYRD

"MY ONLY OBJECTIVE," said Admiral Richard E. Byrd, the man who unlocked Antarctica, "other than the satisfaction in being able to get all these scientists down here to study this last great mystery in the world, is simply that I wish to keep my name so well known by the public that when the time comes for them to choose the inevitable ambassador of brotherly love to the other nations of the world, I shall be that man!"

The world never made him that ambassador, though Byrd kept his name very well known by the world. His achievements were real: though not the first man to fly the Atlantic or to view either pole, he was the first to do all three, and his five expeditions to Antarctica charted territory half the size of the United States. But Byrd's success in part came from his skill as a promoter. During his second trip to the South Pole in 1933 he hooked up radio broadcasts from the ice-locked continent so the world wouldn't forget he was down there. And to keep his wealthy backers happy, Byrd dubbed his discoveries with names like the Rockefeller Mountains, the Ford Ranges, the Walgreen Coast and Sulzberger Bay.

While Byrd was spending his months, sometimes years, in his various ice stations, he left his wife and four children back in Boston, where they lived well in a large home on Beacon Hill. Himself a descendant of one of the most prominent families of Virginia (his brother was a governor and senator), Byrd sent his only son to Harvard. Richard Jr. later married the daughter of a Massachusetts governor and senator. In 1946 he accompanied his father on his fourth Antarctic expedition, earning himself the rank of Navy lieutenant.

After Byrd—debilitated by his frigid missions—died in 1957 at the age of sixty-eight, Richard did not continue to follow in his father's footsteps. Instead, the explorer's son tried to make a career of preserving the tracks his father already had made. "He idolized his father," said his son, Leverett Byrd. "The main focus of his life was to continue what [Byrd] had started, to help people who wanted information about him."

He was not equal to the task. He lived off a trust fund and investments, and talked of building a museum to house the explorer's papers and possessions, but he never found the backing. After his mother died, Richard Jr. became embroiled in a legal battle with his sisters over the fate of their father's papers and the family home on Beacon Hill, where Richard lived but which had fallen into such disrepair that the city issued him a citation.

Richard insisted his parents had wanted him to care for his father's legacy. "That is what I have done all throughout my lifetime. Why should I change now?" he said at the age of sixty, in 1980. Two years later the family home was sold, and in 1985, Byrd's papers were sold to Ohio State University. Richard, who was divorced in 1960 and lost custody of his own four sons, spent his last years in a boardinghouse on Beacon Hill, feeding pigeons in nearby Boston Common.

On September 13, 1988, Richard was put on a train bound for Washington by his son Leverett, where he was to attend ceremonies honoring the centennial of his famous father's birth. But Richard never made it to the capital. He was reported missing and remained so until October 3, when a custodian found him dead in an abandoned warehouse in an industrial area of Baltimore. He was wearing a green worker's uniform and one shoe, neither his own clothes. The custodian said he had chased Richard away from the area a week before he found the body. It was only when the body was examined that officials found a Boston Transit Authority identification card pinned to his undershorts, revealing his famous name. Richard had died several days before from malnutrition and dehydration, and doctors later determined that he had suffered from Alzheimer's disease.

"My father was never 'Richard Byrd,' " Leverett told the *Boston Globe*. "He was always 'the son of the admiral.' It's hard today to imagine the proportion of my grandfather's fame in his day, but it was hard for my father to handle. There was so much expected of him."

DAUGHTER of LORD BYRON

WHEN THE FLAMBOYANT POET Lord Byron fled England in 1816, he left behind an incensed wife and a one-month-old daughter. Lady Byron spent the child's youth seeing to it that the little girl would inherit none of her father's restless randiness. While she kept a portrait of her deserting husband she covered it with a green curtain, told Ada little about her father, and only reluctantly passed on news of Ada to Lord Byron in Italy. The poet died when his daughter was eight, never having succeeded in seeing Ada or even exchanging letters with her.

Byron did not forget his only legitimate offspring (other children have been alleged) during his eight years in exile on the Continent. On his deathbed in Greece, the thirty-six-year-old poet moaned, "Oh, my poor dear child! My dear Ada! My God, could

I but have seen her!" He also wrote of Ada in several poems, including "Childe Harold's Pilgrimage":

> *My daughter! with thy name in this song begun—*
> *My daughter! with thy name thus much shall end—*
> *I see thee not—I hear thee not—but none*
> *Can be so wrapt in thee; thou art a friend*
> *To whom the shadows of far years extend:*
> *Albeit my brow thou never shouldst behold,*
> *My voice shall with thy future visions blend,*
> *And reach into thy heart—when mine is cold—*
> *A token and a tone even from thy father's mould.*

To prevent such a blending, Lady Byron employed mathematics. She thought the discipline of numbers would cause her daughter's life to be orderly as well. And for a time, Lady Byron succeeded beyond what she could have hoped. Ada embraced her mathematical studies so tightly that it was almost unbecoming to a proper Victorian lady. In 1833 Ada met Charles Babbage, a prominent mathematician who had designed what is considered the world's first computer. She later saw Babbage's ungainly machine, called the Difference Engine, with a group of ladies. Wrote the wife of another mathematician, "While the rest of the party gazed at this beautiful instrument with the same sort of expression and feeling that some savages are said to have shown on first seeing a looking glass or hearing a gun, Miss Byron, young as she was, understood its working and saw the great beauty of the invention."

Babbage became Ada's tutor, even as she followed more acceptable Victorian paths. She married William King, ten years her senior, in 1835, and had three children in four years. But although the delicate-framed woman often was ill, both physically and emotionally, she regularly devoted time to her mathematics and to Babbage's plans for his improved computing device, the Analytical Engine. In 1843 Ada published a translation of an Italian article about Babbage's theoretical machine. In addition to her translation, Ada wrote a set of technical notes that turned out to be longer than the original article. Her notes, says biographer Joan Baum, are "considered now to be the world's first explanation of computer programming."

But her notes were not recognized as such at the time, despite Ada's high hopes to achieve in science the fame of her father in poetry. "Like the Prophets of old, I shall speak the voice I am inspired with," she wrote Byronically. "I may be the Deborah, the Elijah of Science, submitting to God and his agents to be used as their vocal organ for the ears of mortals." She wrote of her father, "If he has transmitted to me any portion of that genius, I would use it to bring out great truths and principles."

But unfortunately, Babbage never found funding for his new machine, and Ada Byron's "Notes" were soon forgotten. Also, her health problems grew worse. Her variety of ills were treated with opium and brandy, making her at turns moody and temperamental. Ada grew restless in a manner recklessly reminiscent of her father. Bored with her aging husband, and unsatisfied with her scientific achievements, she had an affair and also gambled heavily on horses. She used one of Babbage's servants to make book and, as her losses mounted, she secretly pawned her husband's family jewels to cover her debts. Her husband was left to settle the mess when Ada, after suffering for months in agonizing pain, died of uterine cancer in 1852. She died at the age of thirty-six, just like her father.

Ada's achievement in computers may make her merely a distant ancestral cousin in the lineage that led to IBM. But in 1980, the U.S. Department of Defense initiated a new generation of programming language for its entire system. In her honor, they named it Ada.

C

SON of ALBERT FRANCIS CAPONE

IF THERE IS IRONY in the downfall of the children of successful parents, certainly the reverse can be just as surprising. One would not, for example, expect the son of Al "Scarface" Capone, one of the most murderous gangsters of the 1920s, to quit his job as a used-car salesman after World War II just because his boss was turning back odometers. But that he did. Unlike his father, who went to prison for income-tax evasion in 1931 and died of syphilis in 1947, Capone Jr., for the most part, followed the straight and narrow.

Capone Jr. was born when his father was still a small-time gangster in Brooklyn. His godfather—the religious kind—was a bigger Brooklyn gangster who sent him a $5,000 bond on every birthday. Capone Jr. was shy as a boy, growing up surrounded by bodyguards and later accompanying his mother to visit his father in prison. But though Capone Jr. didn't enter his father's business (he was only twelve when his father was convicted), Capone Sr. spoke of him with pride. "How the hell can a fat dago like me have a son that good-looking?" the mobster said.

Capone Jr. attended Catholic school in Miami and later withdrew from Notre Dame after his first year when his alias, Al Brown, was revealed. He was working toward a degree in business administration at the University of Miami when his father died in 1947. Soon after, his mother had to sell their estate on an island off Miami Beach to pay back taxes that Capone Sr. still owed. She and her son then opened a restaurant on Miami Beach, The Grotto, where Mrs. Capone ran the cash register and Capone Jr. was the headwaiter. His wife's brother was a detective in the Miami Police Department, and Capone Jr. joined the department's pistol team and the Florida Peace Officers Association.

After the restaurant failed, Capone Jr. moved up the coast to Hollywood, Florida. There, in 1965 at the Kwik Chek Supermarket, he tucked two bottles of aspirin and a box of radio transistor batteries into his pockets. A store detective arrested the gangster's son carrying stolen merchandise valued at $3.50. Capone Jr. pleaded no contest to the charge of petty larceny. He told the judge, "Everybody has a little larceny in him, I guess." He was sentenced to two years' probation.

The next year, at the age of forty-eight, Capone Jr. went into court to change his name because, he said, his father's reputation "pushes me into the glare of publicity for even minor violations of the law." He dropped his indelible last name and became, officially, Albert Francis. Since then, he has managed to stay out of the headlines.

DAUGHTER of GIACOMO CASANOVA

GIVEN THAT Casanova bedded everyone in sight, it is hardly surprising that the premier paramour of the eighteenth century had children. And since his conquests occurred over forty years as he traveled to and fled from nearly all the major capitals of Europe, it is also not surprising that exactly how many children he fathered is uncertain. Even Casanova himself—whose panoramic life included luxury and poverty, imprisonment, spy missions for France, and meetings with Voltaire, Benjamin Franklin, and Catherine the Great (oddly, not one of his liaisons) as well as eleven cases of venereal disease—couldn't take it all in. When he died in 1798 he had written 4,545 pages of his memoirs, *Histoire de ma vie*, and was only up to the summer of 1774.

But Casanova did have one child that he could not forget. During the course of his travels he arrived in Naples in 1761 to take advantage of the hospitality of the Duke of Matalona, whom he had met at a party. He was introduced to the duke's sixteen-year-old mistress, Leonilda, and was so taken with her that, uncharacteristically, he proposed. Leonilda accepted, and all that remained was for her mother to make the daylong journey into Naples to sign the marriage contract.

Casanova was out when Leonilda's mother arrived. He entered his rooms at the duke's palace only to see the woman gasp and faint. Then he recognized her: it was Donna Lucrezia, whom he had loved in Rome in 1744. When she recovered, Lucrezia informed Casanova that his fiancée was also his daughter. "The sudden transition I had to make from carnal to fatherly love caused all my moral and physical faculties the deepest distress," allowed Casanova in his memoirs.

Casanova swore to Lucrezia that he had not slept with Leonilda. Whereupon Lucrezia invited Casanova to join both of them for the night. According to Casanova's fairly graphic memoirs—which were not published uncensored until 1960—he made love to his former lover but did not go as far with his daughter.

At least not that night. Nine years later, Casanova learned that Lucrezia was living in Salerno with their daughter, who had married a marquis. The marquis was sixty years old and concerned that he had no heir. So Casanova, who reasoned that just because Leonilda had been born the appropriate number of months after his affair with her mother didn't necessarily mean that he was her father, obliged Leonilda, and the next year she gave birth to a son.

Casanova apparently met the boy—his son and probably his grandson, who by then had inherited the marquis's title—in Prague at the coronation of Leopold II in 1791. What they said to each other has not been preserved. By that time Casanova's footloose days were over. Ailing and too old to charm his way into new fortunes, Casanova had become a librarian for a count in Bohemia. It was out of boredom with his job that he wrote his memoirs, and his life became legendary.

SON of CATHERINE THE GREAT

THOUGH LEGENDARY in many ways, Catherine the Great is not remembered for having been a good mother. In fact, for all of her lovers, it is not clear exactly how many times the Russian empress gave birth, or who all the fathers were. She is known for certain to have had three children—including two illegitimate, a girl who died in infancy and a son raised by foster parents—but she may have had a few more and several miscarriages. Her only child recognized as legitimate was Paul, but even he may not have been fathered by Catherine's husband, Peter III.

Legitimate or not, Paul was snatched from the birthing room by the reigning Empress Elizabeth, his great-aunt. Since Paul was heir to the throne after Peter—and had more right to it than Catherine, who had only married into the Romanov family—Elizabeth took full charge of the young heir and never even allowed Catherine to visit the boy alone. So when Elizabeth died in 1762 and Catherine staged a coup to kill Peter, she had little motherly interest in preserving the Romanov lineage by installing Paul on the throne. Rather, she did all she could to prevent his rise to power and instead consolidated her own.

Paul, trained by his tutors to rule Russia, couldn't even get his mother to discuss official matters of state with him as he grew older. When Catherine became annoyed with his nagging, she sent him and his wife on a fourteen-month tour of Europe. "We have not even been allowed to choose our own cooks!" Paul whined in 1781. When they returned, Catherine gave Paul Gatchina, an isolated estate fifty miles from Petersburg. Desperate for something to do, Paul created his own little kingdom there. He built his own army, made up of 160 outcasts from the Russian Army, and employed engineers and ballistics experts to help him stage military maneuvers and parades. "Let him enjoy his dolls," Catherine said.

At Gatchina, Paul lost his mind. Having grown up frustrated and suspicious that his mother might do away with him as she had with his father, Paul became moody, paranoid about plots, and subject to wild outbursts. He was worried, rightly, that Catherine was planning to pass him over and name his oldest son, Alexander, as her heir. Catherine had raised Alexander just as Elizabeth had raised Paul. And as Paul's temper grew more erratic, Catherine prepared to formalize Alexander's ascendancy. She had planned to snub Paul officially on January 1, 1797. But she died of a stroke two months before then.

Finally seeing the throne within his grasp, at the age of forty-two, Paul rushed into Petersburg with his Gatchina troops and claimed the palace. For his special revenge, he had the coffin of Peter III exhumed and buried next to Catherine. Almost over-night, he tried to wipe out his mother's legacy. He mobilized a 300-man fashion police who seized men's round hats and cut off their coat collars. Square-toed shoes were to replace boots, Paul ordered, and all traffic had to stop for the night at 9:00 P.M. He fired important government officials at whim, only to reinstate them a few days or months later. "Here is your law," said Paul, pointing at his head.

By 1801, everyone from his leading aides to the British ambassa-dor was conspiring to dethrone Paul. Even Alexander acceded to the plan after he was assured that his father would not be killed. Just before midnight on March 22, twelve officers broke into Paul's bedroom, where they found the barefoot tsar in a nightshirt. At first, they just asked Paul to sign a statement of abdication. But then one officer struck Paul in his temple with the sharp corner of a gold snuff box. More officers jumped on the ruler and strangled him with a scarf.

It was announced that Paul had died suddenly of a stroke, a lie that was not officially recanted until after the Russian Revolution. Alexander took the throne and caused crowds to celebrate in the streets when he announced he would reign "in the spirit and fol-lowing the heart of his grandmother." Catherine hadn't been able to keep her son off the throne, but by destroying his sanity she did manage to prevent him from remaining there for very long.

CHILDREN of CHARLEMAGNE

ACCORDING TO LEGEND, here is how Charlemagne, who ruled much of western Europe from 768 to 814, became a liberal father. It happened one night when his second daughter, Bertha, was visited by her lover, a scholar in Charlemagne's court. By morning it had snowed, so Bertha, not wanting a man's footprints to be seen leaving her apartments, carried him on her back to his own house. Charlemagne, who had had his apartments situated just so he could see all who came and went from the palace, spotted his daughter with the load on her back. Soon after, the king built a house for his daughter and her lover to live openly together.

It was, after all, Charlemagne's fault that Bertha didn't marry the man. Einhard, in his famous biography, *Life of Charlemagne*, explains that Charlemagne wouldn't allow his five daughters to marry because, "He said he could not part with their company." But it wasn't love that the powerful Frankish ruler cherished. What Charlemagne, who also was crowned the first Holy Roman Emperor, couldn't part with was his acquisitions. To marry off his daughters meant giving away sizable dowries as well. Then, too, it meant contending with sons-in-law who might compete with his own three sons for a share of his throne.

Also, because Charlemagne controlled Europe from Rome to Denmark, and from northern Spain to Bavaria, there were few marital alliances that carried enough political benefit to be worthwhile. Charlemagne did promise his oldest daughter, eight-year-old Rotrud, to the ten-year-old Byzantine emperor, but only long enough to keep that powerful eastern state at bay while Charlemagne captured some northern territories.

So Charlemagne, who had five wives, eight legitimate children, and as many as ten illegitimate ones, ended up allowing, even encouraging, his daughters to have affairs. Bertha had two bastard children and Rotrud had a bastard son who became an abbot.

But his daughters' convenient arrangements came to a sudden end after Charlemagne died in 814. The ruler had planned to divide his vast kingdom among his three legitimate sons. But his oldest two sons died before he did, leaving only Louis of Aquitaine to succeed him. Unfortunately, Louis was the least competent of Charlemagne's heirs. He was less interested in ruling the empire than in becoming a monk, and hence was called Louis the Pious. Among his first acts was to send all his sisters to nunneries. Louis also banished Charlemagne's four mistresses and three illegitimate sons, who had lived at court. But he never could match his father's power. The nobles and even Louis's own children rebelled, and within a generation, Charlemagne's empire had crumbled.

CHILDREN of
KING CHRISTIAN IX OF DENMARK

HERE'S A MAN who provided for his kids. Christian IX was King of Denmark from 1863 to 1908, a time by which that nation had long passed its prime. Though once Denmark had controlled the largest kingdom in Europe, including all of Scandinavia, Christian IX ascended the throne of a country that had been reduced by wars to one peninsula and a bunch of scattered islands at the mouth of the Baltic Sea. A year after he was crowned he lost even more territory in a war with Prussia, and it was clear that Denmark had become merely a pawn in the clashes between Europe's greater powers.

With his own citizens clamoring for sweeping restrictions on his monarchy, King Christian's royal future did not look bright, and prospects were even dimmer for his six children. But what his country couldn't do on the battlefield, Christian IX accomplished with wedding bells. It is the tradition of royalty to marry each other, and Christian IX invoked that tradition with élan.

A few months before Christian became king, his oldest daughter, Alexandra, married England's Prince of Wales, who later became King Edward VII. His second daughter, Dagmar, married the man who later became Russia's Tsar Alexander III; she was the mother of the ill-fated Nicholas II. As grandchildren arrived, the Danish royal family's Fredensborg Palace became a center of the European court when Christian held family reunions, which looked like summits.

Christian also did well by his older sons. By agreement with the European powers, his son Vilhelm was named King George of Greece in 1863 and he ruled for fifty years. Christian's oldest son, Frederick, followed him on the Danish throne and that line still is maintained today by his great-great-granddaughter, Queen Margrethe II. Christian's two youngest children married a duke and a princess, respectively. One of Christian's grandsons, meanwhile, was elected King Haakon VII of Norway.

For a man whose family business was in decline, King Christian IX certainly earned the title by which he is remembered: "Father-in-law of Europe."

SON of WINSTON CHURCHILL

"WHEN YOU ARE LIVING under the shadow of a great oak tree, the small sapling, so close to the parent tree, does not perhaps receive enough sunshine." So observed the only son of Winston Churchill, though in Randolph's case a lack of exposure was never the problem. Randolph Churchill, the scion of one of the most prominent and enduring families in Great Britain, who made his first appearance in the society pages as a cute four-year-old page boy in the wedding of the prime minister's daughter, who met the pope when he was a teenager, and who spent Christmases at Blenheim Palace, never doubted the stature he would achieve.

"If anyone had said to me that I wouldn't get into the House of Commons by the time I was 21, or immediately afterwards, I would have thought them absolutely too ridiculous for words," he once said. His famous father felt the same way. "He comes from an important political family. There's been two before—Pitt the Elder and Pitt the Younger—but never three," said Winston, referring to his father, Lord Randolph, and his son at Eton. "He's going to be a great man."

Fortunately, Winston was more perceptive as a leader than as a father. Of Churchill's four adult children, none inherited his prominence and three led troubled lives. His oldest daughter, Diana, committed suicide in 1963, when Churchill was eighty-eight. Sarah, a younger sister of Randolph, had a minor Hollywood career that included a dance with Fred Astaire in *Royal Wedding*, but she was better remembered for a series of widely reported arrests in California and England for public drunkenness in the late 1950s and early 1960s.

So it was clearly Randolph on whom the mantle was to fall. He grew up, by all accounts, spoiled and ill-behaved. Even his silver-spooned classmates thought him too big for his britches. But his father never was too concerned about his son's precociousness and encouraged the young boy to join in after-dinner political discussions with prominent leaders. Randolph was just eighteen when he made his first campaign speech for his father and only a year later—against his father's wishes—left Oxford and embarked on a speaking tour of the United States. Randolph spoke off the cuff and had little to say, but Americans gave him a grand reception as the son of his famous dad.

When he returned to England, Randolph didn't go back to school; instead, he wrote magazine articles, showed up frequently in the society pages, and waited to turn twenty-one. He criticized his nation's elder leaders for not stepping aside and letting his generation take over. That prompted one London newspaper to write, "History proves almost indisputably that major fathers as a rule breed minor sons, so our little London peacocks had better tone down their feathers and start trying to make a name of their own."

Finally in 1935, at the age of twenty-four and behind schedule, Randolph sought a seat in Parliament. It was a by-election and Randolph was not the choice of his own Conservative Party. Despite his father's strong support, Randolph came in third, splitting the Conservative vote and allowing the Labour Party to win the seat. Over the next fifteen years, he lost six parliamentary elections, winning only once in 1940, a few months after his father became prime minister. After his last loss in 1950, Randolph said he realized, "I could do nothing while he [Winston] is alive."

That was an ominous pronouncement, since Winston lived to be ninety-one. And in those last years, Randolph, who never outgrew his youthful leaning toward drunkenness and excess, grew overweight and balding and looked more like Winston's only slightly younger brother. In 1963 Randolph eagerly studied hard for an appearance on the American television game show "The $64,000 Question." He was embarrassingly stumped on the first question when he didn't know that the word "boycott" came from the name of an Englishman.

At his father's request, Randolph had begun writing the biography of the famous prime minister in 1961. He had written other books, but this work, which he planned to fill five volumes, clearly was more important not just as a record of his father's life but also as his own redemption. The first volume, published in 1966 after Winston's death and when Randolph himself was in declining health, was well-received. His second volume also won praise when it was issued a year later. That volume, titled *The Young Statesman,* covered Winston's life from the age of sixteen to thirty, by which time his political career already had far outdistanced his son's future path.

There would be no third volume. Randolph, alone since his second divorce in 1961, died at his country home outside London on June 6, 1968, at the age of fifty-seven. His secretary found him lying on the floor of his bedroom in the morning. He had been bedridden for some time, suffering from cirrhosis of the liver, which had been caused by heavy drinking.

Even in death, Randolph Churchill was overshadowed, this time by the assassination of Robert F. Kennedy the same day. Noted Cyrus Sulzberger: "Poor Randolph Churchill died today, as always a footnote."

SON of GROVER CLEVELAND

PRESIDENT GROVER CLEVELAND was a man of many firsts. He has been the only man to win the presidency, lose it the next term and then win it back four years after that, making him the twenty-second (1884) and the twenty-fourth (1892) president. He also was the first president to get married in the White House and the first to have a child born there. But perhaps Cleveland's most un-precedented achievement was to be the first man to win a presi-dential campaign even after it was revealed that he had an illegiti-mate child.

"Ma! Ma! Where's my pa? Gone to the White House, Ha! Ha! Ha!" So went the ridiculing campaign slogan of Cleveland's oppo-nents in 1884 after the *Buffalo Evening Telegraph*, one of Cleve-land's hometown newspapers, published "A Terrible Tale," that told of Cleveland's wayward affair with a widow back when he was sheriff of Erie County. Ironically, the Democrats had nomi-nated Cleveland, the popular reform governor of New York, be-cause they wanted a squeaky-clean candidate to oppose the allega-tion-plagued Republican James G. Blaine. After the scandal was published in July 1884, Cleveland telegraphed his top supporters, "Above all, tell the truth."

The truth was that the stout, thick-necked bachelor, son of a Presbyterian minister, had kept company with a young widowed mother of two who worked in a Buffalo dry-goods store as head of the cloak department. In 1874, when Maria Halpin was thirty-six and Cleveland was thirty-seven, she gave birth to a boy. She named him Oscar Folsom Cleveland, which was a double blow, because Oscar Folsom was Cleveland's law partner. Cleveland didn't deny that he could have been the father, but claimed that others might have been as well. Still, he arranged to support the child though he didn't see him.

By 1876, Halpin had developed a drinking problem and reportedly was neglecting her baby. Cleveland, through a friend who was a county judge, had Halpin committed to an asylum and had the baby placed in the Protestant Orphanage Asylum for five dollars a week, which he paid. Halpin later tried to get her baby back, but Cleveland's friend the judge denied the request and the child was adopted by a wealthy family in western New York. Cleveland never was in contact with his first son, who grew up to become a prominent physician.

When the tale was told during the presidential campaign, Cleveland remained publicly silent on the matter. Instead, he met with influential religious leaders, confessed his sin, and won their support. "After the primary offense," wrote the Rev. Kinsley Twining, a powerful minister, "which is not to be palliated in the circle for which I write, his conduct was singularly honorable, showing no attempt to evade responsibility, and doing all he could to meet the duties involved, of which marriage was certainly not one."

Many newspapers, in fact, declined to report the story at all, and by the time of the election four months later the issue was not even mentioned. Cleveland married Folsom's daughter, Frances, in 1886. She was twenty-two and he was forty-nine. They had their first child five years later and their last in 1903 when Cleveland was sixty-six. By then he had retired to Princeton, where he served on the Board of Trustees, wrote articles on fishing, and died of a stomach ailment in 1908.

CHILDREN of CONFUCIUS

WHEN CONFUCIUS DIED almost twenty-five hundred years ago, it seemed his family tree would wither faster than his philosophy, which had only taken root among a few devoted disciples. The philosopher, a self-educated orphan who wearily traveled China advocating the traditional Chinese way of life, survived all three of his children and never did fulfill his lifelong search for a government post where he could demonstrate his teachings. His ideas, of course, eventually took hold all over China and much of the rest of the Far East. But what may be just as amazing is that there are still those today who can claim to be the children of Confucius— albeit many, many, many times removed—continuing a family line, which, according to some, can be traced back 2,000 years to the Chinese emperor Huang Tu.

Confucius's only son, Po-Yu, was not one of his better students and had died in 483 B.C., four years before the seventy-two-year-old Confucius. Confucius then adopted Po-Yu's only son, and the grandson became his youngest disciple, assuring his aging grandfather, "You have split the firewood, and I will carry it in." In terms of the family, so he did. Said author Carl Crow in 1937, "With the marriage of the grandson, the descendants of this attenuated line prospered and multiplied like fertile mustard seeds and are now numbered by the tens of thousands." He added, "Though they have engaged in many occupations, it is said that none has ever become a Buddhist priest."

Another author, H. G. Creel, in 1949 found one K'ung Te-ch'eng, "the direct descendent of Confucius in the seventy-seventh generation, who is charged by the Chinese government with the function of maintaining the sacrifices to Confucius." But 1949 also was the year that the Confucian classics were replaced by *Quotations from Chairman Mao*. Confucius, to the Communists, was "a representative of the slave-owning feudal class." So presumably being a member of the seventy-eighth or seventy-ninth generation doesn't carry the prestige of some of the previous descendants.

CHILDREN of JOAN CRAWFORD

HELL HATH NO FURY like a scorned child with a book contract. Joan Crawford, one of Hollywood's most glamorous leading ladies for more than forty years, will, as a result of a shocking book by her adopted daughter Christina perhaps forever be remembered as "Mommie Dearest," the mother who hated wire coat hangers. The star, who in the 1940s was named "America's Most Glamorous Mother," was described in 1978 by her adopted son, Chris, as "the bitch."

Crawford, who won an Oscar for *Mildred Pierce* and acclaim for *What Ever Happened to Baby Jane?* and many other films, had always had a reputation as a driven star. But she deftly softened her hard image by adopting four orphans after she suffered two miscarriages and was told she couldn't bear children of her own. "I don't remember so much happiness coming into my life in one small bundle," she told reporters when she adopted infant Christina in 1939 just after her second divorce. At first, Christina recalls in her book, Crawford lavished her with attention, bathing her, taking her everywhere and even saving her hair when it was cut. But by the time Christina was four or five, Crawford was spanking her so hard that she broke three hairbrushes.

Crawford ran a severely strict household. Her children—she adopted Chris (named Phillip Jr. until she divorced her third husband) in 1943, and two girls in 1947 that she called twins even though they weren't even sisters—were allowed exactly thirty minutes for meals. They were forbidden to get out of bed during the night, even to go to the bathroom, and Chris was strapped to the four corners of his bed for much of his childhood. As Crawford's film career floundered in the 1940s, she began drinking and went into uncontrollable rages. On one night, now infamous, Christina said her mother tore apart the child's bedroom after she found wire hangers in the closet. Another night Crawford chopped down all the rosebushes and an orange tree and made Christina and the cook haul away the debris.

Meanwhile, Crawford would parade her children in front of the cameras as they opened their Christmas presents—most of which they would never see again—or celebrated their birthdays. "There were times," said Christina, "when I just wanted to scream that it was all a fake. There really was no Christmas and this was all a scene from another movie starring Joan Crawford and her four lovely children." Yet Crawford managed to sound like a concerned mother when she told one interviewer, "It is not easy to discipline her, but I am forced to, when she insists on doing things her own way. I find punishing her by hurting her dignity is very effective."

Though it was not mentioned in the press, Crawford's abuse was something of an open secret in Hollywood. Cesar Romero once told her, "My God, Joan, why don't you ease up? They're only kids." "They're only kids!" Crawford barked back. "Well, I was a kid once, and I didn't have a damn thing. Those kids are going to appreciate everything they get."

Crawford's cruelty continued even after she sent Christina and Chris away to boarding schools. Because Chris ran away several times and was sent to juvenile hall at the age of fifteen, Crawford refused to see him for the last nineteen years of her life. Christina said she and her mother continued their stormy relationship until Crawford died of a heart attack in her New York apartment in 1977 at the age of seventy-three. Then, Crawford got in her last word when her will was read. "It is my intention to make no provision herein for my son Christopher or my daughter Christina for reasons which are well known to them." Crawford left the bulk of her fortune, some $2 million, to charity, and gave her two younger daughters, Cathy and Cynthia, each $77,500 in a trust that they would receive over twenty years. At the time Christina's book was published both girls were married and had two children each and they strongly denied Christina's charges. "Our childhood, our feelings and memories of our mother are in complete contrast to those described in Christina's manuscript. Her twisted lies should not be given credence."

But the last word truly belonged to Christina. *Mommie Dearest*, published in 1978, sold over 500,000 copies in hardback and another 3 million in paperback. A successful movie version, starring Faye Dunaway, reinforced Crawford's new image in 1981. Christina, a former actress who also worked in public relations, earned more than $1 million from the book and movie rights. She and her brother, a lineman for a Long Island electric company, also sued for a share in the will. In a settlement in 1979, each received $55,000 from their dear mother's estate.

SON of OLIVER CROMWELL

HAD RICHARD CROMWELL been more like his father, there might be no Queen Elizabeth II or any other member of the Windsor family in Buckingham Palace. Instead we might be keeping up with the descendants of Oliver Cromwell, who ruled England from 1653 to 1658 as Lord Protector after he led troops to depose and execute King Charles I. Though he declined to be named king, Cromwell acted a lot like one. His swearing-in ceremony—complete with a purple robe and golden scepter—looked very much like a coronation. Ambassadors addressed Cromwell's daughters as princesses. And since Cromwell had the right to name his own successor, Richard, his oldest surviving son, was treated like the heir to the throne.

But behind his back Richard was given other names. He was called "Queen Dick," "the meek knight," and "Tumble-down Dick," so dubbed because he had so many accidents while he was hunting or playing sports. Cromwell knew his son made a better idle prince than active ruler and he said he would have preferred Richard and his other son, Henry, "to have lived private lives in the country." But as Cromwell's power grew it became clear that his sons, too, would be expected to take on public roles. He counseled Richard to "take heed of an inactive, vain spirit, read Sir Walter Raleigh's history of the world, and endeavor to learn how to manage your own estate." Instead Richard overspent his allowance and mounted massive debts.

Cromwell tried to force Richard to rise to the occasion, appointing him to a parliamentary committee for trade and navigation and naming him chancellor of Oxford. Still, one pamphlet snidely remarked that Richard was "a person well skilled in hawking, hunting, horse-racing, with other sports and pastimes; one whose undertakings, hazards and services for the cause cannot well be numbered or set forth, unless [one includes] the drinking of King Charles', or, as is so commonly spoken, of his father's landlord's health."

When it was first suggested that the title of Lord Protector be made hereditary, Cromwell scoffed, "Who knoweth whether he may beget a fool or a wise man?" But when the fifty-nine-year-old Cromwell suddenly lay dying in September 1658, probably from his recurrent malaria, he named Richard as his successor anyway. After Cromwell died, everyone at first pledged to support his son, and some even called him Richard IV. But Cromwell's claim to power all along had been somewhat of a balancing act, as there were many who wanted to restore the royal family to the throne. Cromwell had ruled because he had the ability to handle Parliament and because he had the support of the army.

Richard had neither. While he didn't do anything glaringly wrong, neither did he do anything to fortify his command. After seven months the army forced Richard to step down. Rather than fight it, Richard simply said, "I will not have a drop of blood spilt for the preservation of my greatness, which is a burden to me." He resigned after Parliament agreed to pay off his debts, which totaled £29,000. "He was on the point of being arrested by his creditors," recorded one official, "who sent the bailiffs even into Whitehall itself to seize him. But he very wisely shut himself up in his cabinet."

Parliament ultimately reneged on Richard's debts, and the former Lord Protector fled to France, leaving his wife and children behind. He lived in Paris under the name John Clarke and, said one writer, "the whole diversion of him there was drawing landscapes and reading books." Richard didn't return to England until 1680, a few years after his wife had died. He wrote to one daughter in 1690, "I have been alone for 30 years, banished and under silence, and my strength and safety is to be retired, quiet and silent."

Richard, who lived to be eighty-five and died in 1712, had done well to leave the country when he did. After Charles II, the son of the executed Charles I, was returned to the throne in 1660, the body of Oliver Cromwell was exhumed from his grave in Westminster Abbey. The man who but for his ineffectual son might have started a new dynasty in England, was posthumously decapitated and his head perched on a pole atop Westminster Hall.

CHILDREN of MARIE CURIE

IT IS A POIGNANT IMAGE: Marie Curie painstakingly sifting through pile upon pile of pitchblende to extract the source of radiation, winning two Nobel prizes for her efforts, and later dying of leukemia and anemia caused by a lifetime of exposure to the substance that made her famous. Just as affecting is that Curie's older daughter followed in her footsteps—every step of the way.

Irène Curie was born in 1897, the year before her parents discovered radium. Marie would leave their lab to nurse her daughter, and despite her long hours of research she made time to bathe Irène and sew her clothes. Curie's father and governesses eventually took over some of the chores, especially after a second daughter, Eve, was born in 1904, the year after Curie and her husband won the Nobel Prize for physics. As her daughters grew older Curie remained attentive to their education, enlisting her fellow professors at the Sorbonne into a teaching cooperative for their children.

While Eve was more interested in playing the piano, Irène embraced her mother's science with her mother's passion. At the age of seventeen she assisted her mother on the battlefields of World War I in operating newly invented X-ray equipment; in 1918 she became her mother's assistant at the Institut du Radium at the University of Paris. "My mother had just as much confidence in me as she had in herself," said Irène, who remembered giving her mother breakfast in bed so they could spend the time discussing their work.

Irène married a lab assistant, Jean-Frédéric Joliot, in 1926, and they began pursuing their own research, much as Curie and her husband had done thirty years before. For their discovery of artificial radiation, the Joliot-Curies won the Nobel Prize for chemistry in 1935, the year after Marie Curie died at the age of sixty-six. She and her husband also discovered the principle of nuclear reactors in 1939, but they hid their research until after the war to prevent Germany from using it. During the war, the Joliot-Curies were active in the French resistance movement and also joined the French Communist Party. That later led to Jean-Frédéric's dismissal as director of the French Atomic Energy Commission during the Cold War of the 1950s.

Like her mother, Irène spent her life working with radioactive elements, often protected by only primitive shields. And like her mother, Irène died of leukemia in 1956 at the age of fifty-eight. Her husband died two years later after complications from hepatitis. Both their children took on the mantle: Hélène, born in 1927, became a nuclear physicist, and Pierre, born in 1932, a biophysicist.

Meanwhile, Eve, who later wrote that her mother's lack of willingness to push her into a science career left her for a time unable to find her own direction, eventually discovered it as a writer and lecturer. She won the National Book Award in 1937 for her biography of her mother and was a war correspondent for several American newspapers during World War II. Eve married Henry Labouisse, who became the U.S. ambassador to Greece. She still lives in New York City.

D

SON of DORIS DAY

IF THEY EVER make a movie about the life of Doris Day, it won't be a typical Doris Day movie. On-screen, Day was wholesomeness personified—her biggest crisis was whether she should do more than kiss her costar, which of course she never did. The ultimate apple-pie-girl-next-door, she was Hollywood's Number One box office star for five straight years in the late 1950s, with a string of hits like *Teacher's Pet* with Clark Gable, *That Touch of Mink* with Cary Grant, and *Pillow Talk*, which earned her an Oscar nomination for making Rock Hudson do the right thing.

But offscreen, the life of Doris von Kappelhoff has been less snowy. As Day revealed in her autobiography in 1975, her first husband, Al Jorden, a trombone player whom she married at seventeen, beat her when she was eight months pregnant. They divorced and Jorden later shot himself in the head while stopped at a red light. Meanwhile, Day's singing career kept her on the road, so her son, Terry (named for Day's favorite comic strip, "Terry and the Pirates"), spent his first seven years with Day's mother in Cincinnati.

Terry joined his mother in Los Angeles after she became a movie star and just before she married her third husband, Marty

Melcher. Terry had fond early memories of Melcher, who was Day's agent and later adopted Terry. But when Terry was in his teens, he said, Melcher beat him and sent him to military school to keep him away from Day, who by then was the top-earning star in Hollywood. "He didn't want me to talk to [my mother]," Terry recalled in Day's book. "He was afraid I might say something that would upset her. He treated her like a patient of some sort. The number one standing order, before 'God is love' or anything else, was, 'Don't upset your mother.' "

Terry quit college after less than a year and took a fifty-dollar-a-week job at the William Morris Agency. He soon became a record producer at Columbia, where he produced seven gold albums for major groups including The Byrds and Paul Revere and the Raiders. Enjoying a sizable income, especially for someone in his mid-twenties, Terry lived with Candice Bergen in a beautiful home, 10050 Cielo Drive, in the Benedict Canyon. Melcher told him, "It makes me sick, a snotty kid to fall into something like this." Partly because of the way Melcher treated her son, Day left him in the 1960s, though he continued to manage her career and business affairs.

After Melcher died of heart disease in 1968 Terry, as executor of his estate, discovered that Melcher had been more than just an unpleasant stepfather. It turned out that Melcher for years had been putting Day's earnings into bad business deals, including shady hotels, oil wells, and cattle. All told, Melcher had lost $20 million and Day was left $500,000 in debt. (In 1974 Day won a $22.8 million judgment against her lawyer, who had worked with Melcher.) Melcher also had signed Day, without her knowledge, to a television series. Terry produced the show, which ran for five years. Because of his mother's financial problems and the time he devoted to her show, Terry gave up his career as a record producer at age twenty-six.

But the real trauma occurred the next year. On August 8, 1969, Charles Manson and his gang slaughtered five people in the house at 10050 Cielo Drive. Terry had sold the house to director Roman Polanski a few months before and was living in his mother's beach house. In the heated investigation to solve the Manson murders, the police told Terry that they believed he was Manson's intended victim, although this later proved to be incorrect. Terry had met Manson several months earlier at the home of Beach Boy Brian Wilson, where Manson was living, and had agreed to listen to some songs Manson had written. Terry said he was unimpressed by Manson's tunes and had made no promises to produce their music. At first, police believed Manson wanted to kill Terry for revenge. "My guilt was monumental," Terry said. "I felt, 'Why couldn't it have been me? How much easier it could have been.'"

Terry and his mother both hired bodyguards. Terry said soon the stress became overwhelming. "What I was striving to be was a person with my own identity, not somebody's son, and I had substantially achieved that; but Marty's death and the Manson murders had turned me into a movie star's son again." Terry said he began drinking heavily and taking pills. He moved to Idyllwild, a remote town in the mountains near Palm Springs. One day while riding his motorcycle he crashed head on into a car, shattering both his legs. After nearly dying from blood clots, Terry spent six months in the hospital and then moved in with his mother. "Although he was 30 years old," Day said, "it was the first time I had really taken care of him."

Terry now lives with his second wife in a house on his mother's estate in Carmel. He produced Day's brief television show in 1985, "Doris Day's Best Friends." He also had restarted his music career and in 1988 he co-wrote the Beach Boys' hit single, "Kokomo." "Over the years, Mom and I have had problems—doesn't everyone in Hollywood?" Terry said a few years ago. "But we've wound up being very close." Just the sort of happy ending a Doris Day movie should have.

CHILDREN of CHARLES DICKENS

MUCH OF THE ACCURATE DETAIL that Charles Dickens captured in portraying the sorry condition of poor children, especially *Oliver Twist*, he knew firsthand. Dickens's writing again and again reflected the hardship of a brief time during his own childhood when his father was sent to debtors prison and Dickens had to work in a blacking warehouse putting the lids on bottles of polish.

Dickens, who also wrote such classics as *David Copperfield* and *A Christmas Carol*, didn't forget those hard times as he raised his own family. He was the father of ten children born between 1837 and 1852—nine of whom survived childhood—and he drove himself to provide for them. He commanded a strict, perfectly ordered household, aided by his spinster sister. He inspected the house every morning for neatness, down to seeing to it that the little knicknacks were in their proper places and positions.

Besides providing for his own brood, Dickens from the beginning of his success as a writer had to support his parents and his brothers and their families. And the weight only grew after he separated from his wife in 1858 and set up his mistress in her own household. Dickens died in 1870 at the age of fifty-eight partly from overwork, as he continued to give public readings even though he had become partially paralyzed during an earlier exhausting tour. For all his worrying, Dickens left a sizable estate—£93,000.

Many of Dickens's children, especially the sons, grew up overwhelmed by their overbearing father. Kate, one of his few children to remain near him in his last years, said, "The only fault I found with my father was that he had too many children." Dickens agreed. "I can't get my hat on in consequence of the extent to which my hair stands on end at the costs and charges of these boys!" wrote the father of seven sons. "Why was I ever a father! Why was my father ever a father!"

Dickens wrote to his sixth son, Henry, who was at Cambridge: "You know how hard I work for what I get, and I think you know that I never had money help from any human creature after I was a child. You know that you are one of many heavy charges on me, and that I trust to your so exercising your abilities and improving the advantages of your past expensive education, as soon to diminish *this* charge." Maybe because of the threat, Henry the next year won a scholarship. Dickens at first barely reacted to his son's proud news. But later, Henry said, Dickens's eyes filled with tears and he said, "God bless you!"

Henry went on to succeed in government and was knighted. But the rest of Dickens's children fared less well. Dickens firmly directed his sons' upbringing, but then was dismayed when they showed such little drive that he felt compelled to arrange jobs for them. His oldest son, Charles, couldn't find work until Dickens got him a job in a bank, which he left after a few years to get involved in tea trading; he went bankrupt, and also failed in a paper-mill venture. Dickens then took him on at his weekly magazine, *All the Year Round*. Charles did fine until his father died, and then the magazine ran into trouble. Charles then invested in a printing plant which also failed. He had a little success giving public readings of his father's works in the United States, but died in 1896 at the age of fifty-nine, leaving his wife and five children penniless.

If Dickens had a favorite it was his youngest son, Edward, whom he affectionately called "Plorn." But when the boy was sixteen, Dickens decided he was unfit to attain any job in England, so he put him through a course in agriculture and then sent the reluctant youth to join one of his older brothers in Australia. He sent two sons to India, one to join the Bengal Mounted Police and the other to Calcutta, where the unfortunate lad met his end. Edward, after first failing in a sheep-farming venture with his brother, was elected to Australia's Parliament despite his recurring financial troubles. He was criticized for taking advantage of his father's name. Edward's reply said much about the entire family: "Sons of great men are usually not as great as their fathers. You cannot get two Charles Dickens in one generation."

E

CHILDREN of MARY BAKER EDDY

FOLLOWERS OF Mary Baker Eddy, the founder of Christian Science, called her "Mother." Religiously, the term was accurate, but personally, it was quite a misnomer. Like so many aspects of this strong-willed New Englander's life, the image didn't mirror the reality. Eddy, who preached the power of prayer to heal, in fact often took morphine to calm her nervous seizures. She professed full faith in God, but regularly blamed her troubles on black magic, hypnotism and MAM—"Malicious Animal Magnetism."

Eddy gave birth to her only child, George, in 1844, when she was twenty-three, soon after her husband of less than one year had died of a sudden fever. Eddy was often ill—it was her delicate health since childhood that eventually led her to take such an interest in healing powers—and she couldn't take care of her child. George at first was raised by Eddy's mother, but after she died when George was four, the boy was sent to live with his former nurse forty miles away. From then on Eddy rarely saw her son and they lost touch completely when the nurse's family moved to Minnesota when George was ten.

They didn't see each other again for twenty-three years, until 1879, by which time the fifty-eight-year-old Eddy was founding her First Church of Christ, Scientist, in Boston. Now married to her third husband, Eddy had little to say to her son. She was living with her followers in Boston boardinghouses, but kept moving from one house to another because of "evil influences" of a former follower. George, who had traveled all the way from the rough Dakota Territory to see her, tracked down the alleged evil-doer, put a gun to his head and told him if his mother moved one more time, "I will search you out and shoot you like a mad dog." They didn't have to move again. Still, George's act didn't bring him closer to his mother.

Eddy next saw her son eight years later when George arrived with his wife and three children despite Eddy's letter telling him not to come. "You are not what I had hoped to find you, and I am wholly changed," she wrote. "When I retire from business into private life then I can receive you if you are *reformed*, but not otherwise." Eddy chastised her son for being nearly illiterate and scolded him for not giving his children a proper education, though she did pay for her grandchildren to get their vaccinations and over the years she reluctantly gave her son money when he asked for it and built him a house. But, even as late as 1908, two years before she died, Eddy wrote to her son, "I am even yet too proud to have you come out among my society."

For all the distance she kept from her son, Eddy clearly wanted a loving and loyal child. As she built her church she often chose one follower, to play that role. It was always a young man who acted as her special assistant. But with all of them, at some point, she would grow disenchanted, and, becoming convinced that they were evil, she would abruptly dismiss them.

Soon after her disappointing visit from George in 1887, Eddy met Dr. Ebenezer Johnson Foster, a homeopathic physician who had enrolled in her Metaphysical College. "Bennie" charmed Eddy so much that she legally adopted the forty-one-year-old man, bought him a fur-lined coat and a diamond ring and also made him her publisher and president of the church. Foster Eddy, as he was then called, traveled with the aging religious leader. He played piano for her and administered her morphine when she had seizures.

But like the rest, Foster fell out of favor with Eddy. Her other followers, some out of jealousy, told her that her adopted son was corrupt and was trying to replace her. In 1894 Eddy fired Foster from his church posts. "You were governed by hypnotism to work against me and yourself and to take me as your authority for so doing," she wrote him. Foster eventually retired to Vermont and lived on the money he had made while working for his adoptive mother. Eddy, unable to find an heir to her liking, arranged that her church would be governed by a board of directors after her death. Meanwhile, she wrote to the man who replaced Foster as president of the church, "My beloved Son, I must call you so at this time, but will try not to often, it would create such envy."

Eddy spent her last years mostly secluded from her church; this enhanced her saintlike image among her followers but caused others to question whether she was in control or even alive. After his *New York World* newspaper published a series of articles in 1906 revealing that the eighty-five-year-old Eddy was very ill and possibly senile, Joseph Pulitzer himself hired a lawyer to try to get Eddy declared incompetent and appoint a guardian to take over her affairs. The lawsuit was joined by Eddy's son, George, and her adopted son, Foster. But Eddy performed well under psychiatric examination and her two sons eventually settled out of court. George got $250,000 while $50,000 went to Foster. When she died in 1910, Eddy left the bulk of her $2 million estate to the child she really cared about, her church.

CHILDREN of THOMAS EDISON

"IF A BOY has ambition, he don't need to go to college," Thomas Edison said eloquently. With just four years of formal education, Edison became a living example of that statement as he changed the world by inventing the light bulb, the phonograph, and the motion-picture camera, to mention three of his 1,093 patents. Edison figured his six children wouldn't need much education either, though in fact he spent so much time in his lab that he paid little attention to their upbringing.

Edison's breakthrough, the electric light bulb, came in 1879, the year after his third child was born. Especially in those early years, Edison would disappear for days at a time into his laboratory to work on his inventions, leaving his children to be indulged by his first wife, about whom Edison said, "My wife Popsy-Wopsy can't invent." Edison's idea of a toy for his two sons and a daughter was an old alarm clock that he would take apart and encourage them to put back together.

After Edison's wife died and he remarried, his three children were sent off to boarding school, where the boys were not happy. (His daughter Marion, unhappy with Edison's second wife, went to school in Germany, married a German army officer, and lived there until after World War I.) Thomas Jr., at the age of sixteen, wrote to his father, "I feel very badly indeed papa so unhappy I dont know what to do. I have failed in every attempt." Later the boy wrote, "I dont believe I will ever be able to talk to you the way I would like to—because you are so far my superior in every way that when I am in your presence I am perfectly helpless."

Thomas Jr. went to work in a machine shop of his father's booming company. But soon he spent more time among the fashionable crowd in New York City, where he traveled on his father's name. Enticed by promises of money and some prestige of his own, Thomas Jr. allowed a group of investors in 1898 to call their company the "Thomas A. Edison Jr. Electric Company." Among the firm's products was a machine for "photographing thought." Later the inventor's son lent his name to the "Edison Junior Chemical Company," which produced the "Electric Vitalizer," designed to "cure anything from catarrh to locomotor ataxia."

Finally in 1904 Edison sued his son's companies for fraud and shut them down. Edison stated publicly that his son had "never shown any ability as an inventor or electrical expert," and was "incapable of making any invention or discovery of merit." Edison later gave his son a job in his company and bought him a farm. Thomas Jr., who had drinking problems off and on, committed suicide in 1935 at the age of sixty, four years after his father's death.

Edison's second son by his first marriage was scarcely more successful. He frequently obtained money from his father to start businesses—dog breeding, bird raising, a car dealership—that soon failed. Said William, "It's a mighty proud thing to be the son of so great a man but not a happy proposition." Between ventures Edison gave William and his wife an allowance of forty dollars a week. It was William's wife, Blanche, who wrote to Edison, "Do you realize that we are the children of 'The Greatest Man of the Century'—and for them to live, as they should, upon an income of forty dollars per week, takes very much more ability than I can display." Edison replied, "Let your husband earn money like I did." William, who also lived on a farm bought by his father, died of cancer in 1937 at the age of fifty-eight.

While Edison's first three children grew up without a mother or much of a father, his second wife, Mina, kept a firm hand on his second set of three. She insisted that her oldest son, Charles, spend time with Edison, so the boy washed out bottles in Edison's lab. She sent all three children to college: Madeleine, the oldest, went to Bryn Mawr, Charles and Theodore went to MIT, though Charles enjoyed too many parties and dropped out. Still, Charles's mother pushed him up through the ranks of Edison's company so that in 1918 he was named chairman of the board. He gradually took over more responsibilities and finally succeeded his father when he retired in 1927. He went on to work in FDR's administration and was elected governor of New Jersey in 1940.

His brother Theodore was more studious, much to Edison's dismay. "Theodore is a good boy," Edison said, "but his forte is mathematics. I am a little afraid . . . he may go flying off into the clouds with that fellow Einstein. And if he does . . . I'm afraid he won't work with me." Theodore did work for Edison's company, though it was in a separate lab where he could do his own research.

Edison left the bulk of his estate to Charles and Theodore, which prompted William and Madeleine to contest the will. Madeleine felt slighted, since she had been his only child to produce grandchildren. The fact that five of the inventor's six children chose to discontinue their lines of the family surely says something about the parenting skills of their father.

CHILDREN of ALBERT EINSTEIN

You may not often think of Albert Einstein as a babysitter, but here's how one student remembered the century's most important scientist: "He was sitting in his study in front of a heap of papers covered with mathematical formulae. Writing with his right hand and holding his younger son in his left, he kept replying to questions from his elder son Albert who was playing with his bricks. With the words, 'Wait a minute, I've nearly finished,' he gave me the children to look after for a few moments and went on working."

In other words, Einstein's Theory of Relativity, which he introduced in 1905 as the twenty-six-year-old father of an infant son, may have been shown to others covered with baby spittle. It was not unusual to see the revolutionary scientist walking a baby carriage in Bern or Prague and stopping to write down mathematical equations. For the man considered the quintessential absent-minded professor, Einstein was remembered by his son as an attentive father—when he wanted to be. "He would tell us stories," said Hans Albert in 1951. "He often played his violin in an effort to make us quiet. But I also recall my mother saying that even the loudest baby crying didn't seem to disturb father. He could go on with his work completely impervious to noise."

Einstein himself acknowledged his absorption in his work. "I am a horse for a single harness," he said, "not cut out for tandem or team work. I have never belonged wholeheartedly to country or state, to my circle of friends, or even to my own family. These ties have always been accompanied by a vague aloofness and the wish to withdraw into myself increases with the years."

His preoccupation with science ended his first marriage, though Einstein said later it was the bad marriage that caused him to work so hard on his theories. His wife, Mileva, left him in 1914 when he was studying in Berlin and World War I broke out. She took their two sons to Switzerland, but after the war the couple did not reunite and they divorced officially in 1919. Einstein married his second cousin soon after, and had no other children.

By the time his parents divorced, Hans Albert was studying to be a scientist on his own. He said later he never felt overshadowed by his father, who won a Nobel Prize in 1921. "It would have been nerve-wracking if, early in life, I didn't learn how to laugh off the bother of it," Hans Albert said. "Probably the only project he ever gave up on was me. He tried to give me advice, but he soon discovered that I was too stubborn and that he was just wasting his time." Einstein fled Europe in 1933 when Hitler came to power, and Hans Albert followed his father to the United States in 1938. He was a professor of hydraulic engineering at the University of California at Berkeley from 1947 to 1971 and he died two years later of a heart attack at the age of sixty-nine.

Einstein's younger son, however, had a much more difficult time. Eduard was only four when his parents separated and nine when they divorced. Growing up in Zurich, Eduard rarely saw his father, who lived in Berlin, and friends said he took after his mother, whose melancholy had been part of the reason his parents had divorced. Eduard was a talented pianist and ambitiously studied psychiatry and medicine. But in his teens, his letters to his father turned from those of an admiring and eager-to-please son, into angry, bitter accusations of Einstein's neglect.

Eduard suffered a nervous breakdown in 1929. He was diagnosed as schizophrenic, and psychiatric treatment didn't seem to help. Einstein visited his son, and his second wife later wrote, "The sorrow is eating up Albert. He finds it difficult to cope with, more difficult than he would care to admit. He has always aimed at being invulnerable to everything that concerned him personally. He really is so, much more than any other man I know. But this has hit him very hard."

When Einstein left Europe in 1933, he left Eduard behind and never saw him again. Eduard was cared for by Mileva until she died in 1948. He was institutionalized in Zurich and died there in 1965—ten years after Einstein—at the age of fifty-five.

F

CHILDREN of W. C. FIELDS

W. C. FIELDS played a lot of funny men, but the role he got the most mileage out of was that of a henpecked husband besieged by his wife and bratty children. Fields believed he had similar troubles offscreen, though in fact he traveled so much that most of his domestic torment was limited to the mail. He never divorced his wife, a chorus girl he had married in 1900 on the vaudeville circuit, but neither did he see her more than a few times a year and he often told reporters he was single. Still, Fields felt hounded enough to write to his wife in 1944, "Can you imagine my surprise when I read your letter and you said we had gone through life doing nothing for each other? Sixty smackers a week, year in and year out, for 40 years ($124,800.00) you consider nothing. Heighho-lackady. Surprises never cease."

Fields's letters to his only legitimate son—born in 1904—were more considerate, but W. C. Fields, Jr., known as Claude, didn't see his father much more than his mother. "Give all my love to my son and have him write me an occasional line," Fields would write in a letter to his wife. But as Claude was growing up Fields accused his wife—as in his movies—of turning the boy against him. Only after Claude grew older and became a lawyer did Fields and his son become close (Fields, who ran away from home when he was eleven, said his son should make it on his own as he had and refused to pay for Claude's education). It was Fields who drove Claude's wife home from the hospital when his first grandchild was born while Claude was in the service in World War II. During the ride Fields explained to his daughter-in-law how to drink martinis without tainting your breath.

Fields died in 1946 before he saw most of his five grandchildren. And Claude apparently kept his famous father a secret from his children for several years. One of Fields's grandsons, Ronald, said he didn't know Fields was his grandfather until he saw him in a movie on television when he was twelve. Ronald does remember his father saying to him after a spanking, "You're lucky I'm around to discipline you. When I was your age, my father was never home." Claude died of cancer in 1971 at the age of sixty-six, the same age at which Fields had succumbed to his drinking.

None of Fields's grandchildren went into show business. W. C. Fields III was an FBI agent and now is an attorney for Campbell's Soup. Another grandson also is a lawyer and another is an administrator for a defense contractor in San Diego. Ronald has written a book about his grandfather and gives lectures.

According to some biographies, Fields had another son, illegitimate, this one by a Ziegfeld girl. Fields's later longtime mistress, Carlotta Monti, says the fifteen-year-old boy showed up one day at Fields's home in Los Angeles unannounced. The boy, who Monti said closely resembled Fields, told her he had traveled from Newark and had hitchhiked from Albuquerque after he ran out of money.

"Get rid of the boy," Fields said from upstairs, according to Monti.

"He's your son," Monti told him.

"Only because nature played a hideous trick on me," Fields replied.

The boy went away without seeing his father. Monti said she gave him $10,000 from Fields's will, which was contested on all sides. Fields had intended for the bulk of his $800,000 estate to establish the "W. C. Fields College for Orphan White Boys and Girls, Where No Religion of Any Sort Is to Be Preached." But his wife and Claude, who had been left only $10,000 each, challenged the will and won.

SON of ERROL FLYNN

"I LIKE THE WHISKEY OLD and the women young," said Errol Flynn, sounding very much like the swashbuckling characters he played in the movies. And in many ways, the screen idol's life was as exciting as his best roles in the 1930s, which included *Captain Blood, The Adventures of Robin Hood* and *The Sea Hawk*. Born in Tasmania and a descendant of Fletcher Christian who mutinied on the *Bounty*, Flynn was a troublesome kid who got kicked out of school and worked on the wharves of Sydney and mined gold in New Guinea before he made his way to England and finally to Hollywood in 1934. On-screen he happily performed his own stunts. His devil-may-care good luck made him seem larger than life offscreen too, and his arrest on charges of raping a young girl (of which he was acquitted) led to the phrase "in like Flynn."

All of this had its price. Flynn's drinking, use of drugs, and notorious sexual escapades with both men and women left him frequently ill. He suffered from hemorrhoids, hepatitis, high fevers, sinus attacks, malaria, and a wide variety of infections. In 1959 he died of a heart attack at the age of fifty, financially depleted and physically a wreck. His liver, kidneys, and spleen were shot; he was overweight and he suffered from hardening of the arteries and cancerous lesions on his tongue and throat.

Flynn left behind four children by three marriages. Each marriage suffered from his affairs and from his tendency to abandon his wives when they were pregnant. He divorced his first wife, French actress Lili Damita, a few months after she gave birth to his first child and only son, Sean. Flynn saw little of his son as he moved on to other wives and other children—Lili frequently sued him for alimony and child support—but the movie star did offer his unique brand of parental guidance. When Sean was eight years old, Flynn taught him how to smoke a cigar. When he was twelve, Flynn took him to a whorehouse.

Flynn's daughters took after him in a fashion: Dierdre became a movie stunt woman, and Rory and Arnella became models. But it was Sean who grew up to become his father's son. The strikingly handsome, six-foot-three-inch youth went through military and boarding schools in Palm Beach and Hollywood only to be expelled from Duke University in his freshman year. By the age of twenty he had contracted a venereal disease. "I'm indiscriminate," Sean said. "I love everybody." In another interview that his father could have given twenty years earlier, Sean said, "I like to drive fast cars. I like to live it up with girls. I'm what you might call a hedonist, a young man specializing in pleasure."

At the age of nineteen, Sean starred in *The Son of Captain Blood*, a sequel to his father's famous first big film. It was an inauspicious debut, but Sean said he wasn't sure he wanted to be a movie star anyway. "My mother was in pictures and, of course, so was my dad," he said. "I'd like to do something else, or at least try." A few years later Sean visited his mother in Paris. He became a photographer and was sent to Vietnam for a French magazine, *Paris Match*.

Sean clearly loved the adventure. In 1966 the twenty-four-year-old photographer was involved in a gunfight with Viet Cong soldiers while he was on patrol with a band of Chinese mercenaries. "I don't know if I hit a Viet Cong, but I tried," Sean told the *New York Daily News*. "They were so close you could see the muzzle blasts and the tracers pouring out of the machine gun." That same year he was wounded by shrapnel.

Sean later began taking pictures for *Time* magazine and would commute to battle scenes on a motorcycle. In early 1970, he was based in Pnom Penh, covering the battles on the Cambodian border. On April 6, Sean and a free-lance cameraman, Dana Stone, were looking for action near the village of Chiphou, in the Parrot's Beak region near the South Vietnam border. Villagers later said that Sean and Stone drove within three hundred yards of a Viet Cong checkpoint and then returned, complaining they weren't getting any good pictures. They left the village again that afternoon and were never seen again. Some villagers said they had seen twenty-eight-year-old Sean and Stone being led away by Viet

Cong troops. Three other journalists, a French photographer and two Japanese cameramen, also disappeared that day.

It reads like another of his father's swashbucklers. But in this case, the response from the North Vietnamese as to Sean's fate at the end of the war was very real: "There is only the tiniest chance that he is alive somewhere. No one should hope."

DAUGHTER of WILSON FOLLETT

WHEN BARBARA FOLLETT was nine years old, this is how she described a story she was writing: "It is about a little girl named Eeperorp who lived on top of a mountain, Mount Varcrobis, and was so lonely that she went away to live wild. . . . She talked to the animals, and led a sweet lovely life with them—just the kind of life that I should like to lead. Her parents all tried to catch her, with some friends of theirs, and every time she escaped in some way or other." Three years later, in 1927, Barbara's 40,000-word tale, *The House Without Windows*, was published. One critic called it "the profoundest revelation of a child's fondness for beauty yet in American prose." He called the twelve-year-old author, "a lyric artist."

Though such praise is surely unusual for an author so young, it is less surprising that Barbara would be a writer. Her father, Wilson Follett, was in the middle of a prominent fifty-year career as a writer and editor. Best known for his standard-bearer guide to writing style, *Modern American Usage*, the Harvard-educated Follett also wrote books of literary criticism and edited a twelve-volume collection of the works of Stephen Crane, and his articles appeared in prestige publications such as *Harper's*, *The Atlantic* and *Saturday Review*.

In this environment, Barbara began playing with a typewriter when she was four years old. Follett and his wife were proud of the fact that they kept their daughter out of school and educated her at home. By five she was writing full-length, complex stories. She created a secret language for herself, called "Farksoo," and a fantasy world called "Farksolia." When her first book was published, some called her a genius. Her second book, *The Voyage of the Norman D.*, was published when she was fourteen.

That was the same year that her father moved out. Barbara was devastated. She wrote him, "I depend very much on you, and I trust you to give another heave to the capstan bars, to get the family anchor started toward the surface again. After all, you have the strongest shoulders for heaving us all! And really, you don't want the family anchor to remain forever on the bottom, do you?" Follett never came back, and Barbara broke off contact. She wrote to a friend, "But lest you think I'm becoming very despondent myself of late, let me assure you that this is my normal state of mind, when I allow it to come to the surface. That is, I *always* am grieved at the world."

Barbara's parents apparently did not part amicably. Samuel Marx, story editor at MGM studios in the 1930s, later wrote that Lillian Hellman, then a script reader, one day was looking for Follett, also a script reader, to tell him he had won a literary prize. Follett asked Marx to order Hellman not to divulge his whereabouts to the prize committee. "It isn't worth it to me," Follett told Marx. "You see, I've run away from my wife, who is a dreadful termagant. You may be able to understand how I feel about her when I say that in order to be free, I have had to abandon my daughter. But I will never go back. I am living with my former secretary and we are very happy. The [script] reading department provides me with a marvelous refuge because my wife is still looking for me but has no idea where I am." (Hellman later wrote in one of her memoirs, "I knew the girl he had run away with and the fact that she was an ugly girl somehow made the whole story more interesting.")

Barbara, after spending two years traveling the South Pacific with her mother, returned at the age of eighteen and met a young man at a college in Vermont. She stopped writing to her mother and lived with her boyfriend in the New England mountains, camping along the Appalachian Trail. They sailed to Spain and camped in Europe for a while, then returned to Boston, where they were married in 1934, when Barbara was twenty. No longer writing much, Barbara worked as a stenographer and a secretary. She again saw her father, who was now remarried and had new children, and she became a member of a dance group.

In 1939, Barbara's husband told her he was having an affair. She was living alone in an apartment in Brookline when she went out on the afternoon of December 7 and disappeared forever.

Follett refused to believe that his daughter was dead. He wrote a long article for *The Atlantic Monthly* in 1941 entitled "To a Daughter, One Year Lost," which he signed only "From her father." "Did you not leave us because life had come to seem to you unbearably like a promissory note that is perpetually renewed?" he wrote, adding later, "Do not imagine for a minute that I have not had to face and to live with everything that luckier moralists have ever said about the children of divorce."

Follett begged his daughter at least to send some word that she was alive and well. Barbara never sent it. And if, in fact, she did not die soon after she disappeared in the winter in 1939, perhaps she left her clue in one of her last stories, written years before, called "Lost Island."

She wrote: "Jane laughed again, but there was a gleam of danger in her eye. Sometime, not too far off, she would stage another rebellion. It would not be the same kind of rebellion, though. One could never repeat the real adventures. That was why so many people were unhappy, she reflected. They tried to go back and repeat the things that had made them happy before. . . . If only they had the courage to push on, forward, over deserts and swamps and glaciers, they would sometime make new discoveries as bright as the others, or even brighter, perhaps."

SON of BENJAMIN FRANKLIN

WITH CHARACTERISTIC good nature, Benjamin Franklin had this philosophy on raising his son, William: "Pray let him have everything he likes. I think it of great consequence, while the features of the countenance are forming. It gives them a pleasant air and, that being once become natural and fixed by habit, the face is ever handsomer for it, and on that much of a person's good fortune and success in life may depend." Nice though his sentiment was, the Founding Father probably altered his view on child-rearing once his son grew up to become one of the leading Tories of the American Revolution.

William Franklin was illegitimate, though his father never admitted it and the mother's identity remains unknown. The boy was raised by Franklin and his common-law wife, Deborah, whom Franklin couldn't marry legally because she already was married to a man who had left her. Franklin and Deborah had two children, a son who died of smallpox at the age of four, and a daughter, Sarah.

But it was William whom Franklin treasured, so much so that it made Deborah jealous. William was there when Franklin flew his famous kite in 1752. When Franklin was elected to the Pennsylvania Assembly, he made William clerk of the assembly. And when Franklin was appointed deputy postmaster general of North America, he named his son postmaster of Philadelphia. Together the two men—Franklin nearly fifty, William half that age—organized troops to fight Indians in 1755.

Franklin also took his son with him to England when he had to settle some colonial disputes. They ended up staying five years, during which William studied law and was called to the English bar in 1758. Like his father, William also fathered an illegitimate son, William Temple Franklin, in 1759. Meanwhile, the longer William stayed in London, the more he enjoyed his aristocratic friends, much to his father's dismay. When William married the daughter of a wealthy Barbados sugar planter in 1762, Franklin was so disgusted he left England a few weeks before the wedding.

Franklin was further annoyed when William had himself appointed royal governor of the New Jersey colony, though it wasn't the post that bothered Franklin as much as that his son had gotten the job without his help. Still, Franklin and his son maintained an affectionate relationship, writing each other long gossipy letters between William's New Jersey governor's mansion and Franklin's home in London, where he was the royal agent for New Jersey as well as four other colonies.

But as tension mounted between those colonies and England, the warm correspondence between Franklin and his son hardened into debates over colonial rights. Franklin became outspoken in London on behalf of those rights, while William was pressured by the Crown to hold the line in his colony. And as Franklin raised England's ire, William found himself having to answer for it. "The truth of the matter is, having been disappointed in his late attempts to injure my father, the colonial secretary is now endeavouring to hurt him through me," William wrote in 1771. "He has no reason (other than the natural connection between us) to imagine that I entertain the same political opinions with my father."

Franklin urged his son to resign as royal governor, and as he sailed back from England to escape arrest in 1775 he wrote his son a 196-page letter detailing why. Instead, William clung to his post longer than any other royal governor. He also was the last royal governor to keep sending intelligence dispatches to England, many of which were intercepted and published.

William, at no small physical risk, visited Franklin in Philadelphia during the Second Continental Congress in 1775. William had been promoting a compromise to some of the rebel leaders, but his father, at this late hour, would have none of it. The meeting was not successful and it was the last they spoke until after the war. Late that year, Franklin disinherited William and left everything to his daughter and her husband. "I have lost my son," he wrote.

In June 1776 William was arrested after he called his colonial assembly into session to try to dissaude their support for the pending Declaration of Independence. At first Franklin's son was put under house arrest in Connecticut. But after it was discovered that he was still sending intelligence reports to the British, William was sent to Litchfield Prison, one of the most horrible jails of the time. He was kept in a tiny, unfurnished, filthy cell, given little food and harassed by guards and rebels outside. He was not allowed to leave when his wife died. Franklin probably could have gotten his son released or at least held under better conditions. Instead he left for a diplomatic mission to France, taking William's son, Temple, with him.

Only when he was near death was William moved to better quarters at the end of 1777. A year later he was released and he imediately began trying to rally Loyalist support for the British. As the war neared its end in 1782, William finally fled to London. There he lobbied with British leaders to negotiate a peace treaty that protected the Loyalists, even as Franklin, representing the colonies, was refusing to allow such protections.

Finally in 1784, for the first time in nine years, William in London wrote to his father in Paris, asking if they could begin corresponding again. Franklin replied, "It would be very agreeable to me. Indeed, nothing has ever hurt me so much and affected me with such keen sensibilities as to find myself deserted in my old age by my only son." But he went on, "There are natural duties which precede political ones, and cannot be extinguished by them. This is a disagreeable subject: I drop it."

Franklin saw his son one final time before the ailing elder statesman returned to America in 1785. The meeting was civil at best. And when he died in 1790, Franklin's will stated, "The part he acted against me in the late war, which is of public notoriety, will account for my leaving him no more of an estate he endeavored to deprive me of."

William lived out his life in exile in England. He married a rich wife and was given a British military half-pension, though he still tried in vain to regain his American properties until he died in 1813. Meanwhile, Temple, who under Franklin's influence had

begun studying law in Philadelphia, gave up his books and returned to England, where he moved in with his father and stepmother. Like the elder Franklins, Temple fathered an illegitimate
daughter, by his stepmother's younger sister. Temple later left
them for Paris. William, like his father, disinherited his son.

DESCENDANTS of
EMPEROR FRANZ JOSEF
OF AUSTRIA-HUNGARY

A LOT OF THINGS had to go wrong for Otto von Habsburg to become emperor of the Austro-Hungarian Empire. And almost all of
them did. As a distant great-grandnephew of Emperor Franz
Josef, young Otto wasn't even born in the Schönbrunn Palace in
Vienna. But after Franz Josef's only son committed suicide in
1889, and Franz Ferdinand, a nephew of the emperor, was assassinated at Sarajevo in 1914, the two-year-old Otto found himself the
oldest son of the new heir apparent, the emperor's grandnephew
Charles.

Two years later Franz Josef died. He had ruled the Austro-
Hungarian Empire—a powerful sovereignty with roots in Charlemagne's Holy Roman Empire founded one thousand years earlier,
and one that still controlled much of eastern Europe—for an amazing sixty-eight years. But when he died, Franz Josef left Otto's
father, Charles, a crumbling monarchy that was losing World
War I and a depleted citizenry that was rioting for food. Otto, four
years old when he became heir apparent, held that place in line
for just two years before his father was forced to abdicate the
throne and take his pregnant wife and four children to Switzer-

land. Charles twice tried to regain power, with the result that he
and his family were exiled to the Portuguese island of Madeira in
the Atlantic.

So in the end too many things went wrong for Otto von Habsburg to become emperor.

Charles died in 1922 of pneumonia, leaving a wife and nine children who were prohibited from returning to their homeland. They
lived in Spain during the 1920s; then Otto went to college in Belgium and later Berlin. Otto said later that Hitler offered to restore
him to the Austrian throne before the Anschluss. Otto lived in
Washington, D.C., during World War II and tried to return to
Austria after the war, but he was expelled from Innsbruck by the
occupying Soviet troops. At the time he had not yet lost his hopes
of ruling his country. "Yes, I was looking for it," he said in an interview in 1979. "There is no doubt about that. I have always been
in politics and I was very much interested in politics."

Otto, who received sizable compensation for his confiscated
Austrian properties, finally settled in West Germany and married
a minor European princess. They have seven children. He applied
to return to Austria in 1961, but though he was willing to renounce all claims to the defunct throne, his entry became a hot
political controversy that did not cool in his favor until 1966. He
now lives both in West Germany and Austria.

The political ambitions of his birthright may have been quelled,
but Otto has not stayed out of the field. A writer and lecturer, the
would-be emperor in 1979 was elected to the new European Parliament, a quasi-governmental organization. It's no throne, but
it has given Otto a podium from which to press his support for
the unification of Europe. "Numerically we are stronger than the
Americans, we are more numerous than the Russians," said Otto,
a member of Germany's conservative political party. "Our economic potential is very superior. If we were not still living in
the states of the nineteenth century, we would be just as much
a world power as, say, the Americans or the Japanese or the
Chinese."

If that sounds like something an emperor would say, consider
this story that went out over the news wires in 1988. It seems

that Otto was asked if he was going to the Austria-Hungary soccer match.

"No," the heir apparent replied. "But how interesting. Tell me, whom are we playing?"

DAUGHTER of SIGMUND FREUD

"A GIRL'S FIRST AFFECTION is for her father," Sigmund Freud once analyzed. For the youngest of his six children, Anna, that affection never passed. She began working with her father, the famous founder of psychoanalysis, almost as soon as she finished high school. It is almost surprising that any of Freud's children followed in his work, since he didn't apply his psychoanalytic research to raising his children. He even sent his sons to a family doctor to learn the facts of life. (One son became a lawyer, another an architect.)

Anna, at first a schoolteacher, sat in on her father's lectures and took his dictation. She became one of her father's patients in 1918, which was highly unorthodox (many of his colleagues quietly criticized the arrangement) and even Freud might not have approved of how closely it seemed to bind his daughter to him. Still, the sessions also taught her technique straight from the master. By 1922, though she had no formal training as a psychiatrist, Anna was admitted to the Vienna Society, a prestigious group of psychoanalysts.

The next year, when Freud's jaw cancer was diagnosed, Anna became not only his best student but also his nurse. For the next sixteen years, until Freud finally succumbed to the disease, Anna devoted her life to him, growing closer to her father than even her mother was. When he had to be fitted with a complicated prosthesis after much of his jaw was removed, it was Anna who rinsed it regularly. As Freud grew too weak or scarred by his surgeries to travel, Anna became his representative, reading his research papers at conferences and accepting his awards. Most of Freud's friends and professional acquaintances in those last sixteen years were friends of Anna. When Freud's jaw became so damaged he could not talk, Anna conducted sessions with his patients as he looked on.

Much as he was grateful for her devotion (he called Anna his Antigone, the daughter who cared for the blind Oedipus), Freud worried about what would become of her. "She takes things too seriously," Freud said of Anna, who wore dark, grim clothes and short-cropped hair, and never married. "What will she do when she has lost me? Will she lead a life of ascetic austerity?" When Freud decided to die by euthanasia to end his pain, it was Anna, not his wife, that he wanted his doctor to tell.

In fact, Freud's youngest daughter, forty-four at the time, flowered after his death. She continued to be the chief spokesman for Freud's work and tightly controlled his papers. But Anna also made known her own pioneering discoveries in child analysis, research she had pursued during the years she cared for her father. Working out of the home in England where her father had lived after fleeing Nazi-occupied Austria, Anna founded the Hampstead Child-Therapy Clinic. She published many important works on the emotional development of children and eventually was sought after in the scientific community. When she died at the age of eighty-six she was considered, in her own right, the leading child psychoanalyst.

Freud's name has been carried on by other offspring as well. Lucian Freud, the painter, is a grandson. And one of the mental master's great-granddaughters, Emma Freud, became the host of a hit British TV talk show in 1988. The gimmick of "Pillow Talk" is that Emma wears pajamas and interviews her guests in bed. Sigmund might have had something to say about that.

G

SON of CLARK GABLE

FILMED IN the scorching Nevada desert and constantly delayed by the tantrums of Marilyn Monroe, Clark Gable's last movie was a nightmare. The only thing that seemed to perk up the fifty-nine-year-old Gable on the set of *The Misfits* was the news that after five marriages he was going to be a father. Said the film's publicist, Harry Mines, "After he told me about it and we'd all had that time off because of Marilyn, he kind of got a new step, a new manner. He sort of flourished. He kept saying to me, 'Imagine, I'm going to be a father.' His big joke, once everyone knew, was to tell people that his and Kay's combined ages were over one hundred. He kept grinning and saying, 'Must be the altitude.' " Gable even talked of retiring after he did one more movie so he could raise what he hoped would be a son.

It didn't work out that way. On November 16, 1960, soon after filming ended, Gable died of a heart attack. Four months later his widow, Kay, gave birth to their eight-pound boy, John Clark Gable. Kay raised her son on Gable's twenty-two-acre ranch in Encino, near Los Angeles, but for the most part she kept John away from publicity because she was afraid he might be kidnapped. Whenever John's picture did make the papers, it always included comment as to whether or not he looked like his debonair father.

These days, with his eyes set far apart, dark hair, and a thin mustache, his resemblance is fairly clear. "It's strange having a famous father you've never met," John told the *San Francisco Chronicle* in 1987. "I have seen all his movies, read books about him and listened to my mother's stories. So I feel I do know him."

John, whose mother died in 1985, did not immediately follow his father's footsteps into the movies. He turned down movie roles and instead raced off-road vehicles. In 1984 he was voted off-road racing's rookie of the year. "I never wanted anything to do with [acting] anyway," he said, "Whenever I went somewhere, there were the photographers going click, click, click. What a turn off! My God, all I've ever wanted in life is privacy."

But after he got married in 1985 and had a daughter, John said, acting became more tempting as a safer, if not more stable, career. "I never felt ready for it when I was younger. I had a lot of anxieties. Would people expect me to step off a stage and start spouting, 'Frankly, my dear, I don't give a damn'? Then as I matured, I began to wonder, what if . . ."

In 1989 John starred in a western, *Bad Jim*, with James Brolin. He also has signed a three-picture deal with an independent production company. "I'm taking acting one day at a time, seeing what they throw at me," said John, who lives in Malibu. "One thing's for sure, I'm not going to try to be like my dad."

DAUGHTER of GALILEO GALILEI

GALILEO GALILEI was not the first to assert that the earth revolved around the sun. But he was the first to prove it with a telescope, which he also invented. After publishing his discoveries in 1632, the Italian scientist was called before the Inquisition and sentenced by the pope to life in prison. The punishment was softened to house arrest, but he was so shocked by the verdict that it almost killed him. Galileo often is portrayed as suffering his ordeal alone as he stubbornly contradicted the Catholic Church. In fact, he received much comfort from a nun—his daughter.

Galileo never married, but he had three children by a mistress with whom he lived while teaching at the university in Padua. When his telescope got him a position in the duke's court at Florence, Galileo left his son with his mistress but took his two daughters with him. The girls, Virginia and Livia, were raised by Galileo's mother and kept out of public view because he was embarrassed to have illegitimate children. When they were old enough, the girls were sent to a convent in the hills of Arcetri above Florence.

It was a poor establishment. Galileo's daughters were ill-fed and Livia was ill so often she became an invalid. But Galileo's older daughter, who changed her name to Maria Celeste, grew more devoted to her absent father. "And your Lordship may believe that I am speaking the truth when I say that except you there is not a creature who gives me any comfort," she wrote in one of hundreds of letters to her father, who lived on the other side of Florence. According to her letters, Maria cheerfully mended her father's shirts, his aprons, and his dinner napkins. In 1631 Galileo bought a house next to the convent so he could be close to her. And during the months Galileo spent under the pressure of the Inquisition in Rome, Maria wrote to him daily.

At the end of 1633 Galileo returned to Florence under house arrest. He could not go into Florence, could not receive treatment for his deteriorating eyesight, and was allowed few visitors except his daughter. As part of his punishment, Galileo was supposed to recite seven penitential psalms once a week. His daughter took this upon herself. "I began to do this a while ago, and it gives me much pleasure: first, because I am persuaded that prayer in obedience to Holy Church must be efficacious; secondly, in order to save you the trouble of remembering it."

Four months after Galileo returned to his home, Maria Celeste died after a short illness. Galileo wrote that "an immense sadness and melancholy, complete loss of appetite and disgust with my existence, make me feel that I am being continually called by my dearest daughter." Galileo lived another eight years. Though he became blind, he began working again, partly with the help of his illegitimate son, Vincenzio, and died at the age of seventy-seven in 1642.

SON of MAHATMA GANDHI

"MEN MAY BE GOOD, not necessarily their children," wrote Mahatma Gandhi as he tried to explain how his oldest son could have turned out so badly. The pious leader, whose preachments of nonviolence and noncooperation helped sway hundreds of millions of Indians toward their nation's independence, was far less effective with Harilal. Partly, Gandhi blamed himself. "I was a slave of my passions when Harilal was conceived," said Gandhi, who had come to believe that the purpose of sex was purely for procreation, not pleasure. "I led a carnal and luxurious life during Harilal's childhood."

As Gandhi transformed himself from a natty British-educated barrister into a cotton-swathed guru, he became more severe with his four sons as well. During his early battle for Indians' civil rights in South Africa, Gandhi did not want his children to become Westernized, so he refused to allow them to attend the Christian mission schools. But since he couldn't afford an Indian tutor, Gandhi himself taught his sons to read and write. He taught them little else. Harilal at one point stayed behind in India for further schooling, and soon Gandhi heard his sixteen-year-old son had married the daughter of his ward there. "It is well if Harilal is married; it is also well if he is not," wrote Gandhi, who had married at twelve. "For the present at any rate I have ceased to think of him as a son."

Gandhi expected all of his sons to adopt celibacy as he had, and indeed Harilal's three younger brothers waited until they were at least thirty before they received Gandhi's grudging blessing to marry. Perhaps they waited because they had seen what Harilal went through. Harilal reconciled with his father and took his wife to South Africa to join in Gandhi's growing struggle. Gandhi had wanted his son to return, but urged him to leave his wife behind. When she arrived, Gandhi ruled over her like a harsh mother-in-law. He criticized what she ate and wore and kept her apart from her husband most of the time.

They were apart mostly because Harilal was jailed seven times participating in his father's protests. After one arrest when Harilal was charged with selling fruit without a license, Gandhi, as his attorney, urged the court to impose a severe sentence. Harilal spent seven days at hard labor, which Gandhi explained was part of his protest strategy to show the harshness of the system. "I thought it only proper that I should make this experiment in the first instance with my son," he said. "Though I know that the boy, poor child, will suffer, I welcome the news all the same. It will do him good to suffer, and me too."

Gandhi's younger sons were put through the same trials, but they remained obedient to their father throughout his life. Devadas, the youngest son, despite his early lack of education, went on to become managing editor of the *Hindustan Times* in Delhi. Harilal, on the other hand, became fed up with his father in 1911 and abruptly left South Africa to return to India with his family. In one of his infrequent letters to his son, Gandhi wrote, "I will not still give up hope of your reformation even as I do not despair of myself. I was a bad man before you were born. But I have been gradually improving since then."

It was after Harilal's wife died in 1918, leaving him with four children, that he became more than a disgruntled son. He racked up large debts. He used his father's name to put together business deals that failed. He stole 30,000 rupees from a merchant who didn't prosecute because he was a friend of Gandhi's. He also drank heavily and went with a variety of women. Growing sick and impoverished, Harilal wandered from home to home, imposing himself on a friend in Calcutta, a brother in Delhi, and a son in Bombay.

The press followed his every step, especially in 1936 when Harilal publicly converted to the Muslim faith. Gandhi responded by writing a public letter urging Muslims to reject what he considered the false faith of his son. "Everyone who knows my son Harilal knows that he has been for years addicted to the drink evil and has been in the habit of visiting houses of ill fame . . .

Harilal's apostasy is no loss to Hinduism and his admission to Islam a source of weakness to it, if, as I fear, he remains the same wreck that he was before."

He did remain so. When his mother lay near death after fasting with her husband in jail in 1944, Harilal showed up drunk the day before she died. Four years later, after Gandhi was assassinated, Harilal arrived at the funeral after his father already had been cremated. He stood there haggard and unrecognized. Six months later, at a sanatorium in Bombay, Harilal died of tuberculosis.

DAUGHTER of DAVID GARDINER

As FAR BACK as the 1600s, Gardiner was a name to be known on Long Island, and today still Gardiners Island remains in the family. As with all family dynasties, however, there are some members with smaller shares of the fortune. Such was the position of David Gardiner in the early 1800s. Not that he was poor, but Moses Beach's 1842 register of the *Wealth and Pedigree of the Wealthy Citizens of New York City*, which listed Gardiner at $150,000, certainly overstated the case. Gardiner, a lawyer and gentleman farmer, worked hard to keep up the appearances of his grand family name. He married well, and though he served only four years in the New York state senate, he had himself called "senator" for the rest of his life.

Gardiner also had high hopes for his two daughters. After putting them through a fashionable finishing school in New York, he took them to Europe and then to Washington, D.C., where his former activities in Whig politics granted him—and them—entrée into the social circle of President John Tyler. His older daughter, Julia, and her sister received the attentions of many politicians that winter of 1842. So much so that they returned to the capital the next season. The family had its calling card presented at the White House and to all the cabinet members, and soon the Gardiner daughters were attending parties almost every night and listening to debates in Congress often enough to be seen by their suitors. The *New York Herald* referred to Julia as "the beautiful and accomplished Miss Gardiner of Long Island, one of the loveliest women in the United States."

All this praise caught the attention of President Tyler, whose wife had died a few months earlier. The Tylers and the Gardiners had become close, with the two families sharing Christmas Eve dinner and Tyler's sons frequently escorting Gardiner's daughters to parties. But then one evening in February 1843 when the two families were casually relaxing at the White House, the fifty-four-year-old president ended up spending the entire time playing cards with twenty-four-year-old Julia. Two weeks later, at the Washington's Birthday ball, Tyler proposed. Julia at first said no, as she had to several other older, widowed suitors. But she continued to exchange letters with Tyler after the Gardiners returned to Long Island in the spring.

The next winter, David Gardiner and his daughters again returned to Washington. On February 28, 1844, they joined Tyler and many others for an afternoon cruise on the new steam frigate *Princeton.* They all cheered as the biggest naval cannon in the world, the "Peacemaker," was fired for the guests. Afterward, Tyler and Julia and some others were below toasting with champagne when it was suggested that the gun be fired one more time. David Gardiner went up on deck, while Tyler and Julia lingered below. Even after they heard the explosion they didn't realize something was wrong until smoke began to pour into the cabin. The gun had misfired, killing the Secretary of State, the Secretary of the Navy, five others, and David Gardiner.

Four months later, in June 1844, Tyler and Julia were married. "She literally stepped over her father's body into the White House," according to one descendant who was quoted in Walter Cronkite's book *North by Northeast.* Upon arriving at the White House, Julia told her mother, "I have commenced my auspicious

reign and am in quiet possession of the Presidential Mansion."
Indeed, Julia entertained grandly. "I determined upon, and I
think I have been successful in, making my Court interesting in
youth and beauty. Wherever I go they form my train."

But Julia's reign was short-lived. Two months after their marriage, pressures over slavery and the annexation of Texas forced
Tyler to withdraw from the 1844 presidential campaign. Texas
was annexed just before Tyler left office, and Julia is given no
small credit for lobbying congressmen at her fabulous parties.
Tyler and Julia retired to Sherwood Forest, Tyler's 1,600-acre
plantation south of Richmond, Virginia. Julia had seven children
before Tyler died in 1862 at the age of seventy-one.

From then on, the rewards of Julia's fortuitous marriage dwindled. An avowed Confederate, Julia was forced to flee Sherwood
Forest in the Civil War and for years afterward she almost went
broke trying to hold on to the Tyler land. She returned to Washington in 1872, where she converted to Catholicism and sold most
of her inherited New York properties to support herself. She
lobbied Congress for a Presidential widow's pension and finally
in 1881 was awarded $1,200 a year and later $5,000 a year after
President Garfield was shot. And on that she lived comfortably—
though perhaps not as well as her daddy had wanted—until she
died in 1889.

SON of JOHN WARNE GATES

JOHN WARNE GATES was just another unsuccessful thirty-dollar-
a-month salesman until, in 1877, he strung his barbed wire around
the town square in San Antonio and then stampeded a herd of
cattle to prove to skeptical ranchers that the fence would hold. It
did, and Gates became the nation's biggest manufacturer of barbed

wire at a time when the entire West was being fenced in. That was only his start, as Gates poured his millions into countless ventures—including several failed steel trusts he hoped would rival J. P. Morgan's—and played the stock market like a roulette wheel. "There's millions in it!" Gates regularly exclaimed, later earning him the nickname John "Bet a Million" Gates. He was right often enough to amass one of the great fortunes of the nineteenth century.

But unlike many other self-made industrialists of the era, the buoyant but bulky Gates never lost his rough edges. Andrew Carnegie once sniffed, "He's a broken-down gambler." Gates would have taken umbrage only at the broken-down part, for he was most enthusiastically a gambler. He would stand with an associate at a window when it was raining and bet on which raindrops would reach the bottom of the pane first. He would place a lump of sugar on his table in a restaurant and bet on how many flies would land on it. That, of course, was just dabbling compared to his poker games, one of which lasted five days in his suite at the Waldorf-Astoria and involved over $2 million.

Like many fathers, Gates wanted his only child, Charlie, to follow in his footsteps. "I want my boy to feel that his daddy is not only his best friend, but his chum," Gates said, and he spoiled his son no end. "I believe that's the right way to bring up a boy." But Charlie seemed to have inherited only his father's ability to spend money, not his knack for making it. At eighteen, Charlie and his rich friends already were regulars at Chicago's high-class brothels. One night when Charlie came home drunk, Gates told him he would give him $1 million if he would stop drinking until he was twenty-one. Charlie reached his majority sober, collected his million, and then promptly became a bigger playboy than he had been before.

Though married, Charlie continued to frequent brothels and date young actresses. When he showed up late or not at all for work at Gates's office, his father would say only, "Well, a young fellow's got to sow his wild oats, I guess." Gates occasionally had to pay off women who were trying to blackmail his son. Finally the raucous tycoon decided to pull in the reins a little. "I guess maybe I've spoiled him, so it's up to me to see he gets straightened out," Gates said. "New York's not the place, I guess, for a young lad with too much money and too much spirit." So Gates took Charlie to Europe.

But Charlie never did come around. In 1905 he tried to corner the wheat market in Chicago and failed so miserably that his father had to pour in $2 million to bail him out. Gates, meanwhile, finally got permanently squeezed out of the steel industry and the stock market by his rival, J. P. Morgan, and retired to Port Arthur, Texas, where he had made one of his fortunes on the oil industry's first gusher, Spindletop.

Charlie didn't like the isolated oil town, so he began touring the country in his private rail car, "Bright Eyes," gambling and womanizing along the way. "This is a life of speed," he said. "The faster the better." Charlie, in fact, set a speed record on the rails in 1911 when he traveled from Yuma, Arizona, to New York at an average of forty miles per hour. He made the trip to try to reconcile with his wife, who had filed for divorce.

Charlie became known for giving big tips, as much as twenty dollars. He bragged that he gave away $1 million a year in tips alone, earning himself the nickname Charlie "Spend a Million" Gates. "I can't take it with me when I die," he said. "I believe in spending it while I'm alive. I don't know how much it costs me to live." One poker game cost him $40,000. His father said, "He'll learn. He's only doing what I've done. How can I blame him for that?"

John Gates died in 1911 at the age of fifty-six, suffering from diabetes and throat cancer. In an act of rare restraint, he had rewritten his will so that instead of leaving everything to Charlie, his fortune, estimated at nearly $50 million, was put in a trust for ten years to be controlled by both Charlie and Gates's wife.

Charlie never saw the full amount. For a while after his father died, Charlie straightened out. After his divorce he married a Minneapolis society girl, built a $4 million house, and attended the board meetings of companies his father had controlled. But it wasn't long before Charlie was back on the rails in "Bright Eyes." Detectives sometimes were sent to make sure Charlie would attend the stockholder meetings where his presence was required. He drank a lot, explaining, "My old man could take a drink. Why can't I?"

In the fall of 1913 Charlie rode his train out to Cody, Wyoming, to go hunting with his friend Buffalo Bill. He returned to his rail car after a party one night complaining that he couldn't breathe. A doctor examined him, found nothing wrong, and Charlie fell asleep. He never woke up. The thirty-seven-year-old apparently died of a heart attack, but there were rumors that drugs were involved. His mother survived him by five years. She left the millions Charlie never had the chance to spend—some $38 million— to her brother and sister.

CHILDREN of PAUL GAUGUIN

"CIVILIZATION MAKES YOU SUFFER. Barbarism to me is rejuvenation." That statement of Paul Gauguin's shows up in his primitive-style paintings. It also reflects his life.

A stockbroker in Paris, Gauguin lost his job in a market crash in 1883 and then devoted his full time to his art. He soon ran out of money to support his wife, Mette, and their five children, and she took the children to her parents' home in Copenhagen. The one child Gauguin tried to raise in Paris, six-year-old Clovis, became so sick from malnutrition and cold that Gauguin had to borrow money from his sister and put the boy in a boarding school. His youngest son, Pola, remembered meeting Gauguin only once, when he was eight. Of his long-haired father who spoke little Danish, Pola later wrote, "That this was my father was something that was quite beyond my comprehension."

But Gauguin seemed unable to have it any other way. He wrote, "My wife, my family, everyone, in fact, is on my back about this confounded painting of mine. But one man's faculties can't cope with two things at once, and I for one can do *one thing only:* paint. Everything else leaves me stupefied."

Gauguin finally abandoned not only his family—and a pregnant seamstress in Paris—but also most of civilization in 1891 when he sailed to Tahiti, where he found the primitive subjects to form his distinctive Postimpressionist style. He married a thirteen-year-old Tahitian girl, Teha'amana, who became the subject of many of the early paintings that he sent back to his ex-wife Mette in Copenhagen to try to sell. He didn't tell Mette who the naked girl in the paintings really was. When Gauguin returned to Europe in 1893, Teha'amana was pregnant. But when he sailed back to Tahiti two years later, she had married another man after apparently aborting their baby.

By that time the painter was suffering from syphilis, which killed him in 1903, and from guilt at abandoning his first family. After he learned his favorite daughter, Aline, had died, Gauguin attempted suicide in 1898. He lived another five years, but stopped corresponding with Mette. He died out of touch with his European children. One son, Jean, became a sculptor in Copenhagen. Pola was an art critic in Oslo. His oldest son, Emil, was a construction engineer; he died at the age of eighty-one in 1955 in Englewood, Florida.

Gauguin also left two children on the South Pacific islands. Distraught over Aline's death, Gauguin seemed happy to learn his new wife, Pau'ura, was pregnant the next year. "It is a happy event for me, because the child perhaps will lead me back to life, which at present I find so unbearable." But in 1901 Gauguin left Tahiti for a more remote island, where he died after fathering a daughter. The child spent her life among the natives in an isolated valley of Hivaoa Island.

Meanwhile, Emile, his son by Pau'ura, raised by Pau'ura's family in a small village, became a vegetable dealer until about 1950, when he moved to the larger town of Papeete and found he could make money by posing for tourists. A few years later his childish drawings and those of local children he had "inspired" were put on display in Paris. Six were drawn by Emile's children, and one newspaper asserted that Gauguin's grandchildren "revealed striking gifts that only heredity could explain."

In 1960 writer Wilmon Menard saw Gauguin's Tahitian son in Papeete. "I found Emile in front of a waterfront garage in a state of inebriated immobility; he had just been released from jail for vagrancy and drunkenness. . . . Sheets of drawing-paper with crayon scrawls, which he signed GAUGUIN for the tourist trade for one dollar each were fluttering around him. He weighed well over 300 pounds and now retained little resemblance to his illustrious painter-father."

Emile's scribblings later were exhibited in London and sold for up to $1,400. He then visited the United States, where he found some demand for his paintings and tropical-patterned dress material. Emile returned to Tahiti in the mid-1960s somewhat famous and wealthy. But he started drinking again and his fame, once-removed, faded. Far from the civilization his father had hated, eighty-one-year-old Emile died in 1980 in his son's hut in Tahiti.

GRANDSON of JEAN PAUL GETTY

J. PAUL GETTY, long called the richest man in the world, once declared, "There are people who have been destroyed, physically and morally, by their wealth. The same people, born poor, would probably have become alcoholics or thieves." With such an idea of fate perhaps it's no wonder that the oil tycoon paid so little attention to his children. Getty had five sons in five marriages and he rarely saw any of them more than once a year. Even George, his oldest and heir apparent, called him "Mr. Getty." Said Getty's fourth wife and mother of Gordon and Jean Paul Jr.: "He didn't want to hear or smell children. He wanted them for his dynasty but he didn't want to deal with them as babies." By the time Getty died of prostate cancer in 1976, two of his sons were already dead, including his heir apparent, George, who had died of a drug overdose three years earlier—a probable suicide. The other three sons all had either been humiliated or pushed out of Getty's cherished oil company long before.

But the Getty who was most "destroyed, physically and morally" came in the next generation. J. Paul Getty III had a similar relationship with his father, J. Paul Jr., to the one J. Paul Jr. had had with the old man himself. "We have perfect communication," Paul II said of his father. "We never talk. That way we don't fight either." Paul Jr. had been fired by Getty as head of Getty Oil's Italian operation in the mid-1960s, and, after being divorced by Paul III's mother, he proceeded to become a rich hippie and a heroin addict. After his second wife died of an overdose in 1971, Paul Jr. became a recluse in England while Paul III was getting kicked out of boarding schools.

Paul III, who grew up mostly in Rome, dropped out of school when he was fourteen and, like his father, became a regular among Rome's glitterati. Although a Getty, he constantly needed money, since his father was as stingy in supporting his ex-wife as Getty had been with his. Paul III once posed nude for a pornographic magazine to earn the money and, perhaps equally, for the shock value. "He was kind of schizophrenic about being a Getty," said his German girlfriend, Martine, who lived with Paul III from the time he was sixteen and she twenty-four. "He knew who he was, but felt inferior because the one thing he was supposed to have—money—he did not have."

In July 1973 Paul III, on his way home from a discotheque, in the middle of the night, was kidnapped. At first, the police and the press thought it was a hoax because of Paul's record of trouble. When the kidnappers made their ransom demands, representatives of the Getty family tried to negotiate a smaller payment. Getty himself refused to put up a nickel. "Although I see my grandson infrequently and I am not particularly close to him, I love him nonetheless," Getty said in a statement. "However, I don't believe in paying kidnappers. I have 14 other grandchildren and if

I pay one penny now, then I will have 14 kidnapped grand-children."

There it stood until November, when Paul's right ear arrived in a box at a Rome newspaper office. Getty finally agreed to pay $1 million ransom, but only as a loan to his son, Paul's father, repayable at 4 percent interest. After he was released, Paul III not surprisingly remained deeply shaken. "No one really understands what the kidnapping did to him," said Martine, whom Paul married nine months after he was released. "He came back changed. He wanted to get control of himself, but he just wasn't able to." He used more drugs and ran into more trouble with the police. He worked briefly in a hardhat job at a Getty oil field in California in 1977, but he quit after a few months, still upset that in 1975 a guardian had been appointed to govern his debt-ridden finances.

Paul III's final tragedy occurred seven months before it was publicly disclosed. And it might have remained secret if his mother hadn't filed suit against Paul Jr. in November 1981 to try to force him to pay $25,000 a month for his son's mounting medical bills. The medical bills had begun in April when, after a night of swallowing liquor and methadone and Valium, the twenty-four-year-old namesake of J. Paul Getty suffered a stroke and fell into a coma. He regained consciousness six weeks later but was blind, paralyzed, and could not speak.

The judge at a pretrial hearing on the suit against Paul Jr. said, "Mr. Getty should be ashamed of himself. He's spending far more money on court obligations than living up to his moral duties." Paul Jr., who had called his oldest son, "the earless wonder," said later, "I have never failed to meet my obligations toward my children under the legal settlements as agreed and my paternal responsibilities as I saw them." Paul Jr. said he believed the medical bills were too high, but he finally agreed to pay them in 1983.

Meanwhile, as his uncles spent the next few years battling over their father's dynasty and ultimately wound up with about $750 million apiece, Paul III remains barely functional. A few years ago, Martine told Getty biographer Russell Miller that Paul's son (who in 1989 played the lead in a remake of the film *Lord of the Flies*) and his stepdaughter "cuddle up with him in bed and talk to him all the time and tell him what they have been doing. Now they have him all the time and they are happy about that."

SON of
JOHANN WOLFGANG VON GOETHE

JOHANN WOLFGANG VON GOETHE once chided a pastor, "All your ideals will not distract me from being true—good *and* evil, like nature." The German author of *Faust* and *The Sorrows of Young Werther* definitely exhibited both sides.

Professionally, Goethe was a Renaissance man. Besides his famous novels and revolutionary *Sturm und Drang* style, he wrote fourteen volumes on science, discovered a small bone in the human jaw, directed plays, and served on the privy council of the Duke of Weimar.

But all of that work left very little time for his family. Weimar society didn't approve of Goethe's peasant mistress, and though Christiane Vulpius bore him a son, August, in 1789, Goethe kept her in the back of the house and didn't marry her until 1806. During the many months he spent traveling, Goethe rarely bothered to provide a tutor for his young son. In fact he often sent August away to live with friends, though his own house was quite large.

August, who grew up being called "the son of that Vulpius woman," began drinking when he was barely a teenager. After he studied briefly at Heidelberg, his increasingly famous father called him home to be his secretary and accountant. Goethe also arranged for his son to marry Ottilie von Pogwisch, whose respectable position in society was supposed to erase August's illegitimate and peasant roots. In fact, Goethe and Ottilie seemed more interested in each other than in August. The marriage of August and Ottilie was unhappy, but Goethe greatly enjoyed his two grandsons by it, born in 1818 and 1820.

August was something of a writer, though he hid it from his father. In one poem, sounding much like Goethe's young Werther, August wrote of his frustration with his life—"destruction is its certain fate." And during one drinking binge, August told a friend, "You take me for a wild superficial kind of fellow—but here, inside me, it goes so deep! If you threw a stone down you would wait a long time before you heard it fall!"

In 1830 Goethe decided his son needed a fresh start, so he sent him to Rome, where Goethe himself had gotten early inspiration. But August continued drinking and, after a short fever, died. His liver was five times the normal size. He was buried in the cemetery that held Keats and Shelley. Said Goethe, "I was not unaware that I had begotten a mortal."

The following month, Goethe suffered a stroke and was cared for by August's widow, Ottilie. Goethe died in her arms in 1832 at the age of eighty-two after saying, "Little woman, give me your paw." Ottilie was not as devoted as might appear. Even while Goethe was alive, she had many quick trysts with visitors to the house. After he died, Ottilie blew all of her money in Vienna and even mortgaged her sons' inheritance from Goethe. She later died back in Goethe's house, in the attic rooms where she and August had lived.

SON of JAY GOULD

THOUGH IT MIGHT BE redundant to call him a hated robber baron, Jay Gould was a particularly scurrilous specimen of the breed. With his wildly flamboyant partner, Jim Fisk, the reclusive Gould grabbed the Erie Railroad from Cornelius Vanderbilt in 1868, and a year later he and Fisk caused a severe panic when they tried to corner the gold market. Fisk was killed in a love triangle in 1872, but Gould went right on gobbling up railroads, the mighty Union Pacific among them. By 1890 he owned almost 9,000 miles of railroads, including half of all the tracks in the Southwest.

Like any proud father, Gould wanted to pass on his business intact to his children. And from the start he groomed his oldest son George as the heir apparent. George skipped college and went right to work for his father, and by the time he was twenty-one, he was named a director of the company. George proved quite competent under his father's tutelage. The two would sit for hours each night poring over business documents for their latest acquisition. By the time Gould died of tuberculosis in 1892, he trusted George enough to leave him complete control of his gargantuan holdings—including the Western Union Telegraph Co. and the Manhattan Elevated Railroad—worth an estimated $72 million. The trust was split among Gould's six children, but he gave twenty-eight-year-old George voting control and an extra $5 million for, he said in his will, "having developed a remarkable business ability and having for 12 years devoted himself to my business."

Unfortunately, without his father lording it over him, George grew less devoted. Though his father never had time for such things, George threw lavish parties and played polo so often that he is credited with helping popularize the sport in the United States. He also built Georgian Court, in Lakewood, New Jersey, which at the time was one of the most spectacular private homes in the country. It was from his Lakewood mansion, or from one of several uptown clubs in New York, that George would occasionally turn his attention toward business matters.

That wasn't enough to manage his father's vast empire, let alone carry out the needed expansion of the Gould railroad network into a coast-to-coast line that would secure its profitability. George was blocked in the West by E. H. Harriman, and the robber baron's son proved no match for the real thing. Badly hurt in the Panic of 1907, and ganged up on by his father's old enemies on Wall Street, George was forced to give up control of railroad after railroad. By 1918 the name of Gould was not on a single piece of train track. After George lost the Denver & Rio Grande Railroad, Denver's *Rocky Mountain News* wrote, "The king is dead. May there be no more kings."

None of this sat well with some of George's brothers and sisters who were seeing their fortune squandered away. The youngest brother, Frank, filed suit in 1919 and had George removed as executor of their father's trust. At that time, the estate was valued at $66 million, $6 million less than when Gould had died in 1892 but worth far less in real dollars. The lawsuit touched off a barrage of counterclaims by other family members so that, until it was settled in 1927, the Gould railroad dynasty became associated primarily with sensational headlines about poor little rich kids in court.

Meanwhile, George had his own family problems to settle. After his wife of thirty-five years died in 1922, leaving seven children, George promptly married his mistress and acknowledged that he was the father of her three children, born in 1915, 1916, and 1922. George and his new bride spent a long honeymoon in Europe. They were in Menton, France, when George died of pneumonia. His estate originally was estimated at $30 million. But after taxes and more accurate evaluations, it was worth $16 million. George's seven children by his first marriage received less than $1 million apiece.

All of George's brothers, ironically, fared much better. Edwin made excellent investments in New York real estate. Howard, living in England, left a fortune of $60 million when he died in 1959. Even Frank, who had been an alcoholic when he filed the suit against George, gave up drinking and became a very successful casino operator on the Riviera in the late 1920s. The normally savvy Jay Gould, clearly, had put all his money on the wrong horse.

H

DAUGHTER of WARREN G. HARDING

Sometimes her eyes are blue as deep sea-blue,
And calm as waters stilled at evenfall.
I see not quite my child in these blue eyes,
But him whose soul shines wondrously through her.
Serene and unafraid he was, and knew
How to dispel the fears in other hearts,
Meeting an anxious gaze all tranquilly:
These are her father's eyes.

Little did the *New York Times* know, when it published this poem in 1926, that it was printing the first public disclosure of the late President Warren Harding's illegitimate daughter. A year later Nan Britton, the poem's author and also the child's mother, was far more specific in a book called *The President's Daughter.* It seems that when Harding died suddenly during the third year of his presidency in 1923, he left behind more than the most scandal-plagued administration since Grant's.

According to Britton's account, which has been largely accepted by historians, she first had a crush on Harding in 1910 in their hometown of Marion, Ohio, when she was barely fourteen and he was a long-married, forty-five-year-old candidate for governor. She plastered her bedroom walls with his campaign posters, telephoned his home just to hear his voice and talked about him constantly—so much so that a ladies' club felt compelled to discuss it with her mother. Her father, a prominent doctor and friend of Harding's, even brought it up with the politician, who laughed it off and did nothing to dissuade the already well-developed young girl.

In 1917 the persistent Britton, then twenty, wrote to Harding, then a U.S. senator, and asked his assistance in helping her pursue a secretarial career in New York. He promptly wrote back offering to find her a government job and telling her that, as a matter of fact, he would be in New York the very next week and would like to see her. They met at the Manhattan Hotel at 42nd and Madison and soon were in his suite where, she said, "We had scarcely closed the door behind us when we shared our first kiss."

Britton said it was another two months before they shared more. They began to see each other regularly on weekends in New York or in Washington, where Harding would register her at hotels as his niece. He wrote her forty-page love letters, got her a job as a stenographer at U.S. Steel, and frequently sent her hundreds of dollars. Then in early 1919, Britton became pregnant. Harding, childless in his marriage, at first suggested she have an abortion. But when she said she wanted the baby, he gave her a ring and talked of marrying her. Later, the Republican presidential hopeful reduced his offer. "If I'm President, Nan, I'll make you White House stenographer," he told her.

Britton had her baby, Elizabeth Ann, on October 22, 1919, in Asbury Park, New Jersey. Supported by Harding, Britton and their baby eventually moved in with her sister and brother-in-law in Chicago. After Harding moved into the White House in 1921, Britton visited him on several occasions during his term and said they made love in a small coat closet off a waiting room outside his office. Britton pressed Harding to divorce his wife, marry her, and recognize his child, but the president replied, "Nan, darling, you must help me; our secret must not come out. Why, I would rather die than disappoint my party."

Harding and Britton last saw each other in January 1923. She returned to Chicago, where she became secretary to the president of Northwestern University, and later she enrolled as a student there. That summer she went to Dijon, France, to take some classes, which Harding paid for. She was in Dijon in August when she heard Harding had died suddenly, never having seen his daughter, then nearly four years old. Britton returned to New York and waited, she said, for Harding's promised bequest. It never came. In January 1924, Britton married a man who claimed to be a rich Norwegian sea captain but left him when she found out he was broke. She lived with her daughter in dilapidated apartments on New York's Upper West Side, but she could never earn enough from her temporary secretarial jobs to make ends meet.

Finally, in 1925, Britton approached Harding's sisters, who at first seemed sympathetic but later declined any responsibility. It was while she was working as a secretary for an executive of the Bible Corporation of America that Britton, with her boss's encouragement, began writing her book. Several major publishers turned down the manuscript, and Britton finally arranged to publish it privately in June 1927 and sell it through mail order. The advertisement featured a picture of the young Elizabeth. Bookstores at first refused to stock the shocking volume, but as demand grew their qualms disappeared and the book was a bestseller by September.

Britton put most of her royalties into the Elizabeth Ann Guild, which she had founded to protect the rights of illegitimate children. But book sales eventually declined and the guild closed in 1932. Britton returned to Evanston, Illinois, where her daughter, under the name Elizabeth Ann Harding, graduated from Sullivan High School in 1938. Elizabeth Ann married an office-building manager, Henry Blaesing.

Harding's "second family" was back in the news in 1964, when writer Francis Russell uncovered stacks of love letters that Harding had written from 1909–1920 to another mistress, who also was the wife of a prominent Marion, Ohio, businessman. Reporters found Britton still living quietly in Evanston. Elizabeth Blaesing, then forty-four, was living with her husband and three children in Glendale, California.

DAUGHTER of
EDWARD HENRY HARRIMAN

SOME CONSIDERED HIM the last of the great robber barons, others less affectionately called him a "cold-blooded little cuss." Edward Henry Harriman inspired mixed feelings as one of the most powerful railroad men at the end of the nineteenth century, controlling the Illinois Central, reviving the continent-spanning Union Pacific, and battling for a grip on tracks throughout the nation. Harriman's expertise at stock manipulation and hostile takeovers outlasted the public's taste for it, and during the anti-trust crusade of the early 1900s he was branded a greedy, conniving capitalist.

And then along came Mary. Harriman's oldest daughter, as well as his other five children—including future diplomat and New York governor William Averell Harriman—"were brought up without even remotely suspecting that their father was even a moderately rich man," said one of Harriman's biographers. That might be overstating the case, considering that the family lived just off New York's Fifth Avenue, but Mary at least was not spoiled.

When she returned home from her spectacular debutante ball in 1900, she burst into tears at the realization that her scores of bouquets would soon wastefully wilt. The next morning, Mary mobilized her fellow debs and delivered the flowers to local hospitals. The young women were so pleased with their effort that about eighty of them began working regularly in a settlement house. They called themselves the "Junior League." Over the next few years, the idea spread to other debutante classes around the country to the point that charitableness among the daughters of the upper class became downright fashionable, and the Junior

League became an institution. "They were smart, and they made it smart," one socialite said of Mary and her friends.

Mary went to college, which wasn't so fashionable, and her charity work eventually led her to set up consumer's committees under FDR's National Emergency Council. In an interview in 1933, she explained the difference between her father and herself. "His period was a building age, when competition was the order of the day. Today the need is not for a competitive but for a cooperative economic system. When I was a young girl I began to realize that competition was injuring some, and I dreamed of a time when there would be more cooperation."

A year later, Mary, the widow of sculptor Charles Rumsey, died suddenly after her horse stumbled and fell on her during a hunt in Virginia. The *New York Times* called the robber baron's daughter "a pioneer in the now common practice of young ladies working for the benefit of less fortunate persons."

GRANDSON of
GEORGE HUNTINGTON HARTFORD

TEA IS TEA, but A&P founder George Huntington Hartford certainly exhibited a flair for selling it. When customers entered the doors of the Great Atlantic and Pacific Tea Company, which he opened in Manhattan in 1859, they passed through a storefront painted with imported Chinese vermillion and gold leaf. And they entered into a tea shop with crystal chandeliers and clerks who sat in gold pagodas. Not only tea but plenty of other goods sold well, and Hartford's tea shops grew to become the first modern grocery stores. His two oldest sons, George and John, inherited their father's marketing talent and left a legacy of some 4,700 A&P stores by the 1950s.

But what George and John did not leave behind was children. Their younger brother, Edward, had a son, but Edward had broken away from his brothers and started an automotive engineering company. So when his son, Huntington, joined A&P after he graduated from Harvard in 1934, he was relegated to the statistics department far from the family fold. It probably wasn't such a bad decision on his uncles' part. The Newport-bred Huntington already had offended the family by eloping during his sophomore year, and he soon was fired from his statistics job after he left early one day to attend the Harvard-Yale game.

Huntington hardly went hungry. His father had died in 1922, leaving him enough money to become the perfect New York playboy with enough eccentricities—he trotted around town in bedroom slippers and ordered milk at the posh clubs—to make the gossip columns regularly. "I was in my twenties," Huntington told *Forbes* in 1985. "I had $1.5 million in income a year—all the money I needed. I never thought about how I would get a return on my investments."

Occasionally Huntington took on serious tasks, such as when he published a pamphlet in 1951 called "Has God Been Insulted Here?" In it, Huntington lashed out against modern art and literature. He said James Joyce, William Faulkner, and Picasso, among others, were vulgar, and he called for a new movement of realism in the fine arts. That earned the ire of writer Tom Wolfe, who called Huntington "the Martin Luther of modern culture," possessing "the most flagrantly unfashionable taste anybody in New York had ever heard of."

Huntington spent $600,000 to build an artists' retreat in Pacific Palisades, California, but once artists realized his bent, they stayed away in droves. He wrote a play adapted from Victorian Charlotte Brontë's *Jane Eyre;* it starred an aging Errol Flynn, who quit before the show reached Broadway, where it lost $500,000.

But all of this was merely a warm-up. Huntington got his real chance to make his mark after the last of his father's generation died in 1957 and A&P went public. Huntington's 10 percent of the stock was worth $90 million and the heir immediately began selling it to raise cash.

One thing can be said for him: Huntington inherited his grandfather's flair. But unlike the elder Hartford, Huntington had nothing to sell, at least nothing that anyone wanted to buy. He created a flashy magazine called *Show* that featured serious articles between photo spreads of pretty girls. He started a modeling agency to service his magazine, and could be seen standing on Fifth Avenue across from the Plaza Hotel handing out his business card to attractive women. The magazine cost him $8 million before it folded in 1964.

Huntington also spent $11 million to buy a beautiful island in the Bahamas—Hog Island—which he renamed Paradise Island, and another $19 million to build a golf course and an exclusive fifty-two-room hotel. Under his care, the island never became the ritzy retreat he envisioned and he finally sold most of his share in 1966 at a loss of $20 million. The island later became a gold mine for Resorts International.

He tried to self-start his art movement by building his own museum on Columbus Circle in Manhattan, a venture that had cost him more than $7 million by the time it closed. He also lost $1 million on a Hollywood theater and $2 million on a company that was to make automatic car parkers. All told, Huntington Hartford's $90 million has dwindled to about $8 million.

Along the way, Huntington married and divorced four times. His son by his second wife is a writer and his daughter from the same marriage is an artist. His daughter by his third wife testified against him when her mother unsuccessfully tried to get a judge to take over Huntington's affairs in 1986. Huntington, who admitted that he used cocaine "sporadically," testified in his defense, "While most people would not approve of my lifestyle . . . that is my concern and not theirs. If I choose to spend my money in what some people believe is a frivolous manner, or if I choose to give it away, that is my affair." Now, Huntington's own attorney manages his diminished fortune and gives the heir an allowance of four hundred dollars a week. He has lived in a nondescript East Side townhouse since he was evicted from his fashionable Beekman Place home in 1982 after his ex-wife, a former hairdresser, was arrested for tying up a seventeen-year-old girl and shaving her head. That ex-wife, Elaine, still lives with Huntington, who has had great difficulty walking since he broke his hip in 1985. He is nearly eighty.

SON of WILLIAM ANDERSON HATFIELD
(and the McCOYS)

IT CERTAINLY WASN'T the only one and it may not even have been the bloodiest, but the feud between the Hatfields and the McCoys came to define the term. Fought in the Appalachian hills of the Big Sandy River valley, which separated Pike County, Kentucky, from Mingo County, West Virginia, the most famous family feud is thought to have had its roots in the Civil War. Later, in the 1870s, the families accused each other of hog-stealing—no small matter in the hills.

But some historians point to Election Day in the spring of 1880 as the event that propelled the feud into the history books. Election Day in the Appalachians was a social event, with most folks lingering and drinking around the polling place all day long. The Hatfields and the McCoys weren't speaking to each other by that voting day, but they tolerated each other well enough for the gathering to proceed pleasantly.

Then Johnse (short for Johnson) Hatfield showed up. He was eighteen, the oldest son of William Anderson "Devil Anse" Hatfield, father of thirteen children and the leader of the three hundred or so Hatfields in the region. According to one descendant, Johnse arrived "dressed fit to kill—yellow shoes, new mail order suit, and a high celluloid collar. He was ruddy faced, ham-handed, and sandy haired, with a pair of insinuating blue eyes that set the mountain belles' hearts all a-flutter. He was a great fellow for putting on the dog."

Trouble was, Johnse decided to put on the dog with twenty-year-old Rose Anne McCoy, one of sixteen children of Randolph McCoy, the leader of the McCoy clan. In a shocking affront to both families, Johnse went over and offered the beautiful black-haired McCoy some gingerbread. Randolph McCoy raised his rifle and separated the pair, but later on Johnse found his way back to Rose Anne. "By common youthful impulse," said the Hatfield descendant, "they drew away from the others to a more secluded spot where rifles were stacked against a clump of paw-paw bushes."

By the end of Election Day Johnse Hatfield had convinced Rose Anne McCoy to return with him to the Hatfield home, which, like others in the hills, was little more than a primitive and crowded shack. Rose Anne spent her first night at the Hatfields' in a bed with two of Johnse's sisters, and despite pleas from her McCoy relations, she wouldn't go home. Devil Anse didn't much like having a McCoy under his roof, but he did get a kick out of how much it riled her family.

Still, the leader of the Hatfields was not about to let his son marry a McCoy. Johnse grew less interested and Rose Anne became more impatient, and eventually, after several months, moved out. Some versions say Rose Anne had Johnse's child, but there is no record of his or her fate. Rose Anne was not immediately welcomed back into the McCoy clan, and after caring for her ailing mother, she died young. Johnse, meanwhile, took up with another McCoy, this time Rose Anne's cousin Nancy. Despite Devil Anse, they married in 1881.

Johnse's romancing made for a very tense Election Day in 1882. And sure enough, so violent a brawl erupted that one of Devil Anse's brothers was seriously injured, and later died. As revenge, three McCoys were captured and summarily executed. Johnse was one of those indicted for the McCoy deaths—cousins of his wife—but he was never prosecuted.

Johnse became a leader of the Hatfield raids against his in-laws during the most violent years of the feud. He was largely responsible for an attack on the McCoy household on New Year's Day

1888 that killed one of Randolph's sons and one daughter—cousins of Johnse's wife—and left Randolph's wife beaten senseless.

That slaughter apparently finally shocked both families—as well as state law-enforcement officials—into trying to cool the feud. Johnse and his wife, whose marriage was hardly happy under the pressure both faced from their families, decided to leave the valley entirely and move to western Canada. Johnse, in fact, went ahead to British Columbia while his wife and their two children returned to McCoy territory to say goodbye to her parents. At a big farewell party Nancy met Frank Phillips, a part-time sheriff's deputy and part-time vigilante, who had been the only man capable of a successful revenge against the Hatfields. Nancy never went back to her Hatfield husband and instead married Phillips.

That was the end of Johnse's relations with McCoy women. The feuding, as well, became more infrequent. Johnse eventually spent ten years in prison for his role in the 1888 slayings. After his release, he became a land agent for a coal company, a job he held until he died of a heart attack while riding a horse in 1922.

CHILDREN of LELAND HAYWARD and MARGARET SULLAVAN

"I'M THE DAUGHTER of a father who's been married five times," said Brooke Hayward at her sister's funeral in 1961. "Mother killed herself. My sister killed herself. My brother has been in a mental institution. I'm 23 and divorced with two kids."

Ah, Hollywood. On-screen you'd hardly believe it. Offscreen, the story of legendary super-agent Leland Hayward, his wife, actress Margaret Sullavan, and their three children is perhaps the most quintessential tale of the decline and fall of a Hollywood family ever to come out of Tinsel Town.

Hayward's client list defined the era: besides his wife—and two of her ex-husbands, Henry Fonda and director William Wyler—Hayward struck deals for Greta Garbo, Judy Garland, Fred Astaire, Katharine Hepburn, Cary Grant, Jimmy Stewart, Gene Kelly, and many, many more, including such writers as Ernest Hemingway and Dashiell Hammett. Hayward, who later produced such hit plays as *South Pacific* and *Mr. Roberts*, took great delight in juggling several deals at once, and was called the "Toscanini of the telephone."

Margaret Sullavan, meanwhile, was a strong-willed yet seductive actress who was loved by critics both on Broadway and in Hollywood. Best known for the movie *Back Street* and the play *The Voice of the Turtle*, Sullavan was, according to one swooning critic, "consummately, unforgettably the epitome of feminine allure." In a poem about her, Ogden Nash wrote, "The fairest of sights in twinkling lights is Sullavan with an 'a'."

Even their own children were awed. "They were both so alive, so insuperably optimistic," wrote Brooke in her dead-on best-selling memoir, *Haywire*, in 1977. "To watch them both was to strain one's own ability to keep abreast, to tread bottomless water; finally, it was to know the real meaning of exhaustion." The book's title, by the way, was Hayward's cable address.

Brooke, born eight months after Hayward and Sullavan married in 1936, and her younger siblings, Bridget, born in 1939 and Bill, born in 1941, spent their early years as part of the happy Hollywood children crowd. Brooke played with Jane Fonda, Bill was friends with Jane's brother, Peter. They all frolicked through rounds of increasingly lavish birthday parties, attended by their nannies. The Hayward children actually had their own separate house, called the Barn, which was connected to their parents' house by a thirty-foot walkway.

Brooke and Bridget and Bill weren't completely spoiled by the Hollywood star treatment mostly because their mother didn't like it. Sullavan was uncomfortable even signing autographs, and she hated the way the telephone monopolized Hayward's life. In 1945,

Sullavan took her own money and bought a farm in Connecticut. She moved the family there and everyone promptly developed hay fever, poison ivy, and countless allergies.

It was, it turned out, the beginning of the end for Hayward and Sullavan, as he began spending more time back in Hollywood and had an affair. They divorced in 1948, an event from which neither Sullavan nor their children recovered. "It was when my parents split and became terribly alienated that this terrible pressure was put on the children," Brooke said in one interview. "I always liked to fantasize that my mother was still in love with my father. Yet she wouldn't talk to him for twelve or thirteen years, and then when she did it was only because my sister was in a mental institution."

After a few years under their mother's strict rule, all three children went to boarding schools. When Bill had a series of discipline problems at the Lawrenceville School, his father took the drastic step of sending him to the Menninger Clinic in Topeka, Kansas, for psychiatric treatment. He spent two years there and then joined the Army. He later returned to Hollywood to produce films with Peter Fonda.

In 1950 Sullavan married British industrialist Kenneth Wagg, but apparently she never really got over Hayward. She suffered a nervous breakdown in 1956 while preparing to do a television series. More than three years later she was in New Haven, Connecticut, starring in a Broadway-bound play, *Sweet Love Remembered*. She was under a psychiatrist's care at the time and, unknown to almost everyone, for some years she had suffered a growing loss of hearing that she believed was threatening to end her career. On January 1, 1960, Sullavan was found dead in her hotel room of an overdose of barbiturates. She was forty-eight.

Nine months later, depressed by her mother's death and by her own epileptic seizures, which had caused her to be institutionalized for a time, twenty-one-year-old Bridget Hayward died of an overdose in her New York apartment. Leland Hayward died after a stroke in 1971 at the age of sixty-eight.

Brooke Hayward survived all of this. She has been asked often if she is worried for herself by the fate of her mother and sister.

But she has maintained that "I never thought that there was a family curse, that it was genetic."

After marriage and two children, she was divorced in the late 1950s. She tried acting for a while, then married actor Dennis Hopper. They divorced in 1969 after eight years. She is now married to bandleader Peter Duchin, the son of bandleader Eddy Duchin. Hayward occasionally writes magazine articles and is working on a second book.

CHILDREN of
WILLIAM RANDOLPH HEARST

IT WAS NO ACCIDENT that not until the third generation of media mogul William Randolph Hearst did any of his descendants earn a college degree. "A certain kind of good mind does resist education," Hearst, a Harvard dropout, wrote to his wife. Millicent Hearst tried to keep her five sons away from their father precisely because of such attitudes. But it did little good. Hearst, whose insatiable hunger for power helped him build one of the biggest media empires of the early twentieth century and made him the model for Orson Welles's *Citizen Kane,* was just as ambitious in squelching such an appetite in his children.

"We never did a goddamned thing," William Randolph Hearst, Jr., told Lindsay Chaney and Michael Cieply, authors of *The Hearsts.* "We never worked because we never had to. . . . It got to the point where they held a parade if one of the Hearst boys bothered to get up in the morning."

Hearst, who maintained separate quarters at the family's grand New York home after he began his long affair with Marion Davies in 1915, would on rare occasions give fatherly advice to his sons. He wrote to John, "It is better to be a successful workingman than a busted playboy." And he wrote to his sixteen-year-old twins, Randolph and David, "No one knows whether you will inherit anything or not; but if you are not able to make money, you will not be able to keep money."

But Hearst indulged his boys with toys—cars and boats and the like—and William Jr. said his father directly talked him into dropping out after he finished two years at the University of California at Berkeley. "You can read and write," Hearst told him. "If you stay there any longer you're wasting your time." John dropped out of college at nineteen for the lure of a $100,000 salary as president of a Hearst company that published four magazines, including *Town & Country*. His father later cut his pay to $15,000 after the entire Hearst empire suffered losses during the Depression. As each of his five sons dropped out of college, Hearst gave them big-titled jobs in his corporation—oldest son George was named publisher of the flagship *San Francisco Examiner* when he was twenty-five—but he gave them almost nothing to do. The non-family executives who really ran the media properties made no pretense of including the Hearst boys in their decisions.

Little wonder, then, that when he died of a stroke in 1951 at the age of eighty-eight, Hearst left control of his empire not to his sons but to his handpicked, nonrelated executives. His sons, though they were left little of his wealth directly, were entitled to remain in their empty jobs and continue to draw big salaries. Future control of the companies, Hearst said, would pass to other executives who must "be no issue of mine."

Such bequests did not inspire productivity among his sons. George Randolph Hearst, Sr., suffered from alcoholism; he married six times. His brothers finally rewrote their trust document to insulate the family money from George's ex-wives. His drinking compounded his diabetes, and he died in 1972 at the age of sixty-seven. John Randolph Hearst, Sr., drifted away from the family business and dabbled in real estate. He was known for staying in bed past noon, and his heavy drinking, too, caused health problems. John died of a pancreatic attack in 1958 at the age of forty-nine. David was forced to retire at the age of forty-five as publisher of the Los Angeles *Herald-Express* when the newspaper floundered in the late 1950s. He was a near recluse until he died of cancer in 1986.

The remaining two sons, Randolph and William Jr., who won a Pulitzer Prize in 1956 for his interview with Khrushchev, still maintain positions in the Hearst organization, which continues to be run by nonfamily executives. Randolph remained largely out of the public eye until his daughter, Patty, was kidnapped in 1974.

If Hearst left his sons little ambition, he at least didn't leave them empty-handed. After some lean years, the Hearst Corp. now is highly profitable. *Forbes* estimated last year that the family shared $40 million. And William Randolph Hearst III, the first male Hearst to obtain a college degree, today is the active publisher of the *Examiner*.

SON of HENRY VIII

FOR WANT OF A SON, the Church of England was born.

King Henry VIII's first wife, Catherine of Aragon, had produced six miscarriages and one daughter, Mary, when Henry's mistress, Bessie Blount, gave birth to Henry Fitzroy in 1519. At first, the king's bastard was kept a secret. But as Queen Catherine grew past her childbearing years King Henry placed his illegitimate son in line for the throne. Henry publicly announced his son's existence when the boy was six. That same year the King heaped a multitude of titles on young Henry, among them Earl of Nottingham and Duke of Richmond and Somerset, both titles that previously had been granted to future kings. The bastard's new titles carried lands and income of more than £4,000 a year and put him in line for the throne after any legitimate heirs. The king also considered naming the boy King of Ireland.

Young Henry, a good-looking, charming child, was raised to be king. England's best scholars were assigned to educate him; he traveled widely with his father and received part of his schooling in the prestigious French court. As young Henry matured, English ambassadors approached European royalty with proposals of marriage, exclaiming that the boy "is near of the King's blood and of excellent qualities, and is already furnished to the state of a great prince, and yet may be easily, by the King's means, exalted to higher things."

Meanwhile, of course, Henry VIII was proceeding with other plans for producing a legitimate heir. The Catholic Church had refused to grant the king a divorce, though the pope was so eager for a compromise that he considered allowing Henry's bastard son to marry Mary, Henry's daughter by Catherine. In 1533, Henry VIII defied the pope, and married Anne Boleyn. He established the Anglican Church in England soon after. He declared his daughter Mary illegitimate and that Anne's future children would be first in line for the throne. Anne produced only one child, Elizabeth, before she was beheaded on charges of adultery on May 19, 1536. Eleven days later King Henry married Jane Seymour and declared a new Act of Succession, this one making both Mary and Elizabeth illegitimate and giving the king power to name his own successor, undoubtedly young Henry, if need be.

But before such a need arose, young Henry Fitzroy died suddenly six weeks later. Some history books record his death from consumption. But it was widely rumored at the time—and the king himself believed—that the illegitimate heir apparent had been given a slow poison by the doomed Queen Anne. So concerned was the king over the loss of his heir that he ordered his son buried in secret. Young Henry was wrapped in lead, covered in straw, and buried in the far-off town of Thetford.

The next year, King Henry finally got his legitimate son, Edward, though the birth cost the life of Queen Jane. Edward was only nine when Henry VIII died in 1547 and Edward himself died before his sixteenth birthday. Henry's first child, who became known as "Bloody Mary" for trying to restore the Catholic Church to England, ruled five years before she died, leaving Henry's greatest legacy to Elizabeth, who was crowned in 1558 and reigned for forty-five years.

As is always the case with royal matters, history might have been quite different had Henry's bastard survived. "Well it was for Mary and Elizabeth that he was dead," said one chronicler of the time. "Had he lived to survive King Edward VI, we might presently have heard of a King Henry IX."

DAUGHTER of AL HIRSCHFELD

"ONE GOOD LINE in a Hirschfeld drawing is worth a thousand good words," said *New York Times* theater critic Brooks Atkinson. Echoed Brendan Gill: "To be a star on Broadway is to have one's name in lights, yes, but it is also, and more significantly, to be drawn by Hirschfeld." Talk about the power of the pen. Al Hirschfeld's simple black ink drawings have so indelibly captured the essence of this century's performers that it is almost impossible to picture, say, Carol Channing without thinking of the parking-meter-shaped mouth that Hirschfeld lovingly bestowed upon her.

Hirschfeld's drawings—more than three thousand of them in the *Times*—usually appeared before a show opened on Broadway, which meant the artist had to attend an out-of-town tryout performance so he could get a sense of the actors' mannerisms and costumes. In October 1945 he was in Philadelphia watching a preview of the show *Are You With It?* when he received word that his daughter, Nina, had been born. Hirschfeld rushed back to New York, saw his daughter, then went to his studio to draw the sketch of the show he had just seen. Ecstatic over his new daughter, he put a poster in the background of the sketch that showed a baby reading a book above the billing, "Nina the Wonder Child."

And he has never heard the end of it. "It started out just as an innocent gesture heralding her entry into the world," Hirschfeld said. "But it's gotten a little out of hand." Indeed it has. Hirschfeld continued putting NINA in his drawings, but he began hiding it in the wrinkles of shirt sleeves, or the strands of hair or curled fingers. He left his daughter's name out of one sketch and received several hostile letters. It turned out some readers actually had created a weekly pool on the matter. Hirschfeld said he once, at his daughter's request, inserted the name of her friend LIZA instead, only to receive flowers and telegrams congratulating him on his second child.

That, still, was not the end of it. It seems the Air Force took to projecting Hirschfeld's drawings and their hidden NINAs on large screens to train its fighter pilots to spot targets. The Department of Defense also paid a Temple University psychology professor $60,000 so he could conduct a study of eye movement while looking for hidden objects, namely NINAs.

It turns out, though, that however hard it may be to spot NINAs (and the number next to Hirschfeld's name tells you how many you should be looking for), it is nothing compared to finding Nina herself. The woman, now in her forties, with the most sought-after name in the *New York Times* won't give interviews. Her mother says she is married, has a son, and lives in Texas.

DAUGHTER of BIG JIM HOGG

PARENTS CAN DO a lot of things to screw up their kids, but they generally don't do them intentionally. So what could Big Jim Hogg, later the first native governor of Texas, have been thinking when he named his only daughter "Ima"? Later Hogg would insist he had named his daughter in honor of his late brother, the author of an epic Civil War poem called, "The Fate of Marvin," which featured a heroine named Ima. Still when Hogg, a three-hundred-pound populist reformer, was campaigning for governor, he delighted his country audiences when he introduced his daughter and one of her little friends by saying, "This is Ima Hogg and this is Ura Hogg."

For decades the legend remained that Ima Hogg had sisters named Ura and Shesa and a brother named Hesa. In fact, only Ima had been branded. Her three brothers were named Will, Tom, and Mike. Many years later, after everyone diplomatically addressed her as "Miss Ima," the governor's daughter remained sensitive about her name. "Ima I became, and Ima I was to remain," she would say curtly and the subject was closed. She did, however, keep a file of letters from people who wanted to know if her name was real.

Perhaps being stuck with such an early embarrassment, which constantly got her teased at school, gave Miss Ima her strength and determination later on. She was eight when her father was elected governor in 1890, but because her mother was ill and died five years later, Ima soon became her father's hostess. She studied piano at the University of Texas and studied further in New York and Europe, where she also bought paintings by some young unknown artists including Picasso, Matisse, and Cézanne. She returned to Houston, having decided not to become a concert pianist but determined instead to start her own orchestra. She founded the Houston Symphony Society in 1913. To raise money, Miss Ima rang doorbells presenting her rich friends with an open ledger so they could see how much others had donated—and realize that others would see how much they were going to contribute. "I was not going to have a one-horse orchestra," she said.

Ima Hogg really came into her own after 1919, when oil gushed up from a 4,100-acre plantation near West Columbia, Texas, that her father had left to her and her brothers when he died thirteen years earlier. While her brothers handled the business side of one of the biggest early Texas oil fortunes, Miss Ima founded the Houston Child Guidance Clinic and later the Hogg Foundation for Mental Health. She and her brothers built a grand mansion in Houston's River Oaks, called Bayou Bend, where Miss Ima hosted elaborate dinners which became forums for her civic causes.

Ima Hogg donated her early collection of Postimpressionists to the Houston Museum of Fine Arts. She created scholarships in the fine arts and donated land for public parks. In 1968 she moved out of Bayou Bend and turned the mansion, full of her vast collection of American antiques, into a museum. She spent her seventies and eighties overseeing the restoration of historic Texas buildings. And though she had been out of the governor's mansion for well over half a century, "Miss Ima," said the wife of then governor John Connally, "always has been and always will be the First Lady of Texas."

In 1975, the ninety-three-year-old Miss Ima was in London, on her way to the Bayreuth Music Festival in Germany, when she fell getting into a taxi and broke her hip. She developed pneumonia and died of a heart attack in a London hospital. Just before the end, the grand lady with an unfortunate name told friends at her bedside, "Whatever happens, remember that it was the way it was meant to be. I'm doing what I want to do. I'm where I want to be. I have no regrets."

DAUGHTER of VICTOR HUGO

VICTOR HUGO's DEEP insight into the human condition in his classic novels, *The Hunchback of Notre Dame* and *Les Misérables*, made him a literary giant of the nineteenth century. He was just as bold in real life, and his outspoken opposition to the regime of Napoléon III forced him to flee France in 1852. Until Napoléon fell twenty years later, Hugo lived on Jersey and Guernsey in the British-owned Channel Islands. The writer relished his life in exile, which only increased his notoriety.

But for his family, and especially his youngest daughter, Adèle, the banishment was more trying. While her father was busy being a famous exile and her two older brothers worked on writing projects of their own, twenty-two-year-old Adèle was left with no friends her own age and little to do. Hugo restricted her activity even more because his oldest and favorite daughter, Léopoldine, had drowned in a boating accident on the Seine in 1843.

Soon after the family moved to Guernsey in 1856—Hugo had been expelled from Jersey for criticizing Queen Victoria—Adèle had a nervous breakdown. Hugo believed his daughter simply indulged herself in self-pity. But his wife wrote him, "Adèle has given you her youth without complaint, without demanding gratitude, and you say that she thinks only of herself. Who knows what she has suffered, and what she is suffering now when she sees her future escaping her?"

Adèle found her only hope in Albert Andrew Pinson, a young Englishman she met in 1854. Even nine years later Adèle wrote of it in detail. "He saw me for the first time on a bench on the terrace in Jersey. I was sitting down, reading; I was absorbed in my book and I didn't see him. But he saw me, and from that day, which is already long ago, he loved me." Pinson joined the British Army, and after he left Jersey they wrote to each other and met a few times when he was on leave. Wrote Adèle, "His career was to love me, his ambition was to see me." Adèle rejected five marriage proposals at Guernsey while she waited for Pinson to return for her hand. Hugo, meanwhile, told her he would not approve such a match.

Suddenly in June 1863, the thirty-three-year-old Adèle left Guernsey. She gave no word where she was headed, but did leave a letter for her father. "Here I am separated, married without being married, the years will pass, this absence may last for a long while, one cannot wait for a long while at the time of life which I have reached. . . . Who knows the consequences of the troubles of an unmarried woman? What abyss may all this drag me into, drag us and him?"

Finally in August, Adèle sent word to her family that she had joined Pinson, who was stationed in Nova Scotia, and that they had married. "My daughter is becoming an Englishman," wrote Hugo to a friend. "Exile, behold your blows! Adèle is inexplicable. She seems to find pleasure and amusement in creating a false and painful situation for us. We did everything for her, and this is how she thanks us, her mother and me." Nevertheless, Hugo grudgingly had an announcement of Adèle's marriage published in the Guernsey newspaper.

Then in December, the family found out that Adèle had made it up. Pinson had not asked her to join him. When she arrived he had refused to marry her and in fact had asked her to leave. Apparently whatever interest Pinson had had in Adèle was gone. But even after her delusion was revealed, Adèle remained in Nova Scotia. She lived in a rooming house and rarely went out except to wait each day at Pinson's barracks and follow him home without speaking. She once asked her father for 5,000 francs so she could put Pinson to sleep and marry him before he woke up.

When Pinson's battalion was transferred to Barbados in 1866, Adèle followed, supported by small checks from her father. Then in 1870, Pinson married someone else. Hugo finally decided it was time for Adèle to come home. "She will forget, and she will get well. I will give some parties for her . . . I will dedicate books to Adèle. . . . If a fool has the power to dishonour, Victor Hugo will have the power to shed splendour!"

Hugo had his daughter brought back to France in 1872, but he did not make her well. So absorbed was she in her fantasy that she did not recognize one of her brothers. Adèle was put in an asylum, where she remained until she died forty-three years later. She was the only member of the family to outlive Hugo, who died in 1885 at the age of eighty-three. *The Story of Adèle H,* a movie based on her life, was released in 1975.

SON of BARBARA HUTTON

IT'S NOT UNUSUAL for children of the rich to grow up spoiled. But what about *their* children, the children of the spoiled rich? Consider the life of Lance Reventlow. "A seven-and-a-half pound boy was born to Barbara Hutton yesterday," the *Times* of London reported in 1936 under the headline "World's Richest Baby," "and began life with the assets of a European title and the prospect of inheriting a Woolworth fortune."

Poor little rich Lance also began life with a pair of jet-setting, castle-hopping, constantly partying parents. "Nothing infuriates me more than rich people who keep saying they're unhappy because they have wealth," said Hutton, who as the granddaughter of five-and-dime mogul F. W. Woolworth had inherited $25 million when she was twelve. "I always tell them they should go down on their knees and thank God they have money." The son of Barbara's second of seven husbands, Danish Count Court Haugwitz Hardenberg Reventlow, Lance was born in a London home near Hyde Park where the bedroom had been converted into a delivery room, complete with modern equipment from a local hospital.

Hutton had been raised by caretakers after her mother committed suicide over her father's affairs, and the heiress provided the same kind of parenting for her only child. After Hutton and Reventlow split up when Lance was two, he was shuttled back and forth between continents and governesses, depending on his parents' schedule. In August 1938, for example, while Hutton vacationed in Venice, Lance was taken by his governess to Yorkshire. The following January, Lance went to Switzerland with the count while Hutton and her new boyfriend went to Egypt. Hutton, whose later husbands included three princes and Cary Grant, largely left Lance to be raised by others throughout his childhood, though she pursued a nasty custody battle with Count Reventlow that lasted until the boy was fourteen.

Lance later would say, "So you were born with brown eyes. I was born with money. It just makes life more convenient." Indeed it did. He dropped out of college after a semester to get into car racing. But his big break came on his twenty-first birthday in 1957, when he got hold of his $8 million trust fund, which produced an income of $1 million a year. For the same birthday, his mother gave him $1.5 million to build his own house. Lance built one with a swimming pool in the living room and a workshop for his cars. His house became the hangout for many of Hollywood's children, and his parties, which occasionally turned into orgies, earned his manse the nickname "Camp Climax."

Also at the age of twenty-one, Lance hired fourteen auto experts to help him build an American racing car that would rival the Europeans. The next year he did in fact beat Ferraris and Maseratis, winning a race in the Bahamas, the first time since 1924 that an American car and driver won an international road race. He never raced as well again, though his passion for racing was cited as the reason that actress Jill St. John, whom he married in 1960, divorced him three years later.

In 1964, at the age of twenty-eight, Lance married nineteen-year-old Cheryl Holdridge, a former Mouseketeer. But within a few years the marriage cooled, and while Cheryl stayed in Los Angeles Lance hung out in Hawaii and Colorado, where he began throwing wild parties again and replaced racing with skiing, sailing, and polo. On July 24, 1972, Lance and three friends went up in a single-engine Cessna over Aspen to survey some land he wanted to buy. They were in the midst of severe thunderstorms when the plane, piloted by a twenty-seven-year-old student flyer, crashed into a wooded area of the Rockies eight miles from the nearest road. All four were killed. Lance, who was decapitated, was identified by the initials on his shirt. The thirty-six-year-old Woolworth heir left his estranged wife most of his estate, which newspapers estimated at $50 million but in fact totaled about $6 million.

Hutton, who was not close to her son and who had briefly cut off his inheritance in 1962 after Lance grossly insulted her about her relationship with a man younger than he was, did not attend her son's funeral. A friend said later that Hutton, who died of a heart attack in 1979 at the age of sixty-six, was deeply disturbed by her son's death. "It was as if a lifetime's guilt had crystallized around the tragedy. She kept saying, 'If I had only been a better mother, Lance would still be alive. If only he hadn't gone up in that plane, I would still have him." In truth, the tragedy had begun long before the plane took off.

J

SON of ANDREW JACKSON

ANDREW JACKSON will always be remembered as the president whose supporters tracked mud into the White House, and the symbolism is apt. The first self-made man to be president, "Old Hickory" brought a down-to-earth quality to the office that reflected his own hard-won struggle. The popular populist, who, as a young man, supported his study of law by betting on horse races and cock fights, was indeed a practical man. Jackson did, however, have a blind spot—his son.

Andrew Jackson, Jr., was not Jackson's natural son. Andrew was one of a pair of twins born to the brother of Jackson's wife, Rachel. Since Rachel had had several miscarriages, and since her sister-in-law almost died giving birth to the two boys, Jackson and Rachel adopted one of them and doted on him shamelessly.

Jackson was away a lot, building his career as an army general and later a politician. But he wrote to his wife and son often, telling Rachel he felt sure that Andrew Jr. "will take care of us both in our declining years. From our fondness toward him, his return of affection to us, I have every hope, if he should be spared to manhood, that he will, with careful education, realize all our wishes."

Rachel never lived to see if that would come true. She died when Andrew was eighteen, in December 1828, between her husband's election and his inauguration as the seventh president. Jackson, busy in his new job, put young Andrew in charge of the Hermitage, his Nashville homestead and primary plantation. But Andrew did not run things as his father had. He started buying land and materials on credit and soon ran up debts that he couldn't pay. He bought a plantation without his father's approval and pledged the Hermitage's cotton crop toward the first year's payments. Jackson wrote his son and asked him to send a copy of the contract. But, as frequently happened, Andrew didn't reply. Finally, two months later, Jackson demanded the contract or, the president told his son, "you will have trouble."

But Jackson could not remain firm with his only child. "My son," he later wrote, "these things are only brought to your view that you may profit by them hereafter. And there is no certainty that I will live to aid you."

In fact, Jackson lived long enough to practically devote his life to bailing out Andrew. When the president left the White House in 1836 at the age of seventy, he returned to find his Hermitage a run-down mess. Supplies were low, the horses lean, the fields unkempt, and his holdings encumbered by his son's huge debts. Jackson was forced to sell part of his plantation to raise some quick cash. In December 1839, he boarded a steamboat for New Orleans, "struggling on floating ice," he wrote, "in mists of falling snow," to obtain loans from some friends. He suffered a hemorrhage on the boat and wrote to Andrew—now married and the father of two boys—"I have taken this trip to endeavour to relieve you from present embarrassments and if I live to realize it I will die contented in the hope that you will never again encumber yourself with debts that may result in the poverty of yourself and the little family I so much love."

But the Hermitage continued to deteriorate. "Poverty stares us in the face," Jackson wrote, asking a friend to help him sell one of his plantations. "My dear Major, aid me in getting a purchaser and I will die happy." So desperate was Jackson for cash that he sought restitution from the federal government to settle a debt from the War of 1812. That caused his finances to be exposed and debated on the floor of Congress, which his party no longer controlled. The nation itself was suffering economically, and the press implied Jackson deserved his own hard times.

Before Jackson died in 1845, he amended his will to repay $16,000 in loans he had received from friends. He left everything else to Andrew, though some friends had urged him to make separate provision for Andrew's wife and children. "That would show a want of confidence," Jackson said.

Andrew did nothing to prove his father's friends wrong. His investments in iron works and lead mines all failed. He sold many of his slaves South in the middle of the night. He was forced to sell most of his father's land and finally even sold the Hermitage itself to the state of Tennessee, with the provision that he be allowed to continue living there. Ironically, Andrew's twin, who was raised by his natural parents and who was quite a trouble-maker in his youth, ended up running a far more successful plantation than his brother. Andrew, meanwhile, spent his final years hunting. In April 1865, while climbing over a fence on a hunting escapade he accidentally set off his gun and shot himself in the hand. Gangrene set in, and Andrew Jackson, Jr., died within a week. He was fifty-five.

CHILDREN of THOMAS JEFFERSON

"I CONSIDER THE LABOR of a breeding [slave] woman as no object, and that a child raised every two years is of more profit than the crop of the best laboring man." Statements like that by Thomas Jefferson—which seem to indicate that his only interest in slaves was as property—have led many historians to deny an apparent contradiction in the life of the man: that he may well have carried on a thirty-eight-year relationship with a slave woman and fathered as many as seven children by her. Some insist that would have been completely out of character for the highly principled president. But there is more than a little evidence to suggest that Jefferson's character had many facets.

Just before his wife of ten years died in 1782 after her sixth childbirth, Jefferson promised Martha that he would never remarry, so that their children wouldn't be raised by a stepmother. Two years later, Jefferson became minister to France and took his oldest daughter with him. In 1787 the forty-four-year-old statesman sent for Mary, his only other surviving child (the other four died before the age of three). Mary arrived in Paris with her chaperone, a beautiful fourteen-year-old slave girl named Sally Hemings.

Sally was one of 135 slaves that Jefferson's wife had inherited when her father died. It was also well-known that Sally, who was one-quarter black, was also the late Martha's half-sister. Martha's father was responsible for several children by Sally's mother, who also now lived at Jefferson's Monticello. The Hemingses had special status in the household, serving as chief house servants or carpenters or chefs.

By the time Jefferson left for America in October 1789, Sally was pregnant. There is no absolute proof that Jefferson was the father of Sally's first child, who was named Tom. Nor is it certain that he fathered Sally's other six children born at Monticello between 1795 and 1808. But biographer Fawn Brodie, in her book *Thomas Jefferson: An Intimate History*, points out many links between the two. In Paris, Jefferson spent as much on dresses for Sally as he did for his daughters. At Monticello, Sally lived in the main house. She was in charge of Jefferson's "chamber and wardrobe," but visitors said she clearly was the lady of the entire house.

Many of Jefferson's descendants maintained that Sally's children were fathered by two of Jefferson's nephews. But Brodie says Jefferson was at Monticello when all of Sally's children were conceived. And even one of Jefferson's legitimate grandchildren said that Sally Hemings "had children which resembled Mr. Jefferson so closely that it was plain that they had his blood in their veins. The resemblance was so close, that at some distance in the dusk the slave, dressed in the same way, might have been mistaken for Mr. Jefferson." One of Sally's children, Madison Hemings, later wrote that Jefferson had convinced Sally to return with him from Paris—she was considered free in France—by promising to free her children when they turned twenty-one. "We were free from the dread of having to be slaves all our lives long, and were measurably happy," he wrote.

Jefferson himself was never known to have uttered a word on the matter, even after bitter Federalists in 1802 flung several accusations about the new president's slave mistress. They published a song about "Monticellian Sally," to the tune of "Yankee Doodle." The chorus went:

> *Yankee Doodle, who's the noodle?*
> *What wife were half so handy?*
> *To breed a flock of slaves for stock,*
> *A black amour's the dandy.*

Of Sally's seven children, Tom's fate is unknown, and her next two died in infancy. A boy named Beverly, born in 1798, and Harriet, born in 1801, were listed as "runaways" in Jefferson's plantation records. They both went to Washington, where they passed as white. Madison Hemings later wrote that Beverly married a white woman in Maryland. Madison, born in 1805, and the youngest Hemings, Eston, born in 1808, both were freed in Jefferson's will in 1826. Sally was freed two years later by Jefferson's daughter. Madison said he and his brother lived with Sally until she died in 1835. Then Madison, trained as a carpenter, married a black woman and moved to Ohio, where he died in 1877. Eston married a black woman in Virginia but later moved to Wisconsin and passed as white until he died in 1853 or 1854, wrote Madison.

As for Jefferson's legitimate children, only his oldest daughter, Martha, outlived him. Both her husband and her sister Mary's husband were elected to Congress in 1802. Martha's husband, Thomas Randolph, later was governor of Virginia before he lost his mind in the 1820s. Martha died in 1836, leaving twelve children.

L

SON of CARL LAEMMLE

WHEN THEIR CHILDREN turn twenty-one, some parents give them a car, maybe, or a trip to Europe. Carl Laemmle gave his son a movie studio. No small gift. The studio was Universal, a cornerstone of the original Hollywood and the crowning achievement of Laemmle's life.

Laemmle had worked very hard to give it all up so soon. A German immigrant, he spent his first twenty years in America at a long list of jobs—from errand boy to bookkeeper—before he opened a nickelodeon in Chicago in 1906. Within seven years the feisty, five-foot-two-inch scrapper had become a millionaire. He was forty-six.

He waged a nasty fight with the company that had monopolized early movie distributions, and created his own film empire. In some ways Laemmle set the stage for Hollywood as we know it. He is credited with creating the first movie stars, including Mary Pickford and Florence Lawrence.

When Universal's cheap westerns and low-brow comedies made him rich, Laemmle was not one to be stingy. It was estimated that "Uncle Carl," as he was called, had seventy relatives on his studio's payroll, many of whom had recently arrived from his hometown in Bavaria and knew nothing about making movies. Nevertheless, said one writer, "the place was so jammed with relatives that a producer would always say 'sir' to a janitor because the latter would probably turn out to be a second cousin of the big boss's wife's brother-in-law." Cracked fellow mogul Jack Warner, Laemmle was "making the world safe for nephews."

And no one was safer than Laemmle's only son, called "Junior" though he claimed to hate it. Junior went to work at Universal when he was seventeen, producing short films. Less than four years later, on his twenty-first birthday in 1929, Junior became chief of production for the entire studio. And Laemmle seemed ready to pass Universal on to his young son. "I wanted him to go to college," Laemmle said. "He wanted to get into the studio. Then, on our way to Europe that summer, I had my attack of appendicitis. In London, the doctors gave me half an hour to live. And during that half-hour all I could think about was, 'What will become of Junior if I die now?' "

The youngest mogul in Hollywood, Junior immediately set about making his mark. Defying Universal's reputation for cheap two-reelers, Junior announced he would produce high-quality films. And that he did. His first major effort was *All Quiet on the Western Front,* which won the Academy Award for Best Picture in 1930. Junior also initiated Universal's famous horror flicks, including Bela Lugosi's *Dracula* and Boris Karloff's *Frankenstein.*

But, as often happens in crap games and Hollywood, Junior's luck ran out. His high-quality, high-budget films started flopping.

The Depression also hurt the studio's profits, and by 1935, as production of *Showboat* bogged down, Junior had spent nearly all of the studio's money. Only then did his father step back in. As fast as he had given his son the studio, he took it away, passing control to his son-in-law. Laemmle, who had retained his financial interest in the studio, desperately pledged his entire share—worth $5.5 million—to secure a $750,000 loan. But it was too late. Within a year he was forced to sell out for $5 million.

Junior at first seemed to brush off his failure and signed on with MGM. But a few months later, having produced no movies, he resigned. His father died in 1939 and Junior later enlisted in the Army during World War II. Junior was a hypochondriac, so during his military service he lived in a Long Island mansion and had a chauffeur drive him to the base every day. After the war, Junior occasionally announced some new movie deal he was working on, but he never made another film. He was often seen at racetracks with his bodyguard, but eventually he became more and more reclusive, living with his shelves of pills in his father's Beverly Hills mansion and entertaining only at his annual Rose Bowl Party. His father had forbidden him to marry a woman who wasn't Jewish, and Junior remained a bachelor all his life.

In the 1960s Junior developed multiple sclerosis, which confined him to a wheelchair until he died of a stroke in 1979 at the age of seventy-one. He had lived to see Universal collect the Best Picture Oscar for *The Sting* in 1973, the first time the studio had received the honor in forty-three years since his *All Quiet on the Western Front*.

CHILDREN of TIMOTHY LEARY

MOST FATHERS, upon seeing their daughter studying in her room and hearing her say, "Hi Dad. What would you like for Christ-

mas?" would not react by contemplating the "complete vulgariza-
tion of the real situation: two complex trillion-cell clusters, rooted
in an eternity of evolution, sharing for a flicker this unique con-
figuration of space/time. Offered this chance to merge souls and
bring out the divinity in the other, we exchanged Hi-Dad-Hi-Susan
squeaks." But then, most fathers are not Timothy Leary, who,
according to his memoir, *Flashbacks*, was in the midst of an LSD
trip at the time.

Promoting acid and the incantation to "Turn on, tune in, drop
out," Leary was one of the epicenters of the youthful sixties,
though he himself was approaching fifty. Before that, the son of
an army captain had been a clinical psychologist at Harvard. And
among those who witnessed his transformation, few saw it at
closer range than his son and daughter, Jack and Susan.

Leary's children were just eight and six years old when their
mother committed suicide on Leary's birthday in 1955. Leary took
his children to Europe, then was hired at Harvard, where he began
performing experiments in hallucinogenic drugs on graduate students and prison inmates. He conducted much of his research in
his home in Cambridge. His daughter, Susan, recalled, "I remember seeing people lying on mattresses in the living room and
I knew they were taking drugs, because they looked sort of funny—
I mean, the expressions on their faces, sort of smiling, sometimes."

Leary had many prominent supporters, including *Time* founder
Henry Luce and Cary Grant, but Harvard dismissed him in 1963
for his controversial experiments with LSD. He settled in with his
followers and two children at an estate provided by Mellon heirs
in Millbrook, New York. "It was like living in a church with jolly
people," said Susan.

It was, to say the least, hardly your average childhood. Susan
and Jack grew up surrounded by their father's groupies, occasionally accompanying them on their pilgrimages to Mexico to get
psychedelic mushrooms. At eighteen, Susan told an interviewer
from *McCall's* magazine that she already had taken LSD several
times. "Well, you know, it changes your patterns," explained Susan, who was in boarding school at the time. "I get hung up on
my patterns—you know, the way I think, the games I'm playing,

all that—the LSD changes you, gives you new insights, sort of clears you up."

In 1965 Susan was arrested with her father at the Mexican border for the possession of less than half an ounce of marijuana. Leary said in *Flashbacks* that Susan was carrying the dope in her panties, but to protect her, he took responsibility for the drug. After a lengthy court battle, he was convicted of smuggling in 1970 and sentenced to ten years in prison. The judge, citing Susan's "unusual home background," put her on probation.

Six months after Leary went to jail, he escaped and received asylum in Algeria, where he stayed with fugitive Eldridge Cleaver and his Black Panthers. He moved on to Switzerland, where he was joined by Susan, who had married and had a daughter. Leary was arrested in Afghanistan in 1973 and returned to the United States, where he served time in prison until 1976. Since then, he has gone on the lecture circuit, advocating the colonization of space, among other things. Most recently he has designed computer software to help people rate their personalities.

In 1978 Leary's son, Jack, was one of five people arrested in Berkeley, California, for conspiracy to distribute LSD. But since then, Leary's children have moved beyond the drug culture. In *Flashbacks*, published in 1983, Leary said his son was a member of the International Brotherhood of Boilermakers, Iron Ship Builders, Blacksmiths, Forgers and Helpers. His daughter, mother of two, had become a geriatric nurse and a member of the U.S. Army Reserve. Today both prefer to live quietly.

In his memoir, Leary still had high hopes for his children. "In my paternal fantasies, my children are frontier scouts of the Baby Boom," he wrote. "Members of the first shock wave of their generation to hit the entrenched past. They are, in my proud reveries, evolutionary heroes, late bloomers with unlimited potential."

SON of GYPSY ROSE LEE

"THE THINGS THAT GO ON in a strip-teaser's mind, would give you no end of surprise," Gypsy Rose Lee used to tell her audiences. "For example, when I raise my skirts with slyness and dexterity, I'm mentally computing just how much I'll give to charity." The famous ecdysiast flashed more tease than skin during her career. But if illusion was the name of her game, the Queen of Burlesque saved her most shocking fan dance for her son.

Erik certainly had an unusual childhood, spending most of each year touring strip joints with his mother, sleeping on a cot in her dressing room and working as her dresser. For her part, Gypsy—whose story became the smash Broadway musical—behaved like a cross between her own driven mother and Auntie Mame. She could buy a lavish sable coat for herself, but then steal silverware from restaurants and cook meals for herself and her son on a hotplate in their cheap hotel rooms. "I'm a woman alone in the world with a child," Gypsy would say. "I'll do whatever I must to survive."

That was true, but her life as a single mother was her own calculated choice. Gypsy divorced her second husband, art-gallery owner William Kirkland, while she was pregnant with Erik. She always told her son that Kirkland was his father and the two usually spent weekends together. But Erik said later he never believed that Kirkland was his real father. When Gypsy married painter Julio de Diego, Erik told his first-grade classmates that his name was Erik Lee de Diego.

Still, it wasn't until Erik was seventeen, in 1961, that he finally learned who his true father was. His mother finally had retired from stripping in 1957 at the age of forty-two and, again divorced, had moved to Beverly Hills while Erik stayed in their townhouse on East 63rd Street in Manhattan. It was Erik's psychiatrist who told him that Kirkland wasn't his father—after Kirkland called the psychiatrist to tell him he would no longer pay the bills. Erik confronted his mother when she was visiting from California, and at first she refused to tell him the truth. "She really felt that who she had had an affair with eighteen years ago shouldn't concern me," said Erik.

Finally, Gypsy confessed to her son, but only on his promise that he would never try to contact his father. The man was Otto Preminger, one of Hollywood's best and most combative film directors. The Viennese-born director of films such as *Laura, Anatomy of a Murder,* and *Exodus* threw such tantrums on the set that he was referred to as, "Otto the Terrible." This was a man who, on the set of *Exodus,* tried to motivate a group of children to shed tears by yelling, "Cry, you little monsters!"

This was the man that Gypsy Rose Lee chose to father her child. Erik later explained how it happened: "[Producer] Billy Rose had been her big love, and when he left her after a long-time affair, she decided she wanted something—a child—no one could take away. She had a brief affair with Otto Preminger for the purpose of conceiving me. She chose him because she felt that under his gruff exterior he possessed qualities she admired. . . . She literally chose Otto from the available Hollywood 'talent' and she didn't tell him what her plans were."

Preminger said their affair, which lasted only a few weeks, occurred while he was making *Laura* and Gypsy was in Hollywood to appear in another movie, *Belle of the Yukon.* "We had a romance," Preminger said. "Was a very short time, Hollywood, 1943–44. For a time after, Gypsy had disappeared. She had left California. I found her in a New York hospital and asked her, 'How are you, darling?' 'Fine,' she says. 'We had a son this morning.'" Preminger said he offered to help raise and support their son, but Gypsy refused. "She just wanted the baby," he said. "She was a very independent, sophisticated woman, way ahead of her time."

Erik honored his promise not to contact Preminger, who didn't know that his son knew about him. Then in 1966 Preminger found out that Erik had been told and, with Gypsy's blessing, the father and son finally met. Erik, twenty-two, was in the Army, stationed in Germany, and he met the sixty-year-old film director at a hotel in Paris. "Getting to know Erik was just like making friends with someone," said Preminger, who by then was married for the third time and the father of twins. Erik said he relaxed after they got drunk together. "Otto reveled in my life. He always wanted to know who I was seeing—and seemed a little wistful."

After Erik got out of the Army, he joined Preminger's film production company as a casting director and story editor. They continued to keep their relationship secret at Gypsy's insistence. She was hosting a daytime television talk show and was afraid her audience of housewives would disapprove. It wasn't until after Gypsy died of lung cancer in 1970 that Preminger publicly announced that Erik was his son. He adopted the twenty-six-year-old man in 1971.

Erik wrote the screenplay for one of Preminger's films, *Rosebud*, which flopped. He later was associate producer of the comedy hit *The Heartbreak Kid*, and in 1984 he wrote a book about his mother called *Gypsy and Me*. Erik said he wasn't bitter about his mother's decision to raise him by herself. "A friend suggested that the way Mother chose to have me was very selfish," Erik said. "I never thought of it that way. I just thought she was not the kind of person who would want to get into debates about what school I should attend."

SON of ABRAHAM LINCOLN

As THE NATION tried to cope with the assassination of Abraham Lincoln, it was left to Robert Todd Lincoln, the president's oldest son, to hold together his shattered family. Robert, a recent Harvard graduate who was staying at the White House when his father was shot, blamed himself for Lincoln's death, believing that had he been in the box at Ford's Theater he somehow could have stopped John Wilkes Booth. Meanwhile, since his already emotionally unstable mother was incapacitated with grief, Robert had to arrange the funeral service, which he was the only family member to attend.

He took his mother, Mary, to live with him in Chicago, where he became a successful corporate attorney. His career progressed and he began a family of his own, but his mother grew worse. Mary already had lost two of her four sons; four-year-old Edward had died of diphtheria in 1850 and twelve-year-old Willie, her favorite, had died in the White House of a fever in 1862. The fourth son, fifteen-year-old Tad, accompanied his mother to Europe in 1868, and for three years he devotedly took care of her. But Tad developed a chest cold during the chilly ocean voyage back to New York in May 1871, and two months later he was dead.

Mary, who previously had suffered mental breakdowns, began to have hallucinations. Once she left her hotel room partially clothed. She carried $51,000 in securities in a skirt pocket and began spending it on items such as seventeen pairs of gloves and two hundred dollars' worth of toiletries. In 1875, before Mary could squander the small fortune, Robert moved to have her declared incompetent, though he was tormented by the public attention it brought. After the hearing, Mary tried to kill herself by drinking what she mistakenly thought was a fatal drug. Robert placed her in a private sanitarium west of Chicago, but she was released to her sister four months later. After she was adjudged competent a year later, Mary wrote to her only surviving son: "You have tried your game of robbery long enough." Later she referred to Robert as "that wretched young man," but they reconciled in 1881, a year before Mary died.

In his career, Robert declined to follow in his father's large footsteps. He stayed out of national politics until 1880, when he led a move to elect President Grant to a third term. After fellow Republican James Garfield won the election, Robert was named Secretary of War. Four months later, he was at the train station when Garfield was shot, and it was up to him two months later to make the first official announcement of Garfield's death. Robert later served as minister to England under Benjamin Harrison.

But though his powerful namesake led many to talk of nominating him for president in 1884 and 1888, Robert actively sought to defuse his support. "I have seen too much of the wear and tear of official life to ever have a desire to reenter it," said the chubby, five-foot-ten-inch son of the former president, whom he didn't resemble at all. "The Presidential office is but a gilded prison. The care and worry outweigh, to my mind, the honor which surrounds the position."

Robert returned to his corporate law practice in Chicago in 1893, eventually becoming president of the Pullman Car Company in 1901 after its founder died. He retired in 1911, dividing his time between Washington, D.C., and his summer home in New Hampshire, where he played golf. As biographers approached him about his father, Robert kept a tight hold on his father's papers and would not grant interviews except to confirm basic historical facts. In 1919, Robert turned over Lincoln's papers to the Library of Congress with the stipulation that they be sealed for twenty-one years after his own death.

Robert Lincoln's last public appearance came in May 1922 at the dedication of the Lincoln Memorial. Robert, seventy-eight, did not speak at the ceremony, but he was very much pleased with the monument and thereafter would have cab drivers pass by it whenever he traveled around the city. Robert died of a stroke in his sleep a week before his eighty-third birthday in 1926. His wife had him buried in Arlington National Cemetery, but in 1930, he was reburied near his father in Lincoln's tomb in Springfield, Illinois.

CHILDREN of CHARLES LINDBERGH, JR.

FEW HAVE KNOWN the oppressive glare of fame as well as Charles Lindbergh, Jr. After his record solo flight across the Atlantic in 1927, Lindbergh could make headlines just walking out of his house. It wasn't enough for him to build Hopewell, his isolated New Jersey estate, where he tried to insulate his wife and new-born son from the publicity. It was from the upstairs nursery, while the Lindberghs and a nanny were in the house, that Charles Lindbergh III was kidnapped on March 1, 1932. Despite an even bigger barrage of publicity, or perhaps because of it, the baby, not yet two years old, was found dead in a shallow grave two months later.

So when his wife, Anne, gave birth to her second child in August, Lindbergh issued a statement to the press. "It is impossible for us to subject the life of our second son to the publicity which we feel was in large measure responsible for the death of our first. We feel that our children have a right to grow up normally with other children. Continued publicity will make this impossible. I am appealing to the press to permit our children to lead the lives of normal Americans."

His appeal went unheeded. When the car that was hired to drive young Jon to nursery school was ambushed in the middle of the road, the hijackers turned out to be photographers. Following other threats, the three-year-old was pulled out of his nursery school and, under armed guard, played "in a wire entanglement like a tennis court." Soon after, the family fled to England and later to France. Finally, when the family returned to settle in Darien, Connecticut, in 1941, the publicity had died down, and the children—Land was born in 1937, Anne in 1940, Scott in 1942, and Reeve in 1945—could play with the neighbors.

After the glare faded, Lindbergh encouraged his children to take risks. When Jon, whom Lindbergh was prodding to climb a steep cliff, said, "I want to come down," Lindbergh replied, "No, you want to go up." Said one child: "He didn't converse so much as he lectured." But Lindbergh rarely talked about his famous Atlantic flight and only once mentioned the death of the children's older brother.

After World War II, Lindbergh largely stayed out of the public eye. He died of cancer in 1974. His wife still lives in Connecticut. His children, meanwhile, all went in different directions, none related to their father's famous feat. Jon, after three years as an underwater demolitions expert in the Navy, set a world record in 1962 under the sea above which his father had flown; Jon dived 432 feet deep into the Atlantic and stayed down for forty-nine hours. He now lives near Seattle, where he is an independent consultant developing fish farms.

Land is a rancher in Montana. Scott is a primatologist working to reintroduce species of monkeys into Brazilian jungles. Lindbergh's daughters, Reeve and Anne, both write children's stories and other books. It's enough to make a father proud.

DAUGHTER of ART LINKLETTER

ART LINKLETTER was the quintessential television "personality." He couldn't sing, dance or act, but he did have a talent for talking, and viewers felt comfortable having him show up on the screen in their living rooms. He was there for two decades until 1969, hosting "People Are Funny" and later, "House Party." The Canadian-born Linkletter became a very successful businessman, the proud father of five children, and a spokesman for things wholesome and promising. His books, such as *Kids Say the Darndest Things* and *Yes You Can!: How to Succeed in Business and Life,* found a large audience.

His youngest daughter, Diane, seemed to be following in his footsteps, having appeared on a couple of television shows and on tour. In the summer of 1969 Diane and her father recorded a song together that later won a Grammy. It was called "We Love You—Call Collect," and was about a father appealing to his runaway daughter to call home.

Later, Linkletter would say that the song wasn't about Diane, an attractive twenty-year-old girl with a beehive hairdo and pearl necklace. But the press quickly drew parallels after she jumped to her death out of the kitchen window of her sixth-floor Hollywood apartment on Saturday morning, October 4, 1969. She apparently had had a fight with her boyfriend and had taken a large dose of LSD, not for the first time. Just before 9:00 A.M., she called her brother Robert and told him, "I'm going to kill myself. I'm scared. Help." She jumped before Robert arrived. Her boyfriend had tried to grab the belt loops of her dress but he couldn't hold on.

In an interview in the *Los Angeles Times* the next day, Linkletter said he had known for six months that his daughter was taking drugs, but he had been unable to stop her. "It wasn't a suicide," he said, "because she wasn't herself. It was murder. She was murdered by all the people who manufacture and sell drugs."

Linkletter said he wanted to publicize his daughter's death to expose the dangers of drugs. "I think my daughter's death is going to be paid for many, many times by the kinds of things I can say and get done using this as an example," he said. "I want the parents and I want their kids to read about this and be shocked, be frightened at what can happen." About three weeks later he met with President Nixon and congressional leaders, after which Nixon said he had been "so moved" that he called for increased funding for drug abuse education. Three months later the Senate passed a bill to tighten drug enforcement.

Linkletter became a frequent spokesman against drug abuse, and in 1973 he wrote a book about his daughter's death, *Drugs at My Doorstep.* But Diane was not the only tragedy in Linkletter's family. His oldest daughter's husband, distraught over business losses, had shot himself in the head three months before Diane killed herself. And in 1980, his son Robert died after a car crash in West Los Angeles.

Two days after Diane's death, Linkletter said, "I've been as good a parent as I could possibly be, I think. We've been a very close family. We've done everything you do according to the book—taken vacations together, gone on pack trips together, traveled extensively all over the world. We've been a good Christian family. My wife and I have tried to set a good example by being a good example. We have tried to keep our children up to date on what the dangerous things are, but perhaps we did not bear down as hard as we should have."

CHILDREN of JOE LOUIS

JOE LOUIS wasn't just one of the greatest boxers who ever entered the ring. He wasn't just the man who, at six feet one and a half inches and 197 pounds defended his heavyweight title twenty-five times—including his famous two-minute knockout of Hitler's boy, Max Schmeling—and retired undefeated after twelve years in 1949. More than all of that, Joe Louis was America's first black hero. "The Brown Bomber" had plenty of white fans, but it was in the black ghettos that his victories sparked spontaneous street parties. "Louis was the black Atlas on whose broad shoulders blacks were lifted," said one writer. "For in those days, there were few authentic black heroes."

Aware of the delicate status of being a black hero in the 1930s, Louis—born Joe Louis Barrow, the son of Alabama sharecroppers— and those around him made sure his image stayed clean. In public, he followed a list of rules to live by set down by his manager. They included:

- Never have your picture taken alone with a white woman.
- Never go into a nightclub alone.
- Live and fight clean.

In private, Louis managed to find plenty of pleasure that went unreported. During his career and well after, the fighter had many mistresses scattered across the country, including Lena Horne and Lana Turner. The good times had their price. After he retired the IRS went after him for $1.25 million in unpaid taxes and penalties. "I liked the good life," said Louis. "I just don't know where the money went. I wish I did. I got 50 percent of each purse and all kinds of expenses came out of my cut."

Louis had affairs whether he was married or not, which usually he was. The twenty-one-year-old boxer married a nineteen-year-old secretary, Marva Trotter, in 1935, and they had a daughter,

Jacqueline, in 1943. Marva grew tired of her husband's affairs and divorced him in 1945, but they remarried later that year. Joe Louis Barrow, Jr., was born in 1947 before the couple split up for good in 1949. After that, Joe Jr. said recently, he and his sister saw their father only a few times a year, usually at dinners where Louis was besieged by fans. "It always bothered me that we would have to share him with the whole restaurant," Joe said. Louis was married briefly a second time in 1955 and then married Martha Jackson, a Los Angeles attorney, in 1959.

In his autobiography, Louis said that in 1964 he became involved with a prostitute, whom he called "Marie." Louis said she introduced him to cocaine, and then in 1965 told the fifty-one-year-old retired fighter that she was pregnant with his child. Louis told his wife, who decided she wanted to raise the baby. She named him Joseph, despite the fact that Louis's legitimate son was already named Joe Jr. Martha and Marie became friends, and Martha later took in three more of Marie's children, none of them Louis's. "I love the kids and they love me," Louis said in his autobiography. "They make me feel young. Those times when I'm concentrating too much on myself, they come along with some little ache or pain that's so important to them that I had best change my concentration to them."

That's a rosier picture than perhaps existed. Louis was confined to a wheelchair after he suffered a heart attack in 1977. He and Martha officially adopted all four children in 1980, the year before he died, but Joe Barrow, Jr., says his father was in such poor health he may not even have been aware of the action. Years earlier, in 1969, Joe Jr. had had his father committed to a mental institution in Colorado after Louis developed a paranoia that he later said was related to his drug problems. When he recovered, Louis signed on with Caesar's Palace in Las Vegas, where he was paid fifteen thousand dollars a year and given a home with a swimming pool for his services as a "greeter," which basically meant chatting and playing golf with the casino guests.

Since Louis died, his adopted family has scattered. Martha is in poor health and lives in Detroit. In 1988 Joseph was convicted of supplying false information to the FBI after he fabricated a kidnapping in Cincinnati. The three younger children, still in their teens, are living with friends or relatives in Las Vegas or California.

Joe Louis Barrow, Jr., a Denver banker and businessman, recently wrote a biography of his father. Barrow said he learned more about his father by researching and writing the book than he ever had known when Louis was alive. "Joe Louis was my father, but he was a great deal more to those of his own generation," Barrow wrote. "He was a hero. I came to realize they knew him better than I did. Emotionally, he seemed more attached to other people than to the family."

CHILDREN of MARTIN LUTHER

SOMEHOW THE IMAGE of Martin Luther as a rebellious monk doesn't jibe with that of a happy family man. But he was both, and the second image proved to be almost as significant as the first. Luther was excommunicated by the Catholic Church in 1521, four years after he nailed his "Ninety-Five Theses" on the church door in Wittenberg, Germany. What began as a criticism of church corruption grew into Luther's radical notion that man has direct access to God and doesn't need priests to interpret the Bible for him.

The first Protestant set down the basic guidelines for a new church, including the argument that priests should marry and that to remain celibate was unnatural. Luther himself seemed to have no plans to follow that idea until he met Katherina von Bora. He had helped Katherina and eight other nuns escape from their convent in 1523, and had found husbands for all the other nuns except Katherina by 1525. Eventually, Luther said, he decided it was God's will that he "take pity on the abandoned." They married secretly that summer when Luther was forty-one years old. Once the marriage became known, it created a major scandal. Luther's enemies said he began the entire Reformation just so he could get married. In fact, Luther probably married Katherina to set an example.

Though he suffered from chronic depression, Luther became a devoted husband and father. By 1534 he had three sons and three daughters, five of whom survived infancy. None of them became clergymen of Luther's church. His oldest son, Hans, studied law and became counsel to a duke. His youngest son, Paul, became a royal court physician. Luther delighted in his children, calling them God's "little jesters." He wrote them songs and they sang for him as he played his lute. He sent them long, loving letters when he was away. Luther was a strict father but said, "Punish if you must, but let the sugar plum go with the rod." He wrote that sometimes while he was working on one of his essays, "My Hans may sing a little tune to me. If he becomes too noisy I tell him off a bit, and he continues to sing but does it more to himself and with a certain concern and uneasiness. That is what God wishes; that we be always cheerful, but reverently."

Luther's household, which resided in the friary where Luther had been a priest, grew to include far more than his own sizable family. He adopted eleven orphaned nieces and nephews, and his dinner table also was crowded with student boarders. Some of his students recorded Luther's mealtime conversations, which later were bound together in *Table Talk*, a compilation of more than seven thousand pronouncements and musings by the rebel priest.

It is because of his lively "Lutherhaus" that Luther is said not only to have founded Protestantism but also that he presided over the first Protestant parsonage. By the time Luther died in 1546 at the age of sixty-two, his conduct, as much as his essays, had set the standard for the new church.

M

SON of THOMAS MANN

GERMAN NOVELIST Thomas Mann was a writer who enjoyed bountiful success in his own lifetime. The author of a bestseller, *Buddenbrooks*, at twenty-six, and later *Death in Venice* and *The Magic Mountain*, Mann was hailed as the greatest German writer since Goethe. Mann also enjoyed a fifty-year marriage that produced six intelligent children. His oldest daughter, Erika, married British poet W. H. Auden, and his two younger girls married Hungarian and Italian historians. One of his sons also became a historian, as did his youngest son, Michael, after he gave up a career as a concert viola player.

But it was Mann's oldest son, Klaus, who chose the most difficult road of all. Not only did he want to be a writer like his father, he also wanted to be as successful. "I must, must, *must* become famous," Klaus wrote in his diary when he was fourteen. The boy dropped out of two boarding schools that his parents had sent him to, and at the age of eighteen he began his writing career. He wrote his first novel in 1926 when he was twenty, a book about his own pessimistic generation of German adolescents after World War I. His father helped him get it published, but critics were far less kind.

As Klaus continued to try to boost his career by writing plays, reviews, and short stories, the harsh comparisons grew worse. Playwright Bertolt Brecht joked in an essay, "The whole world knows Klaus Mann, the son of Thomas Mann. By the way, who is Thomas Mann?" A satirical magazine published a cartoon in which Klaus says to his father, "You know, of course, Papa, that

geniuses never have highly gifted sons. Therefore, you are no genius." Mann tried to encourage his son and autographed a copy of
The Magic Mountain, "To my respected colleague—his promising
father."

Klaus turned out, in fact, to have a career that would be considered successful by any terms outside the league of his father.
After being one of the first German writers to be expelled by the
Nazis, Klaus founded *Die Sammlung*, a highly respected literary
journal that featured works by other exiles, including Einstein. He
is probably best known for *Mephisto*, a novel about the Third
Reich that was made into a movie and in 1981 would win the Oscar
for best foreign film. After one of Klaus's novels, *The Volcano*, a
book about a frustrated writer who ends up committing suicide,
was published in 1939, his father wrote him, "For a long time
people did not take you seriously, regarded you as a spoiled brat
and a humbug; there was nothing I could do about that. But by
now it cannot be denied that you are capable of more than most."

Klaus's 1942 autobiography, *The Turning Point*, also was well
received. His aim in that book, Klaus said, was "to tell the story of
a character who spent the best time of his life in a social and spiritual vacuum; striving for a true community but never finding it;
disconnected, restless, wandering; haunted by those solemn ab-
stractions in which nobody else believes—civilization, progress,
liberty."

Thomas Mann gained popularity in the United States when he
renounced his German citizenship under Hitler and became an
American citizen. Klaus tried to do the same so he could join the
Army, but the FBI delayed his application because they suspected
he was homosexual. Finally sworn in in 1943, Klaus wrote for
Stars and Stripes.

After the war, Klaus tried to reestablish his writing career in
Germany. But he felt uncomfortable there, though neither was he
happy when he settled in Santa Monica near his parents. He attempted suicide in July 1948. He was successful ten months later
in Cannes, France, where at the age of forty-two he overdosed on
sleeping pills. The *New York Times* reported he had died of a
heart attack.

"I seriously believe that he belonged to the most gifted of his generation and was perhaps the most gifted of all," Mann, who died of a blood clot in 1955 at the age of eighty, wrote of his son. "But a constantly growing, passive desire to do away with himself—overcoming his good intentions and nourished by disappointments—was mixed in him with the general intellectual despair of and for this era."

Playwright Christopher Isherwood said his friend Klaus was "bitterly lonely, despite his many friends and the affection of a large, closely knit family. A wanderer . . . he found no permanent companion on his journey."

CHILDREN of JAYNE MANSFIELD

NOTHING ABOUT the sexpot image of Jayne Mansfield suggested that she was the matronly type. But in fact the 1950s second-string blond bombshell was the mother of five. She saw no contradiction, as she testified when her first husband tried to get custody of their daughter after Mansfield posed nude in *Playboy* in 1956. "I'm a very stainless character, my petticoats are clean," she said. "I read little Bible stories to Jayne Marie every night and she is a well-balanced and intelligent child. Those pictures in *Playboy* magazine I posed for to get milk and bread for the baby."

Sweet as that sounds, Mansfield never let her children get in the way of her career. Just the opposite, actually. Mansfield arrived unknown in Hollywood in 1954 with three-year-old Jayne Marie and a husband who soon went back to Texas, where the two previously had alternated college classes so they could take care of their baby. When Mansfield moved to New York and became a hit in the Broadway play *Will Success Spoil Rock Hunter?* she took Jayne Marie with her. One staff member of the show remembered that Mansfield would send her daughter "to play in the subway at 55th Street. She'd skip up and down the steps. She never gave the kid any attention." Mansfield took Jayne Marie with her on dates, but would leave her with the maid in the ladies' room.

When Jayne Marie fell asleep during one of her mother's performances, Mansfield scolded, "How do you expect to grow up and become a great actress if you don't watch your mother?" Jayne Marie soon began imitating her mother's sex-kittenishness.

As she got older, Jayne Marie became her mother's assistant hairdresser, wardrobe assistant, and bartender. When Mansfield's career started to decline by 1960, she worried that she was getting too old. So to avoid any comparison with her growing daughter, she dressed Jayne Marie to look younger than she was. When Jayne Marie was eleven, for example, Mansfield made her look eight. "One of these days you're going to have to start being my sister," the sex symbol said. Jayne Marie said later, "She didn't get me a bra until I was already very big. I went straight into a 34D."

Mansfield's four younger children were all born after their mother was a star. Mansfield married ex–Mr. Universe Mickey Hargitay in 1958, and their son Miklos was born the same year. Zoltan arrived in 1960 and Mariska was born in 1964. They grew up in the Pink Palace, their mother's Beverly Hills mansion with a pink marble fireplace, thirteen bathrooms with pink fur on the floor, and a heart-shaped swimming pool.

Though Jayne Marie was usually responsible for taking care of the younger children, Mansfield took them with her everywhere. "My children have to get used to being in public so they can always be with me," she explained. When they showed up at a festival in Blackpool, England, with eight-month-old Miklos, the British National Society for the Prevention of Cruelty to Children complained. During a personal appearance at a zoo in 1966, six-year-old Zoltan was severely mauled by a lion and suffered a fractured skull. When he returned home from the hospital a month later on Christmas Day, Jayne presented her son at a press conference to announce his recovery.

Mansfield's family kept growing even as her marriage was dying. Sick of his wife's tireless exhibitionism, Hargitay had moved out before Mansfield became pregnant with Mariska. Mansfield was seeing other men by then, but Hargitay returned for Mariska's birth, though they divorced soon after. Mansfield turned around and married director Matt Cimber, who fathered her youngest son, Tony, in 1965. When, after they separated, Cimber tried to get custody of their son, Jayne Marie testified against her mother, but Mansfield won custody, nevertheless. Jayne Marie then had to take care of the little boy.

Jayne Marie put a further crimp in her mother's publicity-dependent career when in 1967 she showed up at the West Los Angeles police station and said Mansfield's latest boyfriend had beaten her with a belt at her mother's urging. Jayne Marie was sent to live with her father's uncle. She was living there that June when Mansfield was killed gruesomely in a car crash on a dark, foggy highway outside of New Orleans, where she was scheduled to make a television appearance. Mickey Jr., Zoltan, and Mariska were asleep on the floor of the back seat. Mickey broke one leg and arm and Mariska suffered cuts on her face.

Mansfield's death led to numerous lawsuits, as various guardians and fathers sought to control her estate on behalf of the children. The legal maneuvers grew so messy that a judge ordered that everyone stay out of the Pink Palace except the children and guardians appointed by the court. They remained in the deteriorating garish mansion for a year. The estate wasn't settled until 1978—eleven years later—when, after all the debts and lawyers were paid, each child was awarded a paltry $1,700.

Since Mansfield's death, two of her children have made headlines. Jayne Marie, seventeen when her mother died, posed for *Playboy* in 1976, twenty years after her mother. The year before, she had told *Interview* magazine that her mother "said the body is beautiful, sex is beautiful, people are beautiful. You have nothing to hide, it's other people that make you self-conscious."

Mariska Hargitay, meanwhile, was raised by Mickey Hargitay along with Zoltan and Mickey Jr. She was crowned Miss Beverly Hills in 1982 and studied acting at UCLA. She has since appeared in a few movies and in 1987 became a regular character on television's "Falcon Crest." Mariska, who was three when Mansfield died, said she thought her acting career would be different from her mother's. "My mother had to worry about how she looked, how she stood, how to be a *star*. My concerns would be more like those of Meryl Streep: focus and concentration."

SON of THOMAS MANVILLE

"THE FIRST THING I say to a girl is, 'Will you marry me?' The second thing is, 'How do you do?' " For Tommy Manville, that was no idle boast. The son of industrialist Thomas Manville, "the asbestos king," Tommy was married thirteen—count 'em—thirteen times to a total of eleven women. (He married two twice.) His father was a prominent businessman who turned the Johns-Manville Corporation into the world's biggest manufacturer of insulation. That and his charity work got Manville a nice write-up when he died in 1925. But on Tommy's death more than forty years later, the most significant fact that the *New York Times* could offer was "This extraordinary cycle of marriage and divorce was his only claim to celebrity."

Thomas Manville was an admired business leader (this was long before his company filed Chapter 11 in 1982, buried by asbestos-injury lawsuits). But he and his son apparently never got along. Manville often threatened to disinherit Tommy and never considered training him to take over the company that his father had founded.

Tommy demonstrated his real aspirations when he married for the first time in June 1911 at the age of seventeen. He had met Florence Huber, a chorus girl, under a Broadway marquee five days before the wedding. Tommy's father, on returning from Europe, threatened to have the marriage annulled. He didn't, but he did cut off Tommy's money, so the boy took a fifteen-dollar-a-week job in the family's factory in Pittsburgh. It sounds romantic, but apparently it wasn't. Tommy and Florence separated in 1913, though they didn't divorce until 1922.

Next Tommy married his father's stenographer, Lois, in September 1925. Manville died a month later, leaving Tommy and his sister, Lorraine, $10 million each from his $50 million estate. The timing was not good, as it cost Tommy $19,000 per year in alimony when Lois charged him with desertion and divorced him in 1926.

Here is the rest of the honor roll. Note that as Tommy got older, his wives, mostly beautiful blondes, didn't:

• Avonne Taylor. A Follies girl, Taylor married Tommy in May 1931, separated from him thirty-four days later, and divorced him in November.

• Marcelle Edwards. This showgirl married Tommy in 1933. They were together an impressive four years, before she left with a $200,000 settlement.

• Bonita Edwards (no relation). Tommy explained his four-day engagement to this twenty-two-year-old showgirl in November 1941 by saying, "We're glad we waited to be sure." They divorced in January 1942.

• Wilhelmina (Billy) Boze. A twenty-year-old actress, Boze married Tommy in October 1942 and divorced him in February 1943. She refused alimony.

• Macie Marie (Sunny) Ainsworth. They were married in August 1943 and separated less than eight hours later, though the divorce didn't come through until October.

• Georgina Campbell. They were married in December 1945, and although they separated, they were still married when she was killed in a car crash on her way to have breakfast with Tommy in 1952.

• Anita Roddy-Eden. They married in July 1952 and were divorced in August, netting Anita $100,000.

• Pat Gaston. Tommy was sixty-three when he married this twenty-six-year-old showgirl in May 1957. They were divorced in November.

Finally, Tommy married Christina Erdlen in January 1960. She was a twenty-year-old waitress at the time and got a quickie Mexican divorce from her husband, a barber, to marry Tommy. They were still married in 1967 when Tommy suffered a heart attack at his Chappaqua, New York, mansion—where a sign over the entrance read, "Beware: Marrying Manville Lives Here"—and died at the age of seventy-three. Amazingly, he left no children. Christina inherited most of his estate, which had been greatly depleted by his divorces.

Given that eight of his wives fit the category, it was not for nothing that on his death *Newsweek* called Tommy Manville "the patron saint of chorus girls."

CHILDREN of KARL MARX

"THERE IS no greater stupidity than for people with wide-ranging aspirations to marry and thus bind themselves to the trivial miseries of domestic and private life," Karl Marx wrote to his close friend Friedrich Engels in 1858. By that time the philosopher, whose *Communist Manifesto* would revolutionize the world, had seen three of his six children die, at least partly because of the abject poverty in which Marx and his family lived.

Banished from Germany, Belgium, and France for his radical views and activities, Marx raised his children in a tiny two-room flat in London. He called the death of his infant son Heinrich "a sacrifice to bourgeois misery." After his next infant, Franziska, died two years later, his frantic wife had to borrow money for a casket. The other children learned to lie to bill collectors and say, "Mr. Marx ain't upstairs." Marx wrote in 1852, "My wife is ill, little Jenny is ill, Leni has a sort of nervous fever. I cannot and could not call the doctor, having no money for medicines. For the last week I have fed my family on bread and potatoes, but I won-der if I shall be able to buy any today."

Years later, after his circumstances had somewhat improved, Marx wrote to activist Paul Lafargue, who had proposed to Laura, one of his three surviving daughters, "You know that I have sac-rificed my whole fortune for the revolutionary struggle. I do not regret it. On the contrary; if I had my life over again, I would do the same. Only I would not marry. As far as it is within my power I want to save my daughter from the dangerous precipice where her mother's life was dashed to pieces."

Domineering as Marx was, that was not within his power. His three daughters joined his socialist struggle, and they all suffered for it. In 1871 his daughters Jenny and Eleanor were strip-searched by French police on their way to visit Laura, whose husband had fled the country at the fall of the Paris Commune. Jenny, who had written for socialist publications with her father's help, later mar-ried French journalist Charles Longuet, who also was active in the cause. Like Laura and Paul Lafargue, they spent much of their marriage in exile.

Marx had long felt guilty about his family's impoverished up-bringing, and he especially felt it for Jenny, his oldest daughter. "Jenny is already old enough to feel all the burdens and all the misery of our existence," Marx wrote in 1862, "and I think this is the chief reason for her illness. Take all in all, it is not really worthwhile to lead such a lousy life." Jenny, who was ill fre-quently throughout her life, died of tuberculosis at the age of thirty-nine in January 1883, precipitating Marx's death two months later.

Eleanor, Marx's youngest child, born in 1855, had happier memories of her childhood, one in which her father romped with his children, told them stories, and took them on Sunday outings. "Mohr [their nickname for Marx] was not only an excellent horse, he was also something much greater—a unique and incom-parable story-teller. I, personally, of all the countless and wonder-ful stories Mohr told me, loved the story of Hans Rockle best. It lasted months and months, for it was a long story, and in fact never ended."

Because she was the youngest, Eleanor was left to be her father's secretary after her two sisters married, and to care for the aging man after her mother died in 1881. Although she longed to be an actress, and occasionally played in amateur theatricals, Eleanor devoted herself to her demanding father. She suffered a nervous breakdown in 1874 and another one later after her father forbade her to marry a French revolutionary. Marx himself noted in a letter to Laura in 1882 that Eleanor "is very laconic and seems indeed to endure the sojourn with me only out of the sense of duty as a self-sacrificing martyr."

Still, after Marx died, Eleanor wrote to a friend, "If you had ever been in our home, if you had ever seen my Father and Mother, known what *he* was to me, you would understand better both my yearning for love, given and received, and my intense need for sympathy." Eleanor became the mistress of Edward Aveling, an obnoxious playwright and critic who was just as overpowering as Eleanor's father. Eleanor often supported her common-law husband with royalties that had begun to accrue from her father's writings. And as she had with Marx, she spent months nursing him through a long illness in 1897.

The next spring, because of Eleanor's depression and Aveling's illness, the couple decided to commit suicide together. On March 31, Eleanor put on a white dress and took the poison first. But Aveling, instead of following her, left the house and hopped a train to London. He died of kidney disease four months later.

Laura, Marx's last surviving daughter, also did not end happily. Her three children with Paul all died young in the 1870s. In 1911 the couple, aging, poor, and tired of their Marxist struggle, committed suicide together.

But that was not quite the end of Marx's family. Although it was never mentioned while Marx was alive or even for several years after, Marx apparently had fathered an illegitimate son by the family's faithful housekeeper, Helene Demuth. Born in 1851, Frederick Demuth had been removed from the cramped household and raised by a working-class couple. Freddy's schooling was paid for by Engels, who claimed to be the boy's father until he was on his deathbed in 1895. Then Engels summoned Eleanor and told her about her half-brother. Eleanor and Freddy became good friends. She wrote to him two months before she killed herself, "I don't think you and I have been particularly bad people—and yet, dear Freddy, it really seems as though we are being punished."

Freddy, who never knew his father, spent his life quietly as a skilled machinist in London where he, too, fathered an illegitimate son. He died at the age of seventy-eight in 1929—the only child of Karl Marx who lived to see the Russian Revolution.

SON of CHARLES MERRILL

My father, who had flown in World War I,
Might have continued to invest his life
In cloud banks well above Wall Street and wife.
But the race was run below, and the point was to win.

So wrote James Merrill in his poem "The Broken Home." It was an apt description of his father, Charles Merrill, who defined the race on Wall Street by selling stocks to small investors and sent his brokerage firm sprinting toward a larger partnership called Merrill Lynch. Along the way Merrill's firm underwrote such hugely successful ventures as Safeway Stores, Kresge, and Grand Union, making Merrill very rich. Such hardcore financial turf would hardly seem fertile soil for Merrill's son, James, to become one of the greatest American poets of the twentieth century, the winner of a Pulitzer Prize and two National Book Awards, compared by one critic today to "Yeats and Blake, if not Milton and Dante."

James Merrill, the only child of his father's second marriage, grew up in surroundings appropriate to the son of a Wall Street financier. He spent his first five years in a townhouse in Greenwich Village (that some forty years later would be blown up accidentally by the radical Weathermen) and later resided in South-ampton, Palm Beach, and, after his parents divorced when he was twelve, the Lawrenceville boarding school. Charles Merrill's son by his first marriage, meanwhile, became headmaster of a St. Louis private school and Merrill's daughter married the chairman of Safeway.

James decided even in high school that he wanted to be a poet. Later, when he was at Amherst College, he said, his father "wrote to my professors and asked them if I should be allowed to make a career of poetry. When they said that I should be encouraged to do so, he accepted the idea, suggesting that I go about it in the most serious way possible." That, James said, meant "I should rent an office in Manhattan and go there every morning like a businessman."

His father paid to have a collection of James's poems printed when he was a senior in college. Five years later, in 1951, James got published on his own. "People thought I must have paid to get my poems published, which used to bother me," he said in 1983. "I suppose I was eager to achieve something of my own, but I don't worry about that anymore." Critics immediately admired his skill-ful technique, but many said he had been limited by his upbring-ing to produce poems with cold, elitist themes. In more recent years, however, as James Merrill's poems have become more ex-plicitly autobiographical, those critics have been converted. He won the National Book Award in 1967 for his collection *Nights and Days*, and the Pulitzer in 1977 for *Divine Comedies*.

That collection included the first part of a trilogy based on lengthy communications that he and his companion of thirty-five years, David Jackson, had with a Ouija board in after-dinner ses-sions over several years. He was dubbed the "Ouija poet" because of it. Merrill's second installment, *Mirabell*, won another National Book Award in 1979. The complete 15,000-word trilogy, *The Changing Light at Sandover*, was published in 1982. In 1986 Mer-rill was named the first poet laureate of Connecticut.

Unlike most poets, James Merrill has been able to pursue his craft full-time because his father, who died in 1956 at the age of seventy-one, left him well-cushioned. "I felt that in a way I was

set apart from [struggling writers]," Merrill said, "and that therefore I had to try even a bit harder than they were trying to prove
myself. It's possible also that people might not take me seriously—
just the way I myself don't take rich people seriously because I
have a feeling they're out of touch with reality."

SON of A. A. MILNE

RUN ACROSS A COPY of *Now We Are Six* or *Winnie the Pooh* and
you will probably recall with fondness your childhood delight as
you read about the playful adventures of a little boy named
Christopher Robin. But the real Christopher Robin, the son and
literary subject of author A. A. Milne, looks back quite differently.
"People sometimes say to me today, 'How lucky you were to have
had such a wonderful father!', imagining that because he wrote
about me with such affection and understanding, he must have
played with me with equal affection and understanding," wrote
Christopher in his fairly bitter memoir, *The Enchanted Places*, in
1974. "My father was a creative writer and so it was precisely
because he was *not* able to play with his small son that his longings
sought and found satisfaction in another direction. He wrote about
him instead."

A. A. Milne himself, who was deeply frustrated that his adult-
oriented plays and essays were nowhere nearly as successful as his
children's books, would not have disputed his son's assessment. "I
am not inordinately fond of or interested in children," he wrote
in his autobiography in 1939. "I have never felt in the least sentimental about them, or no more sentimental than one becomes for
a moment over a puppy or a kitten." In fact, Milne didn't even
mention his son as he commented on his children's stories in his

autobiography, though he wrote the stories in the 1920s while Christopher was growing up.

Christopher, who was raised in London and spent weekends at a country house called Cotchford Farms, where many of Christopher Robin's and Pooh's adventures occurred, says he grew up feeling closer to his nanny than to his parents. And although he played with his favorite stuffed animals long before his father adopted them as Pooh, Piglet, and Eeyore, Christopher came to believe that later gifts—Kanga and Tigger—were "carefully chosen not just for the delight they might give to their new owner, but also for their literary possibilities." Both characters showed up in the Pooh sequel, *The House at Pooh Corner*, in 1928.

Christopher says that as a child he was mostly unaware of the fame that his fictional self had brought him, but as he got older, he grew to resent it. "In pessimistic moments when I was trudging London in search of an employer wanting to make use of such talents as I could offer," he wrote, "it seemed to me, almost, that my father had got to where he was by climbing upon my infant shoulders, that he had filched from me my good name and had left me with nothing but the empty fame of being his son."

That was in 1947. Soon after, Christopher married and opened a bookshop. A few years later, feeling constricted in the city where his father was published, he and his wife moved their shop from London to Dartmouth, a small town on the southwestern coast of England. A. A. Milne died in 1956, and it was at his memorial service that Christopher saw his mother for the last time. He rarely wrote to her, though she lived another fifteen years.

But even after he had moved away and was out of his parents' reach, Christopher, now in Devon, has been followed by the fictional little boy. "However hard I tried to play down Christopher Robin, however little space I allowed on my shelves to the Pooh books," he wrote, "people would inevitably think of mine as 'The Christopher Robin Bookshop.' "

CHILDREN of JOHN MILTON

GREAT MEN often can be hell to live with, and John Milton is a good example. The seventeenth-century English writer and statesman who penned the classic epic poem *Paradise Lost* saw his first wife leave him a few months after they were married because she was bored with Milton's rigid routine and fed up with his picky eating habits. She later returned and gave birth to three daughters, the second of which grew up to say, upon hearing that her father was getting married a third time, "that that was no news to hear of his wedding but if she could hear of his death *that* was something."

Such was Milton's home life as he gained fame for his radical writings on politics and religion and served under Oliver Cromwell in the Civil War against Charles I. It was while composing a long Latin essay supporting Cromwell's government that Milton went blind in 1652. Thereafter he grew even more dependent on his family and his admirers to help him carry out his work.

He rose by 4:00 or 5:00 A.M. and liked to have the Bible read to him in Hebrew before breakfast. That task fell to Milton's two younger daughters, once they were old enough, since his oldest daughter, Anne was slightly retarded. Mary and Deborah were taught to *read* in Latin, Greek, and Hebrew, but they were never taught what the words meant, so for hours each day they were required to recite to their father what to them must have been gibberish. After Milton's imprisonment in 1660 following the Restoration, he devoted his full time to composing *Paradise Lost*, and usually it was his daughters who were summoned to record his new lines as he dictated them.

When Milton married a third time, in 1662—his first two wives had died in childbirth—his daughters, already sick of their demanding father and motherless most of their lives, did not take kindly to their stepmother, Elizabeth. While the poet, whose wealth had been severely diminished by the Restoration, was moving his family into a smaller house in 1663, his daughters secretly sold much of his library and pilfered housekeeping money as well. The situation finally deteriorated to the point that Milton, in 1670, threw them all out of the house at Elizabeth's urging. According to one contemporary writer, Milton's daughters—Anne, age twenty-three, Mary, twenty-one, and Deborah, seventeen—"were sent out to learn some curious and ingenious sorts of manufacture, that are proper for women to learn, particularly embroideries in gold or silver."

Milton, who had complained that he "had spent the greatest part of his estate providing for" his daughters, had not softened his view when he died of gout in 1674 at the age of sixty-five. To his three daughters, "they having been very undutiful to me," Milton left only the unpaid dowry from his first wife's family. Anne and Mary contested the will, but dropped their objections after Milton's widow gave them one hundred pounds each.

Anne married and died in childbirth in 1678. Mary never married and records indicate she died by 1694. Deborah became a companion to a woman who took her to Ireland; she married there and had ten children. She later became a schoolteacher and returned to England, where she was discovered living in poverty in 1727. A public appeal was made to support the daughter of Milton, who by then was acclaimed to be one of England's greatest poets. Several contributions were made, including fifty pounds from Queen Caroline; Voltaire said Deborah "became rich in a quarter of an hour." But not for long, as she died later that year. Her children, Milton's grandchildren, spent their lives in bare subsistence, even as the poet's stature—and profits to his publishers—increased.

SON of MARIA MONTESSORI

PUT AWAY lifeless dolls and give children toys they can learn with, Maria Montessori believed, and kids will surprise you. Indeed they did. Her simple games involving blocks and beads helped preschool children in a Roman slum learn to read and add so quickly that, within a few years after she opened her first school in 1907, Montessori represented a worldwide educational movement that continues to this day. The first woman to graduate from medical school in Italy, Montessori made the then bold assertion that children shouldn't be treated like children. "Children sleep too much," she said, "chiefly because their parents want them out of the way."

How ironic that the woman most associated with a child's earliest education sent her own son away at birth. In fact, Montessori never publicly acknowledged that Mario was her natural son, and throughout her life—even in her obituary—he was referred to as her adopted son, or, sometimes, her nephew.

Mario, the product of her affair with a colleague, was born when Montessori was doing research at the University of Rome. Both families discouraged a marriage. Since Montessori was something of a celebrity from her medical school days, she rightly feared that being an unwed mother would destroy her career. So she sent Mario to a wet nurse and later to be raised by a family outside Rome. Montessori, who later would speak of the "spiritual nourishment" that was vital between a mother and child during the early years, rarely visited her son, and Mario wasn't told that she was his mother.

Montessori, meanwhile, was building her movement, "aided," according to one writer, "by a little group of devoted disciples, young Italian women who live with her, who call her 'mother,' and who exist in and for her and her ideas, as ardently and wholeheartedly as nuns about an adored Mother Superior."

It wasn't until he was fifteen, Mario said later, that he saw his mother during a trip to Rome with his boarding school class and he went up to her and said, "I know you are my mother." He moved in with her soon after, and began accompanying her on her lecture tours, including a trip to the United States in 1915. Despite their years apart, Mario became Montessori's closest companion, helping her organize seminars and preventing too much publicity from hindering her work. After Mario married and had four children, Montessori would try out her new teaching methods on her grandchildren.

Montessori and her son took their work to India after Mussolini closed her schools in Italy. Once the war began in 1940, Mario was interned along with all other Italians in the British territory. But two months later, on Montessori's birthday, Mario was released, along with a note from a British official that said, "We have long thought what to give you for your 70th birthday. We thought that the best present we could give you was to send back your son." It was the first time Mario was publicly referred to as Montessori's son.

After the war, Montessori settled in the Netherlands. She continued to lecture, but as she approached eighty her son occasionally spoke for her. It was at what turned out to be her last appearance, in 1951, that Montessori spoke of the "spiritual nourishment" between a mother and her child during its early years. She died after a stroke in 1952 at the age of eighty-one.

Montessori left everything to her son, including her own acknowledgment of his birthright. In her will, she wrote that she hoped "that the world will render him the justice due his merits, which I know to be so great . . . and that my friends and those who labor in my work should feel their debt to my son—my son!"

Mario Montessori was director of the Association Montessori Internationale, which licenses schools and trains new supervisors, until he died in 1982. His daughter, Renilde, is director of a Montessori training center in Toronto and his son, Mario Jr., is a psychoanalyst and works with Montessori schools in the Netherlands.

SON of WOLFGANG AMADEUS MOZART

FOR TWO CENTURIES the rumor mill has churned over Mozart's early death at thirty-five. Many have speculated the great Viennese composer was murdered and many suspect Mozart's primary contemporary musical rival, Antonio Salieri. If Mozart was, in fact, poisoned, the medical evidence has yet to appear. And—though admittedly this is circumstantial evidence—if Salieri did kill Mozart, doesn't it seem odd that he later gave singing lessons to Mozart's youngest son?

Franz Xaver Wolfgang Mozart, one of only two of Mozart's six children to survive infancy, was born just four and a half months before Mozart died. But his mother, Constanze, decided very early that it was on Franz that Mozart's mantle would fall. "Little Wolfgang once tuned his crying to the note played by his father on the Fortepiano," Mozart's widow boasted, "whereupon the latter declared that the child would become a true Mozart."

That is all the more interesting considering the speculation that little Franz was, in fact, not Mozart's son. Nine months before Franz was born, Mozart had been away from home for five weeks. Meanwhile, one of his students, twenty-four-year-old Franz Xaver Süssmayr, was staying in his house. Some historians have pointed to the fact that little Franz was given the same name as Mozart's student, and the fact that Mozart's biographer took great pains to declare how much Franz looked like Mozart, as evidence that perhaps Franz wasn't born with the composer's talent.

Whatever the case, Constanze, left impoverished by her husband's death, took full advantage of her son's surname. She pushed Franz to perform very early, much as Mozart's father had done with him. Franz was just four when he sang a song from his father's opera *The Magic Flute*. To make sure there was no mistake as to his legacy, his mother began calling him Wolfgang Amadeus Mozart the Younger.

It worked. Raised partly by family friends in Prague and trained by the best—including Salieri—Wolfgang Jr. began regularly performing his father's work when he was seven. He wrote his first opus at the age of eleven and gave his first major concert at thirteen, which drew an unheard-of box office of 1,700 florins. He was much more financially successful than his father, but still his mother was not satisfied. She wrote to her other son, Karl (who became a bureaucrat in Italy), "Although he gets help on all sides, he does almost nothing unless he is forced. Do me a favor and ask him how many works he has composed this year, and whether he works thoroughly at orchestration." Just how much of a stage mother Constanze apparently was can be seen in a letter Wolfgang wrote in 1819 after seeing her for the first time in eleven years: "I have found my mother kind beyond all expectation. All the past is forgotten. She is to me an affectionate and tender mother, which certainly she has always been without disclosing it to me."

Wolfgang was sixteen when he was hired as a music tutor for a count. He got the job on the recommendation of Salieri, who said the boy had "a rare talent for music," something Salieri wouldn't have been caught dead saying about the boy's father. Salieri also predicted that the young Mozart's career would be "not inferior to that of his celebrated father," which may or may not have been a compliment. Wolfgang went on to a very popular tour of northern Europe. His father's name clearly helped, though one critic said his mistakes in his own compositions "would have made his father Mozart stamp irritably."

After the tour, Wolfgang was invited to become the court composer for the king of Württemberg, which could have given him the security and reputation to develop his own serious work. Instead, he moved to the small town of Lemberg and became a piano teacher. Later in his life, Wolfgang turned down a job as Konzertmeister of a major church and in 1842 he declined to compose a piece for the unveiling of a memorial to his father in Salzburg.

Though he had never known his father, Wolfgang seemed intimidated by Mozart's reputation, which had grown greater since his death. He complained to his mother in 1828 that giving piano lessons left him little time to compose. "If only I were master of my time for a couple of years," he wrote, "father in his grave would be pleased with me." Over the years Wolfgang did write a few piano concertos and a violin sonata. But apparently he lacked either the talent or the confidence to in any way rival his father.

A painter who had met the young Mozart in 1822, when he was still full of promise, saw him again in 1834 and wrote, "No more did one see the brilliant and enthusiastic eyes of the artist, no more the gay face with its Apollo-like brow margined by luxuriant dark curls and gracefully smiling mouth. The figure appeared shrunken, the eyes dull and with an expression of profound melancholy."

The young Mozart gave his last public performance at the Salzburg memorial in 1842. Two years later, having suffered from a stomach ailment for years, Wolfgang died at the age of fifty-three. His last words were said to have been "I am looking forward to seeing my father again." His epitaph read, "May the name of his father be his epitaph, as his veneration for him was the essence of his life."

CHILDREN of BENITO MUSSOLINI

THE IRON GRIP of Benito Mussolini may have made Italy's trains run on time, but his hand was somewhat softer on his five children. Though his Fascist government banned American jazz music, the dictator's son Romano remembers that the children "played jazz at home all the time and my father liked some of the records." Mussolini's only public displays of grief came when his youngest daughter, Anna Maria, nearly died of polio, and after one of his sons, Bruno, was killed while testing a new airplane bomber in 1941.

But his greatest affection was said to be reserved for his oldest daughter, Edda, whom the British press called "the only human being in the world who can talk back to Benito Mussolini." The glamorous woman with bleached blond hair and persuasive charm made the cover of *Time* magazine in 1939 for playing no small part in cementing Italy's ties with Nazi Germany. Edda, born in 1910, had double influence: through her father, and through her husband, Galeazzo Ciano, who, after she married him in 1930, rose quickly through the Fascist ranks to become Mussolini's foreign minister in 1936. Ciano was then considered to be the heir apparent to Mussolini.

But whatever plans Mussolini might have had changed as Italy began to lose World War II. Mussolini dumped Ciano from his inner circle early in 1943. Later that year, on July 25, Ciano helped return the favor by joining eighteen other members of the Fascist Grand Council in dismissing Mussolini as Italy's leader. Mussolini was arrested and sent to a remote hotel in the mountains to prevent him from mounting a comeback. But a crack unit of German soldiers rescued him and helped him return to power— what was left of it—by the end of the year. Mussolini, who had long been criticized for favoring his son-in-law, now had Ciano arrested and sentenced to death.

All of Edda's pleading could not save her husband from her father, who in Ciano's final days refused to see her. Ciano was shot (it took three bullets) on January 11, 1944. Edda fled with her three children to Switzerland, and never saw her father again; he, too, was executed April 28, 1945. She returned to Italy after the war and was banished to the small island of Lipari. She later fought to recover her husband's estate and by 1959 was reported living in a luxury apartment in Rome, with a villa on the Isle of Capri. She wrote a book, *My Truth*, in 1977, which seemed to show that much of her bitterness toward her father had dissipated.

Mussolini's oldest son, Vittorio, born in 1916, also fled Italy after the war. He settled in Buenos Aires, where he continued working as a journalist, and much later returned to Italy. He wrote *Mussolini: The Tragic Women in His Life* in 1961. Mussolini's youngest daughter, who never fully recovered from polio, died from complications of chicken pox in 1968 at the age of thirty-eight.

Only one of the dictator's children seemed to benefit from his name. Mussolini's youngest son, Romano, born in 1927, also was sent into exile after the war. He later earned a degree in economics, went into the lumber business, and became a poultry farmer before he embarked on the career he truly loved, that of a jazz pianist. "The Romano Mussolini Jazz Band" toured the world and the dictator's son played with greats like Dizzy Gillespie. Critics were kind, but interest mainly seemed to be in his name—and the fact that he married Sophia Loren's sister.

Romano said that for a while after the war he changed his name when he performed in jazz clubs in Italy. "But since then I have always used my name. It has helped me—in Italy it has helped me," he told the *New York Times* before a performance at New York City's Town Hall in 1972. He remains a popular jazz pianist in Italy and occasionally performs in the United States. His older daughter, Alessandra, also has kept the family name as she pursues an acting career. In his book, *Apology for My Father*, Romano said he didn't see the darker side of the dictator. "My father was very kind, very gentle with me." Mussolini, his son said, instilled in him "the sense of honesty, and to be good with people."

N

SON of NAPOLEON III

FROM THE MOMENT he was born, Napoléon Eugène Louis Jean Joseph was groomed to carry on the Napoleonic Dynasty in France. As the son of Napoléon III, who was the nephew of the original Napoléon and who had made himself emperor of France in 1852, the Prince Imperial learned to ride a horse before he could walk. "Loulou," as his father called him, gave military salutes from his baby carriage and could march the goose step at the age of four.

But suddenly when he was fourteen, the heir became much less apparent when his father lost a war with Germany and the family fled in exile to England in 1871. Young Napoléon had been with his father on the losing battlefront and escaped only by being disguised in peasant robes and smuggled into Belgium. The press widely noted that the Prince Imperial's only exposure to the battle had been to pick up a spent bullet and carve his initials in it.

After his father died in 1873, the still exiled prince became the last hope of the simmering Bonapartist movement in France. On his eighteenth birthday the following year, nearly 6,000 Frenchmen traveled to Kent, England, to celebrate his coming of age. "Vive l'Empéreur!" and "Vive Napoléon IV!" they shouted, and he responded, "If the name of Napoléon should emerge an eighth time from the ballot boxes, I am ready to accept the charge imposed on me by the will of the nation. . . . Carry my remembrance to the absent—and to France the prayers of one of her children. My courage and life are hers."

But France did not call and "Napoléon 3½" or "The Imperial Baby," as the French press dubbed him, settled in with the British party set. He grew restless, and finally decided that in order to restore the reputation of his name he needed a few military victories under his belt. Trouble was, he had no country to fight for. He was rejected by Austria when he offered to aid its fight in the Balkans. And England too turned down his application to join in its colonial war in Zululand, later called South Africa.

When young Napoléon received word of his rejection by the British, his mother saw him burst into tears for the first time since he was a child. The widowed empress went to her friend Queen Victoria, and soon the Prince Imperial was on his way to Africa. "He *must* be very careful not to expose himself unnecessarily, for we know he is very venturesome," ordered the Queen. Napoléon was assigned to a general's staff as an observer. He was to be accompanied by a British officer at all times and was to be kept in out-of-the-way positions, but still the Prince Imperial was elated to be among the troops. "When one belongs to a race of soldiers," he wrote when he arrived in Africa in March 1879, "it is only with sword in hand that one gains recognition."

Napoléon did not stay away from the front lines for long. On June 1, he joined five British horsemen on a reconnaissance mission. A British officer, Lieutenant Carey, was supposed to be in charge, but the prince acted as if *he* were and Carey allowed it. He had the band of men dismount in mid-afternoon to rest near a river, not far from some tall grass. Carey warned that spot was vulnerable to an ambush, but the prince insisted on resting. Carey soon suggested they leave, but Napoléon said to wait a few more minutes. Carey later wrote a distraught letter to his wife about that night. "Only a few minutes before our surprise, he was discussing politics with me and the campaigns of 1800 and 1796, criticizing [the original] Napoléon's strategy and he talked of Republics and Monarchies. Poor boy!"

The men were finally just mounting their horses when suddenly forty or fifty Zulu warriors, armed with rifles and spears, jumped out of the tall grass. The British soldiers panicked and tried to ride away. Two were shot dead and fell off their horses. Napoléon's horse was already running as he tried to vault into the saddle. It was a trick he had performed often and well enough to finish first in his riding class at the British Royal Military Academy. But this time a strap on the saddle snapped, and the Prince Imperial was kicked hard as he fell into the dust.

As the remaining British soldiers rode away, Napoléon got up and began running from the Zulus, who chased him for 250 yards before he turned and drew his pistol. He fired once, missing, before a spear pierced his thigh. He pulled it out and tried to thrust it at the enclosing warriors. He fired once more, missing again, but then he was overcome. When British soldiers returned the next day, they found his body stripped except for a small gold locket that had been worn by French monarchs since Charlemagne. He had been stabbed eighteen times, all in the front, and five of the wounds were considered fatal. When returned to England on July 11, his body was so torn and decomposed that he was unrecognizable and was only identified by a dentist who had put a gold filling into one of his teeth.

The death of the last Napoléon caused outrage in France, where even those who had shown no great affection for him now blamed the British for not taking care of him. Some were so hostile as to accuse Queen Victoria of arranging his alleged murder. More than 35,000 attended his funeral in London. Lieutenant Carey withstood a court-martial, but the controversy lingered. "To savour the situation fully," wrote Donald Featherstone on the subject in 1973, "one must try to visualize what would occur if Prince Charles, heir to the throne of Britain, were permitted, at his own insistence, to go to Vietnam, and was then killed in an ambush having apparently been abandoned by a young American officer."

DAUGHTER of CARRY NATION

YELLING "MEN, I have come to save you from a drunkard's fate!" as she stormed into a saloon, smashing whiskey bottles and windows with the ax that became her trademark, and then leaving with the words, "God be with you," prohibitionist Carry Nation was a woman many people thought was nuts. And they probably were right. She was the daughter of an illiterate Kentucky planter (he meant to spell her name "Carrie") and a mother who spent her last three years in the Missouri State Hospital for the Insane. Mental illness ran rampant on her mother's side and Carry exhibited her own peculiarities at an early age as she lay bedridden from stomach and nervous disorders and would sit up long enough to preach about God to her father's slaves before she retreated into a mystic spell.

She married Dr. Charles Gloyd, a handsome Union Army captain and doctor, against the wishes of her parents, who turned out to be right when Gloyd showed up drunk at the wedding. Carry later wrote that she thought her love would reform him, but she left Gloyd after a few months and returned to her parents; she was pregnant with Charlien at the time. Gloyd died six months later.

Carry would later blame all of her daughter's troubles on Gloyd's drinking, and likewise made it the justification for her crusade. She wrote in her autobiography, "This my only child was peculiar. She was the result of a drunken father and a distracted mother. The curse of heredity is one of the most heart-breaking results of the saloons. . . . If girls were taught that a drunkard's curse will in the nature of things include his children . . . they would avoid these men. And men will give up their vices before they will give up women."

But Charlien's troubles were not entirely preordained. When Charlien was about ten, she refused to go to Sunday school or read the Bible, which touched off a series of traumatic fights, with Charlien going into violent tantrums that caused Carry to lock her daughter in her room. Carry said she prayed for God to give her daughter some affliction that would show her God's power, much like what she believed had caused her own conversion at the same age. Sure enough, a few days after Carry said she began her prayers Charlien developed a large sore on her face. Within a week her entire right cheek had rotted away, exposing her teeth and jaw. "Something told me," Carry wrote, "that this was in answer to my prayer." For a while near death, Charlien recovered, but her jaw remained locked for eight years until a surgeon corrected the problem.

In 1877 Carry married David Nation, a lawyer and preacher, and took her daughter to live on a farm in Texas, where they nearly starved. Nation later took his wife to Medicine Lodge, Kansas, where he had been assigned to preach and where Carry began her crusade. She started mildly, merely greeting public officials with such pleasantries as, "Hello, you rum-soaked Republican rummy." Later, dressed in black, standing nearly six feet tall and weighing 175 pounds, Carry began conducting prayer meetings in front of illegal saloons to get them shut down.

She wasn't yet using her famous ax when she visited her daughter, who had remained in Texas with her husband and was pregnant with what would be the fourth of her eight children. Upon visiting, Carry discovered that her daughter and her son-in-law had become alcoholics. It was after she returned to Kansas that she began splitting open kegs of whiskey with an ax, a stunt that became very popular; as she conducted her "hatchetations" around the country, Carry raised money by selling souvenir miniature axes.

Carry's crusade quickly flamed out after her rousing national tour in 1901, during which she was arrested nearly thirty times and suffered several beatings. She continued to lecture and occasionally wielded her ax, but she also played the New York stage for a while as the forlorn mother of a drunken son in a play called *Ten Nights in a Bar Room*. Meanwhile, Charlien's husband had Charlien committed to a sanitarium in 1904. Carry later had her released from the State Lunatic Asylum in Austin, though Charlien continued to have her troubles.

When Carry Nation died of a stroke in 1911 at the age of sixty-four, her will provided her daughter sixty dollars a month, "so long as she is not confined to an insane asylum." How long that was didn't make the history books.

SON of PAUL NEWMAN

"PEOPLE EXPECT more out of me," Scott Newman once said, and it was a daunting prospect that haunted the only son of Paul Newman. Scott didn't grow up in a movie star's home; his parents had long been divorced by the time Newman really became a screen idol. Still Scott, who was good-looking but not as attractive as his blue-eyed father, felt pressured by the constant comparisons and tried to separate his life as much as he could from that of his father. He dropped out of college after two years to become a "career parachutist." Later he cut trees in the Sierras for ski runs and dug ditches for three dollars an hour.

As he drifted he also wandered into trouble with alcohol and drugs. In 1974 he threw a violent fit when police tried to arrest him for drunkenness, adding several charges to the crime. The same year, his father arranged for him to get a small role in *The Towering Inferno*, in which Newman was starring. After a couple of other small roles, Scott seemed happy. "It's a brand new world," he said in one interview. "I love it, and I'm good at it. I know what I want to do now. When I was a punk kid I felt that I was entitled to everything my father gave me. But for the past four years I've made and paid my own way, except for the help he gave me when I got in that scrape with the law."

Scott went on to other acting roles, including a lead performance in *Fraternity Row* in 1977. But when he was interviewed, the same question always came up. "The only thing my dad helps me get is my foot in the door," he replied. "But no one in his right mind is going to hire somebody to handle a part just because he's somebody's son." As if to prove that, Scott performed in nightclubs under the name William Scott.

Scott spent Sunday afternoon, November 19, 1978, watching football games at a friend's house in Los Angeles. He was drinking rum and apparently was upset. About 9:00 P.M., he called the psychology clinic where he had been undergoing treatment. His father had arranged to have someone on call there whenever his son needed it. An associate of Scott's doctor picked him up and took him to the Ramada Inn where Scott was staying in West Los Angeles. They had dinner. Scott drank some more and took some Darvon that his doctor had given him to ease the pain of an injury from a recent motorcycle accident. Later there were reports he also took some Quaaludes and cocaine in the bathroom.

The doctor stayed as Scott went to sleep. At about midnight, the doctor noticed that Scott was barely breathing. By the time paramedics got him to a hospital, he was pronounced dead. Some initial reports said Scott had committed suicide. But doctors said his death was caused by an accidental overdose of drugs and alcohol.

Newman has barely spoken about his son's death in interviews. He founded the Scott Newman Foundation to sponsor drug abuse education programs. In 1981 he directed a film, *Say No,* urging youths to avoid drugs and alcohol. On one occasion he said, "I had lost the ability to help him . . . we both backed away." He told *Time* in 1982, "We were like rubber bands. One minute close, the next separated by an enormous and unaccountable distance. I don't think I'll ever escape the guilt."

O

SON of MADALYN MURRAY O'HAIR

MADALYN MURRAY O'HAIR made a career out of being an atheist by saying things like this: "With its poisonous concepts of sin and divine punishment, [the church has] warped and brainwashed countless millions," she told *Playboy* in 1965. "It would be impossible to calculate the psychic damage this has inflicted on generations of children who might have grown up into healthy, happy, productive, zestful human beings but for the burden of anti-sexual fear and guilt ingrained in them by the church."

Although church teachings were not ingrained in him, O'Hair's son, who was the subject of the landmark 1963 Supreme Court case that banished prayer from public schools, does not remember either a happy or a zestful childhood. In fact, so far have William Murray and Madalyn O'Hair (her name by a later marriage) diverged that Murray even disputes the circumstances of his own birth. He and his younger brother, Jon, were, Murray says, illegitimate, and he says his mother never married the Mr. Murray who was his father. Murray remembers being raised mostly by his grandparents and as for his mother, "her image was so indistinct I didn't know clearly until I was in grade school that she really was my mother." Despite his mother's later godless reputation, Murray said in his 1982 memoir that both he and his brother were baptized. The family also had a regular Christmas tree, but his mother called it a "Solstice tree," he said.

Murray said the whole controversy over whether or not he should join the rest of his Baltimore ninth-grade class in prayer wasn't just a religious matter. His mother had been with her sons in France, where she had tried to advance her application to become a Soviet citizen. When that failed, they returned to Baltimore. "I honestly believe that prayer was removed from public schools because the Soviet Union rejected my mother," Murray said later.

Murray said he went along with his mother in the court battle to try to please her, but actually he hated the harassment he faced at school and the pressure he faced at home. "I wanted to run away from the school and its prayers, from the city of Baltimore, from the state of Maryland and—most of all—from my family and the house at 1526 Winford Road." As his mother—who holds a law degree and had served on General Eisenhower's staff in World War II—turned the lawsuit into a national movement, Murray spent much of his time helping her publish the *American Atheist* newsletter.

At the age of seventeen, the same year the Supreme Court ruled in his favor, Murray began living with his girlfriend in the basement of the house he occupied with his mother and grandparents, an event that was reported by the press. He married the girl when he was eighteen, and they had a daughter, Robin, in 1965. By then they were living in Hawaii, partly to escape a criminal complaint filed by the girl's father over their relationship. "I became convinced that I was being persecuted," Murray said. "I was regarded by the entire community as a close accomplice of Madalyn Murray—who was already called 'the most hated woman in America.' "

A few months after his daughter was born, Murray left Hawaii with another woman. His daughter was raised and later adopted by O'Hair, who moved her atheist cause to Austin, Texas. Murray drove a cab for a while in Hawaii and later worked as a ticket agent for Braniff Airlines in Dallas and New York. He ran for Congress from Austin in 1976 and lost with 46 percent of the vote. He remained active in his mother's atheist organization until 1977, when he walked out on her during her national debate tour with a popular television evangelist, saying the event was a publicity gimmick.

Shortly thereafter, Murray said, he became an alcoholic as a series of his business ventures failed. It was during later meetings at Alcoholics Anonymous, Murray said, that he found God. "There had to be good, because I had looked into the eyes of evil," he said in his memoir, *My Life Without God*. "There had to be a God, because I had held hands with the devil."

In 1980 Murray wrote a letter to his old hometown newspaper, the *Baltimore Sun*, apologizing for his Supreme Court case, which he said had contributed to the moral decline of the nation: "Being raised as an atheist in the home of Madalyn O'Hair, I was not aware of faith or even the existence of God. As I now look back over 33 years of life wasted without faith in God, I pray only that I can, with His help, right some of the wrong and evil I have caused through my lack of faith." He now calls his Supreme Court case "a criminal act."

Murray has become an evangelical Baptist. He tours the country giving sermons, holding prayer vigils, and distributing hundreds of thousands of pamphlets—containing the Lord's Prayer and the Ten Commandments—to schoolchildren. In 1984 Murray pressed school officials in a New York town to let him preach in the school auditorium. They turned him down, citing his famous Supreme Court case.

Murray's younger brother, Jon, now runs their mother's American Atheist Center in Austin. Murray's daughter, Robin, is editor of the group's magazine and was jailed briefly in 1987 for refusing to take the juror's oath, which included the words, "so help me God."

Murray, who also runs Freedom's Friends, a Dallas group that sends medical supplies to the Nicaraguan contras, has not talked to his mother, who turned sixty-nine in 1988, since their fight in 1977. But, he says, "I pray daily for her deliverance."

CHILDREN of EUGENE O'NEILL

IT WAS A STORY about Eugene O'Neill's younger son, Shane, but writer Elizabeth Sergeant could have been describing the playwright's relationship with any of his three children: "I remember one afternoon when I found [Shane] sitting listlessly on the dock," Sergeant said. "He was so delighted when I asked if he'd like to come inside and have me read to him. Neither Gene nor Agnes [O'Neill's second wife], as far as I could see, paid much attention to him. Gene once told me he didn't know how to talk to children and he felt he couldn't have any connection with him until he grew up."

The four-time Pulitzer Prize–winning playwright dealt compassionately and honestly with human tragedy in his plays such as *The Iceman Cometh* and *Long Day's Journey Into Night*. But O'Neill showed almost no ability to deal with his children. After leaving his first wife very soon after he married her, O'Neill didn't see his oldest son until the boy was twelve. O'Neill suggested to his second wife, Agnes, that they move Shane's crib to the basement so the baby wouldn't distract him. And one by one, after he finally established relationships with each of his two sons and daughter, O'Neill found reasons to reject all of them completely in the last decade of his life. "Children in squads," O'Neill said, "even when indubitably my own, tend to get my goat."

O'Neill found out he was a father for the first time when a bartender in New York showed him a newspaper announcing it. The child grew up with the name Richard Pitt Smith, after his stepfather, and wasn't told who his real father was until he was twelve and O'Neill had become a successful playwright. The boy then changed his name to Eugene O'Neill, Jr., and began spending part of his summer vacations with his father and O'Neill's other two children, Shane and Oona. Eugene Jr. and O'Neill even grew close as the son became a noted Greek scholar at Yale.

But after his second divorce, Eugene Jr. became like a character in one of his father's plays. He drank heavily and slept with many women even as he maintained a stormy relationship with one woman, Ruth Lander. They lived in the bohemian artist community of Woodstock, New York, after Eugene had left Yale because he found it too confining. Eugene said in a 1948 interview, "Being the son of a great writer made me feel obligated to do well whatever I did. Naturally I haven't always succeeded, but I regard the stimulus of having a famous father as a very valuable influence in my life."

Eugene was deeply hurt when O'Neill's third wife, Carlotta, prevented him from seeing his father. Eugene was even more distraught when Ruth Lander left him. On September 25, 1950, after drinking all night with a boyhood friend and his wife, Eugene was found dead on his living-room floor. He had gone home, climbed into the bathtub, and in classic Roman fashion slashed his left wrist and ankle. From the trail of blood, the police surmised that Eugene then had stumbled down the stairs and tried to use the telephone, which had been shut off for nonpayment. Beside an empty bottle of bourbon he had left a note which said, "Never let it be said of O'Neill that he failed to empty a bottle. Ave atque vale [Hail and farewell]." O'Neil didn't attend Eugene's funeral, and Carlotta said the playwright only mentioned his son once again before he died in 1953.

Shane spent his early years near his father, though he was raised mostly by a maid at their seaside home near Provincetown. After O'Neill divorced Agnes, Shane's mother, in 1928, she sent Shane to a military boarding school in Florida to correct his discipline problems. Instead they grew worse. After leaving school, he drifted from job to job. He drank heavily and tried to commit suicide more than once. Through a lawyer, he asked his father for money, but was turned down. Shane married in 1944 and became a father the next year. Three months later the baby, named Eugene O'Neill III, died in its crib, and medical officials said there were signs of neglect.

After that, O'Neill never saw Shane again. But in 1948 after Shane was arrested for heroin possession, the playwright said, "Much as I hate to say it, my son Shane is a complete rotter." O'Neill wrote him out of his will and Shane rotted further. He was committed to a mental hospital for a few months in 1956, so malnourished that his teeth had fallen out. He and his wife and four children got by on an inheritance from her family. Later Shane was able to gain his late father's copyrights, and his family lived on the royalties of O'Neill's plays. In 1977, separated from his wife, Shane jumped from the fourth-floor Brooklyn apartment of a woman with whom he had been arguing. He died the next day at the age of fifty-seven.

O'Neill's relationship with his only daughter, Oona, was shortest of all. Oona was only three when O'Neill divorced Agnes in 1928, and she didn't see her father again until she was eleven. Vivacious and pretty, Oona was a childhood friend of Gloria Vanderbilt. As a teenager she started showing up on the society pages and decided she wanted to be an actress, both of which made her father bristle. Oona was staying with her mother in a Hollywood apartment when she met Charlie Chaplin in 1943. A few months later the barely eighteen-year-old girl married the fifty-four-year-old movie star. It was Chaplin's fourth marriage and he already had two sons, one Oona's age.

Needless to say, O'Neill never mentioned Oona again and wrote her out of his will as well. But unlike her brothers, Oona didn't take after her tragedian father. She and Chaplin remained married until Chaplin died in 1977. They had eight children, the last born when Chaplin was seventy-three.

O'Neill, suffering from Parkinson's disease, died in 1953 at the age of sixty-five. A year earlier he had been hospitalized with a broken leg and a nurse remembered, "Sometimes he'd talk to me about his older son's suicide. He never mentioned his daughter directly, but he gave the impression, in his ramblings, that his entire family had gone wrong."

P

SON of GEORGE S. PATTON

IT WOULD HAVE BEEN ironic if the son of the ruthless and arrogant Lieutenant General George S. Patton had grown up to be a peace activist, or perhaps a methodical diplomat. But that didn't happen. The son of "Old Blood-and-Guts" grew up to be Blood-and-Guts Jr. The son of the man who said, "Kill every one of the goddamn bastards," grew up to say, "I do like to see the arms and legs fly." The son of the general who was never seen without his two pearl-handled revolvers once attended a party wearing a peace medallion around his neck and carrying the bullet-scarred skull of a Viet Cong soldier.

Patton's son entered West Point just as World War II was starting. "Well we are real proud of you for the first time in your life," Patton wrote him. "See to it that we stay that way." George III had to repeat a year at the military academy, but so had his father. George didn't graduate until after the war, but Patton had assured his wife that George "need not worry about missing a war. The next is on the way."

Indeed, Patton's son served in Korea and Vietnam, earning many high honors though his father, who died after a car accident at the end of World War II, was not around to take pride in his son. George III attained the rank of major general in 1973, and, in 1975, was put in command of the Army's 2nd Armored Division, the same unit that Patton had driven through North Africa. Before he took command, George visited the base chapel. "While there," he told *Time*, "I not only felt the presence of God, I also felt the presence of my father. This happens to me from time to time. Every once in a while I see my father sitting at the corner of a building, sort of gazing at me."

Clearly proud to be his father's son, George said, "His reputation is not in any way a handicap. In fact, I enjoy the hell out of it." George, who retired from the Army in 1980 and raised peacocks on his Massachusetts farm, is now a military consultant.

George had two older sisters, both of whom married West Point men. Ruth Ellen's husband fought in Italy in World War II. The husband of Patton's older daughter, Beatrice, fought with Patton in Tunisia but was captured in 1943. Patton arranged to keep track of his imprisoned son-in-law, Lieutenant Colonel John Waters, Jr., through General Eisenhower and others. And at the end of the war, when Patton was pushing through Germany, he defied his fellow generals and commissioned a special task force to break away from the path of the Allied troops and free Waters, who was being held in a prison camp in Hammelburg. The task force was wiped out, but the camp was liberated a week later. Patton, with uncharacteristic humility, said the raid was "one of the two mistakes," he made during the war.

CHILDREN of ADMIRAL ROBERT PEARY

EXPERTS STILL ARE ARGUING over whether or not Admiral Robert Peary made it to the North Pole in 1909 as he had claimed. But if he did not plant the American flag precisely on top of the world, the indefatigable explorer did leave something else behind in the Arctic—two Eskimo sons. The winters are, after all, long and dark in northern Greenland, and Peary weathered many of them during his several attempts—beginning in 1891—to reach the Pole.

Actually, Peary's American wife, Josephine, accompanied him on his early ventures, and their daughter, Marie, was even born in the Arctic in 1893. But Josephine stayed home during Peary's later explorations. She found out about her husband's Eskimo mistress when she showed up in Greenland unannounced in 1900. Aleqasina was, Josephine said, "unquestionably pretty." The Eskimo woman had recently given birth to her first child by Peary, named Anaukaq. Later, when Peary's claim to the Pole was challenged by Dr. Frederick Cook, the sensational controversy got so nasty that Cook published a photograph of Aleqasina and her son above the headline "Polar Tragedy—a Deserted Child of the Sultan of the North and Its Mother." Peary denied the relationship.

Anaukaq died of a perforated ulcer at the age of twenty-seven. But Peary's second Eskimo son, Kali, born in 1906 on Peary's ship, the *Roosevelt*, still lives in the northern Greenland town of Qaanaaq just south of the 78th parallel. According to a fascinating series of articles in the *National Geographic* in 1988, Kali, a hunter, is the patriarch of some forty Eskimo descendants of Robert Peary. Kali's daughter, Pauline, is mayor of the four hundred residents of Qaanaaq and used to be a member of Greenland's parliament. Kali's son, Peter, was the only man to reach the Pole twice by dogsled.

Peary's Eskimo descendants were visited in 1987 by one of Peary's American grandchildren, Edward Peary Stafford, who is Marie's son. He saw Peary's seven-year-old Eskimo great-great-granddaughter, Taufinguaq, whose "light complexion and dark blond hair," Stafford said, "suggested to me that even after four generations the Caucasian genes can still reveal themselves with pronounced effect."

Another legacy of Peary's Arctic years lingers in the marriage of one of his great-granddaughters, Kista, to Kitdlaq, a grandson of Matthew Henson, Peary's assistant, who received almost no credit for helping Peary reach the Pole because he was black. Like Peary, Henson left behind a son, also named Anaukaq, born within a few days of Kali in 1906. But unlike Peary, who eventually received great honor and countless awards for his trek before he died in 1920, Henson ended up working as a messenger in the Federal Customs House in New York and died in 1955. Still, today there are more than thirty darker-skinned descendants among the Eskimos of northern Greenland.

Anaukaq Henson died in 1987, three weeks after he returned from his only trip to the United States. He and his best friend, Kali Peary, went together and were greeted by the president of Harvard University at a "North Pole Family Reunion." "For the first time in my life," Kali said, "I feel like a Peary."

Also during the trip, Kali met his half-brother, Robert Peary, Jr., the admiral's only surviving child after Marie died in 1978 at the age of eighty-four. Robert Jr. visited the territory of his father's fame only twice, in 1926 and 1927, and never did any exploring of his own. He became a civil engineer (his father's profession before he began his northern explorations) and helped build San Francisco's Golden Gate Bridge. Robert says his father, who died when Robert was sixteen, rarely talked about his adventures. But Robert, now retired in Maine, dismisses recent reports challenging Peary's claim to the Pole. "Of course he got there," says Peary's son. "I know he did. He said so."

SON of GREGORY PECK

GREGORY PECK has made a career out of being a good father. Whether he actually played a parent, as in his Oscar-winning performance in *To Kill a Mockingbird*, or not, Peck became a movie star by giving his characters a paternal moral strength and wisdom. And unlike many Hollywood personas, Peck took his image home with him. "We weren't typical actor's kids," said Peck's oldest son, Jonathan. "We were never part of the Hollywood jet set. My father's home life was very important to him. When he came home after a day at the studio, he wanted to relax, and that meant not talking about his work."

Peck, the son of a California drugstore owner, had three sons in the 1940s before he was divorced in 1954. When he remarried the next year, to a French journalist, Peck and his new wife bought a house just a few doors from his ex-wife so he could be near his sons. Relations were good enough that Jonathan lived with his father during high school.

Jonathan grew up to look very much like his handsome father. That annoyed him, and was part of the reason he didn't become an actor. "I seriously considered an acting career when I was in high school and college, but I'm not star material," he said. Instead, after becoming a California state track champion in college and spending two years in the Peace Corps in Tanzania, Jonathan decided to become a reporter. He wanted to work in television, but with no experience he had to start in radio, first for United Press International and later for a station in Los Angeles.

Finally in 1975 Jonathan was hired by KCOY-TV, a tiny television station in Santa Maria, California, north of Los Angeles. His beat was the much larger city of Santa Barbara, where he was supposed to come up with three stories a day by 1:00 P.M. Jonathan told his father he felt he couldn't keep up the pace. His station didn't even send him enough film, he said. Peck promptly had twelve cannisters sent to his son.

But Jonathan had other troubles. His girlfriend had committed suicide in 1970. His more recent girlfriend had declined to move in with him. And a doctor had told him that he had an enlarged heart and, though he was barely thirty-two, his arteries were hardening. On June 28, 1975, Jonathan didn't file any stories. A friend went to check on him and found Peck's son dead in his apartment, where police said he had shot himself in the head.

Peck, who was in France at the time with his wife, said later, "If only I had been here in this country, then I'm sure Jon would have called me and said, 'Dad, I'm at the bottom of the barrel; I need help.' And I would have said, 'Sure, come on. Let's go up in the mountains, let's go to Tahiti, let's talk it over.' But I wasn't here, and he didn't call."

Peck's other four children have sought diverse careers. Steve, a Marine lieutenant in Vietnam, makes documentary films. Carey, Peck's youngest son by his first marriage, ran for Congress in California in 1978 and 1980. Peck and former Governor Pat Brown chaired his campaign. Peck's two children by his second marriage, Anthony and Cecelia, both have pursued acting careers.

Peck has said he has wondered what went wrong with his oldest son. "When you look back on your life, there are a number of things you say you might do differently," he said. "But with Jon, if he were born tomorrow, I would raise him the same way." The trouble with children isn't always their parents. Sometimes it's that they grow up. "Who knows," said Peck, "how good a father any man is?" Or can be.

SON of
KING PETER OF YUGOSLAVIA

OFTTIMES IT'S TOUGH to feel sorry for deposed royalty. Sure, they've lost their crowns, but usually they've managed to slip away with enough money to settle into another castle beyond hostile borders. King Peter of Yugoslavia was a bit different. His father was assassinated by a Croat terrorist when he was ten, but Peter did not become king until age eighteen, in 1941, when he ousted his pro-Axis regent cousin. But he ruled only eleven days before Hitler invaded and he was forced to flee to England. Peter didn't exactly live poorly in England. A great-great-grandson of Queen Victoria, he was also a cousin of King George VI.

Peter soon married, and in 1945 his only son, Alexander, was born at London's Claridge's Hotel. As a male heir (and godson of the future Queen Elizabeth), Alexander brought brief hope that Peter could regain the Yugoslav throne at the end of World War II. Instead, England and the United States backed Marshal Tito's regime and Peter was left without a country and with little money of his own. He moved with his wife and son to New York in 1948 and tried to establish himself as a consultant on international politics. Within a year he was bankrupt.

He then returned with his wife to Europe to try to solicit money from relatives, while Alexander was left with his Irish nanny in New York. Shortly thereafter he was given over to the care of his grandmother, a Greek princess, in Venice, and then attended boarding school, where Prince Charles was one of his classmates.

Peter, meanwhile, never became accustomed to his life in exile. He returned to New York in the 1950s to try his hand, badly, at public relations. In the 1960s he became a director of a California savings and loan—where he was addressed as "Your Majesty"— with duties to attract European investments. He was not successful, and his other schemes, ranging from plastics to real estate, failed as well. He inherited some money from his mother in 1961, but it was not enough and the deposed ruler seemed never to be able to contain his lifestyle within his means.

Peter separated from his wife and developed a drinking problem. Then, soon after he underwent treatment at a hospital in New York in 1970, he disappeared. He was found a week later at Delmonico's Hotel. Unable to pay his bills, depressed, he died of cirrhosis of the liver on November 3 at the age of forty-seven.

Prince Alexander, who has never seen his kingdom, has had an easier time giving up the crown he never wore. After seven years in the British Army, where he specialized in intelligence and antiterrorism, Alexander became an insurance agent. From 1981 to 1984 he worked for the Fred. S. James Co. in Chicago and Washington, designing group insurance plans. "I inherited no wealth from my father," he said during that time. "That means I have to earn my living like anyone else."

Now working for an insurance firm in London, Alexander doesn't like to be addressed by his royal title. "I like to go into a company and be on a first-name basis with everybody," said the prince, whose distant cousin is actress Catherine Oxenberg. He and his wife, who would be a Brazilian princess if that country's royalty had survived, occasionally attend functions in their royal roles, but Alexander doesn't even speak Serbo-Croatian, the language of his country.

SON of FRANKLIN PIERCE

WITH THE PROSPECT of a civil war already tearing the country apart, perhaps no man elected president in 1852 could have made it into the history books with a favorable record. But Franklin Pierce entered the White House carrying an extra burden from which he, and to some extent the nation, never recovered.

That Pierce even became president was a quirk of fate that doesn't happen anymore. A former congressman and senator for ten years, during which time he did absolutely nothing to distinguish himself, Pierce resigned his Senate seat in 1842 to spend more time with his family in New Hampshire. His wife was frequently ill and hated Washington. And they had a new baby, Benjamin. He was their third son, but the only one who survived early childhood, and Franklin and Jane Pierce lived for Bennie. Pierce took him to the Congregational church twice a day. When Pierce didn't come home from his law practice at the usual hour, Bennie would run down to his office to retrieve him.

So it might have continued, except that the Democrats, divided by the slavery issue, could not settle on their nominee in 1852. On the forty-ninth ballot, they chose Pierce, who had remained active in New Hampshire politics. Pierce made no campaign speeches but was elected president anyway. If Pierce was a reluctant leader, his family was even less enthusiastic about his post. After his father was nominated, Bennie had written his mother, "Edward brought the news from Boston that Father is a candidate for the Presidency. I hope he won't be elected for I should not like to be at Washington and I know you would not either."

After Pierce was elected the family spent New Year's in Boston. On January 6, they boarded a train to return to Concord, New Hampshire. A mile out of the station, their train car derailed and rolled down an embankment and into a field. The president-elect and his wife were barely hurt. But they saw their eleven-year-old son mangled to death. Bennie was the only fatality.

Pierce and his wife, both deeply religious, tried to understand why God had let this tragedy happen. Jane decided it was God's way of freeing her husband to devote his full attention to the presidency. To Pierce, that meant she blamed him. Pierce said in his inaugural address, "No heart but my own can know the personal regret and bitter sorrow over which I have been borne to a position so suitable for others." Pierce dodged most of the inaugural parties while his wife secluded herself upstairs in the White House and penciled notes to Bennie, apologizing for not loving him enough.

Pierce wrote to a friend, "How I shall be able to summon my manhood and gather up my energies for the duties before me, it is hard for me to see." No one can say exactly how big a role Bennie's death played in Pierce's failure as president, but his administration never got off the ground. Congress ignored his proposals as it fought over whether to admit Kansas and Nebraska as free or slave states. By the time the Democrats rejected Pierce as their nominee in 1856—the first time a party had turned down its own president—bloody border wars were raging in Kansas.

Pierce and his wife toured Europe after they left the White House. Jane carried Bennie's Bible and a box that contained locks of hair from each of her three dead sons. They retired to New Hampshire, where Jane died in 1863. Pierce, who had had an occasional drinking problem back in his congressional days, became an alcoholic and died, in obscurity, in 1869.

CHILDREN of TYRONE POWER

SWASHBUCKLING and incredibly good-looking, Tyrone Power didn't become one of the hottest screen idols of the late 1930s and early

1940s by being a father figure. And Power, who in films like *The Mark of Zorro* and *The Razor's Edge* reaped millions for Darryl Zanuck's 20th Century–Fox, wasn't much more paternal offscreen either, though he had three children. "We didn't really have parents," said Power's younger daughter, Taryn. "Mother and Father had their own lives and interests. We didn't miss them. We didn't know any better and we loved Blanca," their Mexican grandmother.

Actually, Power enjoyed the height of his fame childless. It wasn't until his second marriage, after he divorced his first wife, Annabella, for Lana Turner but instead married Linda Christian, an MGM contract player, that Power fathered his first child, Romina, in 1951. He and Linda split soon after, but reconciled long enough to produce Taryn in 1953 before they finally divorced three years later. His third wife was pregnant in 1958 when Power, while filming a sword fight on the set of *Solomon and Sheba* in Madrid, collapsed and died of a heart attack at the age of forty-four. His widow gave birth to their son, Tyrone Power IV, on January 22, 1959.

Power was in fact the fourth generation of his family to become an actor—his great-grandfather was famous on the Irish stage, his father was popular on Broadway—so it isn't all that surprising that his children have followed suit. His only son, whose godfather was Rock Hudson, was featured in the hit *Cocoon*, with Raquel Welch's daughter, Tahnee. He also appears in the sequel *Cocoon II* and another film, *Shag*.

Tyrone IV has never met his two half-sisters, Romina and Taryn, who grew up in Mexico City with their grandmother and later in Rome, where their mother carried on well-publicized affairs. Romina modeled and acted in some European films before she married twenty-seven-year-old Italian pop singer Al Bano in 1970 when she was eighteen. Parents of two daughters, Romina and Bano have had singing hits together in Italy.

Taryn starred in a Mexican film, *Maria*, when she was eighteen, and later moved to Los Angeles. She appeared in *The Count of Monte Cristo*, with Richard Chamberlain, and in a movie with John Wayne's son, Patrick. Taryn married photographer Norman

Seeff six weeks before their daughter was born in 1978. They divorced in 1982 and Taryn moved in with Tony Sales, a rock musician and son of Soupy. They have two children. Now Taryn is looking for acting roles again. "I talked about this to Rory Flynn, Errol's daughter, a year ago," she told *People*. "We said, 'It's bizarre. Here are you and me, and we're the daughters of who we are, and we can't get a job in this town.' "

Taryn, who doesn't remember her father, said in 1986, "He'd be 72 now, and my whole life would have been different if he had lived." Maybe.

CHILDREN of JOSEPH PULITZER

JOSEPH PULITZER was mighty proud of the newspaper empire he had built. A Hungarian immigrant who came to the United States to join Union troops in the Civil War, Pulitzer bought the near-defunct *St. Louis Dispatch* in 1878 for $2,500 and turned it into a major voice in Missouri politics. That he was practically run out of town after his chief editorial writer shot and killed a prominent lawyer in 1882 turned out to be a good thing, as Pulitzer moved to New York and bought another ailing newspaper, the *New York World*. There he applied his brand of yellow journalism to jump circulation from 15,000 in 1883 to a Hearst-rivaling 1.5 million in 1898. Even after Pulitzer went blind in 1887, his aggressive zeal and competition with Hearst drove the *World* to huge profits and, later, respectability.

So it wasn't surprising that upon his death, Pulitzer forbade the sale of his creation. Said his will, "I particularly enjoin my sons and my descendants the duty of preserving, perfecting and perpetuating *The World* newspaper in the same spirit in which I have striven to create and conduct it, as a public institution from motives higher than mere gain."

It was a tall order for his sons, who, as Pulitzer frequently reminded them, had done nothing to demonstrate their ability to fulfill it. Pulitzer was especially disappointed in his two oldest sons. Their school marks were poor and when they grew up they didn't embrace his newspapers with enough enthusiasm.

When his oldest son, Ralph, showed more interest in writing thoughtful editorials than in learning how to run the newspapers, Pulitzer wrote, "Fix upon your mind the idea that I am dead and that you are president of the company in my place with supreme powers—an hypothesis most natural and presumably not remote." He told his son to keep a daily diary of his observations about managing the *World* and be "ready to send when I telegraph." Pulitzer demanded such detailed accounts from all his sons as he spent years traveling the world seeking relief or cures for his blindness and many other ills.

Pulitzer's second son, Joseph Jr., at least seemed to enjoy journalism. But after Joe didn't show up for work one day at the *World*, Pulitzer fired him and sent him to the *Post-Dispatch* in St. Louis. "This is my son Joseph," Pulitzer wrote to the editor. "Will you try to knock some newspaper sense into his head?"

Pulitzer seemed pleased only with his youngest son, probably because Herbert was too young to have failed the way Pulitzer thought Ralph and Joe had. Pulitzer believed Herbert to be his brightest boy and said he could be president of the United States some day. Pulitzer saw that Herbert's daily routine was strictly scheduled—even his playmates were screened—and he took Herbert on many of his world travels. "It is not that he loves me," Pulitzer wrote, "but he is useful to me because I can love him. That is why I have carried him around like a woman who wears a crucifix or talisman."

So when Pulitzer died at the age of sixty-four in 1911, it was fifteen-year-old Herbert who received the biggest share of the empire. After providing trusts for his wife and two daughters—and money to start the Pulitzer prizes and a journalism school at Columbia University—Pulitzer left Herbert three-fifths of the stock in the *World* and *Post-Dispatch*. He left Ralph one-fifth and Joe only one-tenth. The actual control of the company was left to outside trustees until Pulitzer's sons came of age—which for Joe meant thirty and Herbert twenty-one. Ralph, thirty-two at the time, was left out.

Still, it was Ralph who took the largest active role in the newspaper after his father died. When Herbert was older, he did some reporting in Europe, but Pulitzer's best hope for an heir turned out to be more interested in hunting big game at his lodge in Scotland. The *World* lost money and morale. In 1930 Ralph resigned because of ill-health and Herbert finally took control. Within two months he began negotiating with Scripps-Howard and sold the *World* for $5 million in 1931, nineteen years after Pulitzer forbade it.

Ralph died in 1939 at the age of sixty. Herbert died at the same age in 1957 after a life of hunting and deep-sea fishing. His son, Herbert Jr., also called Peter, made his own headlines in 1982 during his much-trumpeted divorce trial in Palm Beach. Meanwhile, Joe Jr., whom Pulitzer had banished to St. Louis with the smallest share of his empire, turned the *Post-Dispatch* into one of the most respected newspapers in the country. He died in 1957, and his son, also called Joseph Jr., is now the chairman of the Pulitzer Publishing Company.

R

DAUGHTER of RASPUTIN

RASPUTIN, the debauched monk who became the powerful adviser to Russian Tsar Nicholas II, is not often thought of as a family man. That's partly because he left his wife and three children back on their farm in Siberia while he wandered the countryside, showing off his mysterious healing powers and engaging in wild orgies as well. Once he gained the ear of the tsar, Rasputin did bring his two daughters to St. Petersburg so they could study in the best private schools.

Maria, Rasputin's older daughter, later wrote that she and her younger sister, Varvara, were aware that their father was surrounded by more and more enemies as the Russian Revolution neared. On the night that Rasputin was brutally murdered, Maria said she and her sister had hidden their father's boots and she had begged him not to go out into the dangerous night. " 'Do not worry, Maria,' " Rasputin had told her. " 'God will protect me. Go to bed now.' " The next time Maria saw her father, it was to identify his stabbed, bullet-ridden, rope-bound body after it had been pulled frozen from the Neva River.

Soon after, Maria married a Russian soldier. They fled to Paris in 1920, where her husband died of tuberculosis four years later. Her sister died in Russia the same year. Maria later wrote that her mother and brother were taken prisoner during the Revolution and she never heard from them again.

Until the end of her life, Maria maintained that her father was a good man who had been misunderstood and destroyed by his enemies. "His power came from belief in God," she told the *Los Angeles Times* in 1967. "He healed by power of prayer." He was not evil, she told *Esquire* magazine in 1974, but "simple, deeply religious and just lusty." Maria recounted just how lusty in her 1977 memoir, *Rasputin: The Man Behind the Myth*. In stories passed on to her mostly by her father's mistress, Maria describes her father's sexual exploits in such detail that even Rasputin himself might have blushed.

Maria never was able to regain privileged status either for her father's memory or for herself. After her husband died, she became a cabaret dancer in Paris, where her notorious maiden name didn't hurt. She later was working in a European circus when an agent for Ringling Brothers and Barnum & Bailey Circus signed her to train wild animals in the United States in 1935. She gave up the circus two years later after she was mauled by a bear in Peru, Indiana.

Maria later married an electrical engineer, moved to Los Angeles, and was divorced. She went to work in a shipyard in 1945, became a skilled machinist, and then worked in factories until she retired in 1965. "Lathe, drill press—I operate them all," the daughter of the legendary Russian told the *Los Angeles Times.* "You name it, I do it." Maria continued to live on a pension in a small house in the Los Angeles suburb of Silverlake, where she did volunteer work at the nearby Russian Orthodox church. In 1977, she called a neighbor to say that she was having trouble breathing. She was found soon afterward dead of a heart attack in her home, surrounded by walls covered with pictures of Rasputin and Russian aristocrats.

SON of PIERRE-AUGUSTE RENOIR

IN HIS LIFETIME, Pierre-Auguste Renoir was hailed as one of the greatest painters of the nineteenth century. Had any of his three sons chosen to follow Renoir in his craft, they undoubtedly would have faced the heavy burden of being compared to the master French Impressionist. None of Renoir's three sons did try to make his mark on canvas. But his middle son, Jean, found fame nearly as great as his father's. Jean's medium was not canvas but celluloid, on which he created such classics as *Grand Illusion* and *The Rules of the Game,* earning a reputation as one of the greatest international film directors. None other than Charlie Chaplin called Jean Renoir the greatest of them all.

Auguste Renoir was forty-four when his first son, Pierre, was born, and he was nearly fifty when he married Pierre's mother in

1890. By the time Jean was born in 1894, Renoir already was suffering from the rheumatism that would later cripple him. When Claude was born in 1901, the sixty-year-old painter walked with a cane and his hands were stiff and swollen. Later Renoir would paint some of his most famous works by wrapping the brush to his fingers with a piece of cloth. Remembered Jean, "His twisted fingers gripped rather than held the brush. But until his last breath, his arm remained as steady as that of a young man."

Renoir was not a healthy man, but he adored fatherhood nonetheless. Jean, in his 1962 memoir, said his father would file down the sharp corners of marble mantels and wooden tables throughout the house so his children wouldn't hurt themselves. He boarded up lower window panes and banned bleach from the house. Renoir was not a demanding father, Jean said, except that he did require his children to sit fairly still while he painted them, which he did often.

Renoir taught his two younger sons, Jean and Claude, to make pottery, which had been the start of Renoir's artistic career. And Jean, in fact, planned to start a ceramics factory with the son of Paul Cézanne after World War I, in which both Jean and Pierre were seriously wounded. But instead Jean, enthralled with early films he saw, wrote a screenplay in 1923 for his wife, who had been one of his father's last models before he died in 1919. His brother Pierre, a film actor, introduced Jean to some friends and the film was made.

Jean's early films were commercial flops, but by the end of the 1920s he was a successful director in France. He directed his two acknowledged masterpieces, *Grand Illusion* and *The Rules of the Game*, in 1937 and 1939, before he fled France during the Nazi occupation and resettled in Hollywood. Jean never had similar phenomenal success in America, but his work in France is credited as one of the major influences on French New Wave directors, including François Truffaut and Jean-Luc Godard. He was awarded a special Academy Award in 1975.

Though the mediums of Auguste Renoir and his son were different, critics often looked for similarities anyway. They compared Jean's occasional soft focus and romantic touch with the Impressionist brush strokes of his father. Jean discounted the comparisons, though he admitted, "When I started to make films I went out of my way to repudiate my father's principles; but, strangely, it is precisely in the productions where I thought I had avoided Renoir's aesthetics that his influence is most apparent."

Jean Renoir, who in later years was bereft of the beautiful strawberry-blond curls that his father loved to paint when he was a child, made thirty-six films during his fifty-year career. His brother Pierre, who became a well-known character actor, appeared in some of them and Claude often was his production director. He died of a heart attack in Los Angeles in 1979 at the age of eighty-four.

CHILDREN of PAUL REVERE

"LISTEN MY CHILDREN, and you shall hear of the midnight ride of Paul Revere," wrote Henry Wadsworth Longfellow. But the poet didn't tell the whole story. Revere's ride appears even more heroic when you consider that the man who galloped through the Boston countryside in 1775 shouting that the British were coming was in fact the forty-year-old father of nine. And fighting in the Revolution didn't stop him from fathering seven more children before his second wife gave birth to their last when Revere was fifty-three. With two wives who gave him a total of sixteen children—eleven of whom survived infancy—it's no wonder that Revere worked so hard to become a prosperous silversmith.

Revere's first child was born seven and a half months after he married Sara Orne in 1758. A new baby arrived every two years after that until Sara failed to recover from her eighth childbirth in 1772. With six living children, Revere remarried five months after Sara died, and his new wife, Rachel Walker, gave birth to her first child the next year. The last arrived in 1787, a year after Revere had written, following his fifteenth baby, "I now begin to think that I shall have no more children."

To support his burgeoning brood, Revere did much more than make silver bowls. He cleaned and replaced teeth; fit eyeglasses; designed clock faces, surgical instruments, and branding irons; and cast bells. After the war he supplied the copper bolts and pumps for the USS *Constitution*, "Old Ironsides." Revere was successful enough to provide his sons excellent educations, including tours of Europe. But his responsibilities didn't end when his children grew up. He paid the rent on the house of his oldest son, Paul Jr., who had seven children of his own. He also took in three grandchildren after his daughter Frances died and her husband went insane. Even during his last years Revere shared his house with five of his children and three grandchildren. Some of his children did quite well on their own. John became a professor of medicine at New York University. Deborah, his oldest daughter, married Amos Lincoln, a cousin of Abraham's father. When Deborah died, Amos married one of her sisters. And Amos's brother also married a Revere girl.

Paul Jr., Revere's only son by his first marriage, also became a silversmith, but he never was as successful as his father, probably because he came of age as an apprentice while Revere was fighting the Revolution. Instead Revere, who lived to be eighty-three, passed on his trade to Joseph, his third son by his second marriage. Joseph's descendants kept Paul Revere & Son alive until 1900, when the company was merged with other copperworks. So Revere's hard work did pay off.

SON and GRANDSON of
RICHARD J. REYNOLDS

IMAGINE IF Henry Ford's son had promoted bicycles, or if the son of beer-maker August Busch, Jr., had joined the Women's Christian Temperance Union. Such is the dynastic revolt that exploded in the Reynolds tobacco family a few years ago. Company founder Richard J. Reynolds sold so many millions of cigarettes that he left his four children a very comfortable $100 million when he died in 1918. Today, grandson Patrick travels the country saying, "My grandfather helped popularize smoking in America. And I want to do everything I can, now that we know how dangerous it is, to help people stop."

Patrick isn't the first rebellious Reynolds. His father, R. J. Reynolds, Jr., spent a brief time in a cigarette factory before, at age seventeen, he ran away to work on a tramp steamer. He returned to become a New York society playboy in the 1920s, only to disappear in 1927. He was found eleven days later in St. Louis eating chop suey, and said merely that he was "tired and fed up with New York." He fled to England, where he spent five months in jail for killing a man while driving drunk.

R.J. Jr. settled down somewhat after his brother Zachary died in a questionable shooting accident in 1932. He married a tobacco heiress and they had four children. With his inheritance of $25 million, R.J. Jr. and his wife became known among the racing and yachting set as "Dick and Blitz." R.J. Jr. became mayor of Winston-Salem, North Carolina, in 1940 and treasurer of the Democratic National Committee in 1941.

It was while R.J. Jr. was in the Navy in World War II that he met movie starlet Marianne O'Brien. He divorced Blitz and married O'Brien in 1946. They had two children, the younger one Patrick, before they divorced in a splashy trial in 1952. R.J. Jr.

went on to another messy divorce and a fourth marriage before he died.

When Patrick was nine—not having seen his father since he was three—he wrote him a letter, Patrick recalled. It said, "Dear Dad, I want to meet you—I'm your son Patrick. Where are you? Love, Me." Patrick's father sent for him. "The moment of meeting him was a wonderful thing," Patrick said, "except for one thing— he had sandbags on his chest to exercise his lungs. They thought he had been taken by asthma, but it turned out to be emphysema."

R.J. Jr. died at the age of fifty-eight in 1964 when Patrick was fifteen. Four years later Patrick started smoking, he said, for the usual reasons, "wanting to attract girls and so on." He quit in 1984, five years after he sold all of his Reynolds stock, worth several million dollars. Patrick became an actor for a while, appearing in *Nashville* and *Airplane* and starring in *Eliminators* in 1986.

That same year Patrick testified before Congress, urging the legislators to ban all cigarette ads. Since then, he has appeared in commercials for the American Lung Association and recently created the Reynolds Stop Smoking Program, a series of cassettes and books that sells for $19.88. He has encouraged families of smokers who die to sue cigarette makers, including the company that still provides hefty stock dividends to many of Patrick's relatives. "Some people say I'm biting the hand that feeds me," says Patrick, who in 1989 co-wrote *The Gilded Leaf*, a biography of his family. "I say the hand that fed me—the tobacco industry—has literally killed millions of people and may kill millions more unless smokers wake up."

Patrick's siblings have been less than pleased with his crusade against the family legacy. Said his half-brother John in 1986, "I just wish the kid would straighten up and not take this stand himself. Let him pay someone else to do it." John also said, "Our father and grandfather are probably spinning in their graves." But Patrick doesn't think so. "I like to think my grandfather is in heaven, not concerned with making a profit anymore and saying, 'Grandson Patrick, you're doing the right thing.'"

SON of REMBRANDT VAN RIJN

REMBRANDT's SON is best remembered as the young Christ, Daniel, and other young biblical boys for whom he served as a model in his father's famous paintings. But the son of Rembrandt van Rijn also played a more important role on the business side of his father's art. Depending on which account you read, Titus either saved his father from financial ruin, or was a willing pawn in the Dutch master painter's unscrupulous business dealings.

It is more certain that Rembrandt got into trouble. He was a successful painter early on, in his twenties, and became financially secure when he married the heiress of a wealthy lawyer, who brought with her a dowry of forty thousand guilders. The beginning of his decline came when he bought a huge house in Amsterdam in 1639. He paid off half the price promptly, but then he stopped making payments and cavalierly allowed the interest debt to mount. Meanwhile, his commissions fell off, apparently because his wealthy customers tired of his arrogance, especially after he put some of his patrons in a dark background of *The Nightwatch*.

His wife died in 1642, leaving, from four births, only one surviving child, nine-month-old Titus. According to her will, half her dowry—some twenty thousand guilders—was to pass on to Titus when he came of age. Until then, Rembrandt controlled it. With fewer commissions and a mistress to support, Rembrandt ran through all of his wealth and most of his son's. Buried by the debt of his house, Rembrandt was declared bankrupt in 1656 by the Orphans' Chamber of Amsterdam, which stepped in to protect young Titus. Rembrandt lost his house and was faced with being forced to sell all of his possessions, including his personal collection of his paintings. But before that happened, a partnership was formed between Titus and Rembrandt's mistress to acquire all the paintings and protect them from creditors. Rembrandt was made an employee of the firm and his only responsibility was to continue to paint, for which he received free room and board.

Some historians have portrayed Titus as his father's savior who took over the business side of things so Rembrandt could continue to paint masterpieces. Some also believe that among Rembrandt's later works are some still lifes that Titus painted and the master merely touched up. But others say the painter—who got himself into financial trouble by blatantly ignoring his creditors in the first place—was behind it all. Rembrandt may have designed the partnership that protected his works and he may also have been the author of a will made by Titus that gave everything back to the artist.

That will helped the painter only a little. Titus died in 1668 and Rembrandt died the following year. Whether Titus protected his father or was used by him, either way the painter couldn't have done it without him.

SON of EDWARD G. ROBINSON

"So EFFECTIVE was [Edward G.] Robinson's interpretation of the gangster," wrote the *New York Times*, "that many of the underworld characters found themselves affecting the Robinson character—chomping on cigar butts while snarling threats and orders out of the sides of their mouths." Starting with his classic role in *Little Caesar*, the Rumanian immigrant whose real name was Emanuel Goldenberg did indeed set the standard for movie mobsters. His scowling face sustained his career for more than forty years, in one hundred movies and forty Broadway plays.

Even Robinson's son, Edward Jr., used to imitate his father's snarl when he was a little boy, and would sometimes impersonate Robinson on the telephone. But Edward Jr., called Manny, didn't mean to flatter his father. He just wanted some attention; Manny had discipline problems almost as soon as he could walk and talk. Writing his autobiography in 1973 Robinson said of himself as a father, "I have discussed these matters endlessly with analysts and psychiatrists, and I am prepared to admit, in the late afternoon of my life, that I did everything wrong."

With his father busy making movies and his mother under treatment for depression, Manny was raised by governesses. His father's spurts of attention were brief, if spectacular. For Manny's sixth birthday, Robinson threw a party at which even Hollywood gawked. Invitations were delivered by a man in a police uniform. Children were picked up for the party in paddy wagons. There were trains and horses to ride and a little jail in keeping with Robinson's screen image. Manny, meanwhile, was seen peeing in the ice cream. Robinson wrote in his autobiography, "I turned to bribery via magnificent and thoroughly unsuitable gifts: a shining bicycle when he was too young to use it . . . when he wanted to play baseball, a set of gloves and masks and bats and uniforms that the Yankees would have envied. I confess it. I gave him everything but myself."

Manny was shuttled in and out of several schools, always leaving after he got into trouble. Robinson said his son was bullied by other boys who wanted to prove they could beat up the son of the famous movie gangster. By thirteen Manny was drinking, and by the time he was sixteen, his parents gave up and sent him to New York by himself to study acting. He married before he was twenty, then divorced soon after he became a father. Manny's drunken tantrums made sensational news, especially after the movie gangster's son was arrested and charged with holding up two cab drivers. The jury couldn't reach a verdict. In 1956 Manny tried to overdose on sleeping pills and a few months later he rammed into a parked car and was convicted of drunk driving, spending sixty days in jail.

In 1958, Manny wrote his own autobiography, *My Father, My Son.* "To be born into such a family is to be raised like a prince, the way I was raised," he wrote. "To be born into such a family gives you all the rights, privileges, duties, and obligations that

your family has, except the gimmick which keeps royalty in business—the right of succession." Manny's mother, Gladys, who had
divorced Robinson, was so upset by her son's book that she criticized him publicly. Robinson shrugged it off and continued to try
to get his son acting roles. The two of them appeared as a father
and son in a television drama in 1959.

Manny had other small television and film roles, and he even
stopped drinking for a while. But his career never took off. Once
he became so frustrated that he walked into his agent's office wav-
ing a gun. When Manny's mother died in 1972, she left Manny
only a tea set, a baby chair, and a painting of him, "because of his
unbearable misconduct toward me." The next year, when Robinson died at the age of seventy-nine, he was more generous. He left
his only child one-quarter of his estate, including his famous five-
million-dollar art collection. But it all was put into a trust on the
condition that Manny behave. Shortly before he died, Robinson
had told his son, "All of us Goldenbergs live to our eighties. You've
got forty-one years more. Enjoy yourself, but make it work for
you."

Thirteen months later, Manny's third wife found him vomiting
in the bathroom of their West Hollywood home. He died on the
way to the hospital. Doctors said the forty-year-old man died of
natural causes.

DAUGHTER of JOHN D. ROCKEFELLER

WHEN JOHN D. ROCKEFELLER learned that after four daughters
he finally had a son, tears came to his eyes. If he had known then
how his youngest daughter, Edith, would turn out, his gratitude at
the birth of John Jr. might well have caused the ruthless oil baron
to bawl like a baby.

There was, of course, no question that John D.'s only son would inherit the Rockefeller oil dynasty. So the daughters dutifully married. The two older girls found fine husbands (a third had died in infancy). But it was Edith, a Sunday school teacher, who turned marriage into a merger when she exchanged vows in 1895 with Harold McCormick, son of Cyrus McCormick, who invented the reaper and founded International Harvester. John D. wound up with some $30 million in Harvester stock and Edith became one of the richest, and therefore leading, ladies of Chicago.

Edith filled the role beautifully, patronizing the opera and wearing extravagant jewelry—one necklace contained 10 emeralds and 1,657 diamonds. She possessed a dog collar and tiara worth $1 million. But Edith also had an eccentric side. She sometimes signed letters Edith de La Rockefeller and, apparently not satisfied to be merely the daughter of one of the wealthiest industrialists of her day, believed she was the reincarnation of the bride of King Tut.

John D. Rockefeller had been a warm and deeply religious family man and a caring father; Edith treated her four children differently. They were required to make appointments through her secretary to see her. When a member of her staff broke her iron-clad rule and interrupted one of her lavish pre-opera dinner parties to inform her that her oldest son, three-year-old John, had died of scarlet fever, Edith nodded and continued eating with her guests.

While her husband dallied with other women, Edith sailed to Europe in 1906 to undergo a new type of treatment, psychoanalysis, with the then little-known Dr. Carl Jung. She remained in Switzerland fifteen years and returned to Chicago only after her husband convinced her to divorce him so he could marry an aspiring opera singer. Edith came home estranged from her three children as well. Her son Fowler, who was John D.'s favorite grandson, married the mother of his Princeton roommate and later became president of International Harvester. Edith's daughter Mathilde, when she was seventeen, married her forty-seven-year-old Swiss riding instructor. And Edith's younger daughter, Muriel, married the "ghost" of a lieutenant who had been killed in World War I. She later "divorced" him and married an older, invalid war veteran.

Meanwhile, Edith was determined to bring psychoanalysis to Chicago. She gathered her own patients and offered her own brand of the treatment. She also was seen frequently with Edwin Krenn, an architect without a portfolio, whom she had met at Dr. Jung's clinic. They spent many days going to movies, which scandalized Chicago society, though it was never certain that their relationship was more than platonic.

Edith also had the idea to build her own legacy. She took her Standard Oil stock and began building Edithton, a city for the wealthy on the shores of Lake Michigan near Wisconsin. She and Krenn drew up plans for grand Spanish mansions, and a marina actually was dredged for big yachts before the stock market crashed in 1929. Edith's Rockefeller trust fund, pledged against her now worthless real estate venture, was wiped out. John D., who had been silently embarrassed for years about his daughter, sent his son to move Edith out of her Lake Shore Drive mansion and into the Drake Hotel, where she was given an allowance of $1,000 a day. By contrast, her older sister Alta, who also was given 12,000 shares of Standard Oil in 1917, by 1930 held stock worth $18 million.

Edith did not live in comparative poverty for long. She developed liver cancer and in 1932, not quite sixty years old, she died— five years before her father.

SON of JOHN ROEBLING

WITHOUT JOHN ROEBLING, it might have been decades before anyone thought up the Brooklyn Bridge. Without his son Washington, the Brooklyn Bridge probably would not ever have been built. And without the bridge, both men probably would have lived longer, or at least healthier, lives. Rarely have a father and son been bound into one monumental undertaking such as this. Washington wrote later in his life, "Long ago I ceased my endeavor to clear up the respective identities of myself and my father. Most people think I died in 1869," the year his father died.

John Roebling was the visionary. A German immigrant engineer, he began making his fortune in the 1840s when he developed twisted wire cables to haul canal boats. He later used his cables to build four suspension bridges in the 1850s and 1860s. It was after the Civil War that John Roebling got the idea for his biggest suspension bridge of all, one that would span the East River and connect Manhattan to Brooklyn. "The completed work," Roebling said with enthusiasm that matched his lack of modesty, "when constructed in accordance with my designs, will not only be the greatest bridge in existence, but it will be the greatest engineering work of the continent, and of the age."

But while John Roebling created the conceptual design for the 1,595-foot bridge, the sixty-three-year-old man left most of the practical work to Washington, the oldest of his nine children. Washington, also an engineer, supervised most of the detailed drawings and made most of the measurements at the Brooklyn and Manhattan landings.

On June 28, 1869, John Roebling joined his son at the Brooklyn water's edge to determine the exact location for one of the bridge's two cathedral towers. The father was standing out on a ferry pier, perched on the wooden pilings and calling out measurements, while a ferryboat was docking. As the boat pressed against the pilings, Roebling's boot was caught between the pilings and his toes were crushed. The old man continued to shout directions until he collapsed in pain.

Roebling was rushed to a doctor, who amputated his damaged toes without an anesthetic, at Roebling's request. A man with strong views on health—he believed a cold bath could cure almost anything and he regularly drank a mixture of raw egg, charcoal, and turpentine—Roebling fired his doctor and stuck his foot in cold water. Soon, lying in a bedroom of his son's home in Brooklyn Heights, Roebling developed tetanus. He suffered lockjaw and later fell into a coma. Three weeks after the accident, Roebling was dead.

There was little question that thirty-two-year-old Washington should take over his father's work as chief engineer. He knew more about the bridge's design than anyone else and had spent months in Europe studying similar engineering methods. His expertise was especially important for the use of a pneumatic caisson, a huge wood-and-iron box—bigger than half a city block—that would be sunk to the bottom of the East River so that men could dig the foundations of the two bridge towers.

Besides the obvious threat of flooding, the most dangerous aspect of the caisson was the compressed air that had to be pumped in to keep out the water. Often, men who worked in the compressed air came out suffering "the bends," which sometimes meant a mild case of stomach cramps or painful joints, but could also mean vomiting, nosebleeds and incoherence, and severe cases could be fatal. Doctors at the time thought the bends were caused by spending too much time down in the caisson. Only later did they realize the problem was caused by exiting the compressed air too quickly.

Of hundreds of men who descended into the caisson in the East River, Washington Roebling perhaps suffered the most. Not only did he spend much time inspecting the underwater operation, but he climbed in and out several times a day as he checked on various problems. In 1870, when the caisson caught fire, Roebling spent so much time going in and out of the caisson that he finally collapsed, his legs paralyzed. A few days later and only partly recovered, he went down again.

In 1872 the younger Roebling suffered a more serious attack of the bends that left him painfully near death. Even after the worst symptoms went away, his arms and legs were partly numb; he felt nauseated and tired very easily. By the next spring Roebling took a leave of absence from the bridge and went to Europe to try to recover. But he returned no better and moved to Trenton, New Jersey, where his father's cable business still operated.

From his mansion there, Roebling directed the construction of the Brooklyn Bridge, making specific alterations in the design of the bridge he could not see. He suffered almost constant pain in his stomach and joints, could barely write, and had a nervous condition, probably caused by anxiety over his work load and his illness. Roebling later moved back to the Brooklyn waterfront, where he monitored the bridge's progress through a pair of binoculars. Through the years, it was Roebling's wife, Emily, who made almost daily trips to the bridge to deliver and oversee her husband's directions. There were rumors that the unseen Roebling was an invalid or insane, but he held on to his post as chief engineer until the bridge was completed.

In 1883, shortly before the great monument opened, Roebling was driven in his carriage to inspect the Brooklyn terminal building. He didn't get out. When the bridge was inaugurated on May 24, Roebling watched the spectacular celebration from his bedroom window. Later, more than 1,000 guests arrived at his home, but after he greeted President Arthur, the exhausted engineer, not quite forty-six, retired upstairs.

Washington Roebling lived another forty-three years, but he never built another bridge or anything else. His health slowly improved, but he remained mostly secluded, devoting himself to his impressive collection of rare minerals, which grew to 15,000 samples and is now in the Smithsonian. In his last years, after several of his sons and grandsons had died, Roebling went back to running the family's cable business, riding the trolley every day to work. When asked why he would take on such a demanding position so late in life, the eighty-three-year-old man replied, "Because it's all in my head. It's my job to carry the responsibility and you can't desert your job. You can't slink out of life or out of the work life lays on you."

DAUGHTER of THEODORE ROOSEVELT

"LISTEN," President Theodore Roosevelt told a visitor after his oldest daughter had interrupted their meeting three times. "I can be President of the United States, or I can control Alice. I cannot possibly do both." The trust-busting builder of the Panama Canal might have carried a big stick, but he was helpless when it came to headstrong Alice, who later would proudly display a pillow in her Washington mansion embroidered with: "If you can't say something good about someone, sit right here by me."

Seventeen years old at the time her father became president, Alice said that her reaction had been one of "utter rapture" when she learned of his appointment in 1901, even though it came as a result of William McKinley's assassination. Alice actually was fairly distant from her father, who was raising five children by his second wife; his first wife had died when Alice was born. But on her arrival at the White House with her blue macaw and her green snake, she was embraced by Washington, and especially by the press, who dubbed her "Princess Alice" and occasionally even granted her more and better coverage than her father, the president. Stated the White House usher: "It would be a wizard indeed who could state just when she went to bed." She was the subject of a popular song, "Alice, Where Art Thou?", and after her smashing debut at the White House in 1902—to which even the *New York Times* devoted half its front page—"Alice Blue" gowns became the rage.

The regal treatment continued when she married Nicholas Longworth, an Ohio congressman, in 1906. And it did not subside after her father left the White House in 1908, nor when he died in 1919. Alice again made big news in 1925, when at the age of forty-one she gave birth to her only child, Paulina, after almost nineteen years of marriage. It was no secret that Alice and Nick, who was fourteen years her senior and became Speaker of the House that year, led separate lives, and it was widely rumored that Paulina's real father was William Borah, senator from Idaho. That was never confirmed, but according to Carol Felsenthal's recent biography, Alice chose the night before Paulina's wedding in 1944 to tell her daughter she was illegitimate.

Alice's wicked charm made her a hit socially, but it was entirely inappropriate for motherhood. She seemed to take little interest in her daughter except to criticize her. Paulina, who was raised by a nanny and sent to boarding school after Nick died in 1931, grew up very, very shy and awkward and spoke with a stutter. She married, but her husband, Alex Sturm, became an alcoholic and died in 1951 of cirrhosis of the liver, leaving Paulina overwhelmingly depressed with a four-year-old daughter. She later suffered a nervous breakdown and in 1957 her daughter, then age ten, found her sitting on the living room couch, dead of an overdose of sleeping pills at the age of thirty-one. Alice was heartbroken by her daughter's death, but she never let on in public. She spent the rest of her life trying to make up for it by raising Paulina's daughter, Joanna, and friends said she proved to be a better grandmother than mother.

But family tragedies or responsibilities did not keep Alice from successfully fashioning herself as one of Washington's grande dames, perhaps its greatest. She had attended every Republican and Democratic presidential nominating convention since the beginning of the century and had found something to say about nearly every candidate, including her fifth cousin, Franklin, whom she bitterly opposed. "Can you imagine anything more distressing?" she declared. "Along comes Franklin, called by many in the family 'Feather Duster,' and hops into the Presidency."

Every president after FDR went out of his way to pay his respects to Alice, and despite her staunch conservatism she became very good friends with the Kennedys and President Johnson. Nixon called her "the most fascinating conversationalist of our time." Her mansion near Dupont Circle became the most sought-after salon in the capital. After rising each day at 2:00 P.M. (having partied or read through the night until about 6:00 A.M.), Alice served tea at 5:00 P.M. to Washington's elite. Like a chemist, she mixed political adversaries and admitted she would seat enemies next to each other in hopes of witnessing a good fight.

She carried on this way, hopping up stairs two at a time, well into her late eighties, until her health and her sharp wit began to fade. Alice died of pneumonia at ninety-six, having outlived all four of her younger half-brothers and her half-sister. A few years before she died, Alice had a few deprecating remarks for herself. When told she was considered the closest thing to royalty in the United States she replied, "Oh pish! Utter nonsense! It's just like they said in England about Queen Victoria . . . When you get old enough, people begin to like you. I'm a relic of the past. I'm an old fossil, a cheerful fossil. I have no contemporaries."

CHILDREN of
JULIUS and ETHEL ROSENBERG

THE DEBATE HAS ENDURED over whether Julius and Ethel Rosenberg were guilty of passing the secret of the atom bomb to the Soviets. But while the electric chair sealed their fate in 1953, their children have suffered much longer.

Julius, an electrical engineer who served in the U.S. Army Signal Corps during World War II, was accused by Ethel's brother, David Greenglass, of providing the Soviets with critical information that Greenglass obtained while he worked on the atomic bomb project in Los Alamos, New Mexico. The case against the Rosenbergs—Ethel was charged as her husband's accomplice—immediately became the cause célèbre for both sides in the postwar Red Scare, with anti-Communists calling for broad investigations and civil libertarians decrying the death sentences that resulted.

Caught in the middle of all of this was young Robert, three, and his older brother, Michael, seven, who remembers listening to "The Lone Ranger" on the radio when his father was taken away in the summer of 1950 from their home on New York's Lower East Side. After Ethel was arrested a month later, the two boys were sent to live with Ethel's mother. She couldn't handle them, and they were sent to the Hebrew Children's Home in the Bronx, where they slept and ate separately. "I felt I must have done something wrong; being there was my punishment," Michael said in the memoir he wrote with his brother, *We Are Your Sons*.

It was more than a year after the Rosenbergs were arrested before Michael and Robert were first allowed to see them. During their monthly visits the boys saw their mother and father separately. By then their parents had been convicted and were on death row at Sing Sing prison in upstate New York. Michael says he doesn't remember being afraid of the visits: "It was probably on the first visit that I asked if we could see the electric chair. On the same visit we even insisted the guards frisk us. I don't know if they did."

Their father had a different view. Among his *Death House Letters*, published after he and Ethel were executed, he wrote that during their second visit, Michael "kept on asking about the appeals and what if finally we might lose then death faced us. I kept on assuring him but I could see he was terribly upset over it. He then looked at the sergeant and said you'd better watch me for I don't want my mother and father to die, for if they do I'll kill Dave [Greenglass]."

Robert has almost no memory of his parents before their arrests. "It is from these visits [to prison] that he gets his strongest idea of our parents, of their warmth, good feeling and love," Michael wrote. In the autumn of 1951 the boys were sent to live with friends of the Rosenbergs in Toms River, New Jersey. Once their identities were revealed, the school board expelled them on the grounds that their guardian, the Rosenbergs' lawyer, wasn't a local taxpayer.

Michael and Robert then became part of the publicity campaign to save their parents. Their pictures were spread worldwide in pamphlets and magazine articles that criticized the death sentences, especially Ethel's, whose death would leave the two boys orphans. Michael was photographed delivering a letter to the White House that asked President Eisenhower, "Please let my mommy and daddy go and not let anything happen to them. If they come home Robby and I will be very happy we will thank you very much." The FBI used a handwriting expert to confirm that a child actually had written the letter.

Michael and Robert last saw their parents for two hours on June 16, 1953; Michael was then ten, Robert was six. A few hours before the Rosenbergs were executed on June 19, Ethel wrote to her children, "Always remember that we were innocent and could not

wrong our conscience." She left them a Ten Commandments religious medal and her wedding ring. That evening, Michael was
sent outside to play baseball. When it got dark, he went inside and
found out his parents were dead. "I didn't respond," he wrote. "I
didn't cry. I just sat on the couch and stared at my hands. I couldn't
react. I was not to cry emotionally for six years."

Many people offered to adopt the Rosenberg children, and their
lawyer chose Abel and Anne Meeropol, a songwriter and nursery
school teacher who lived on Riverside Drive in Manhattan. After a
judge dismissed charges by anti-Communists that the children
would be raised as Communists by the Meeropols, the couple
adopted the boys in 1957.

As they got older, both Michael and Robert were active in the
civil rights marches and antiwar protests of the 1960s. Both joined
the radical SDS—Students for a Democratic Society—and Robert
lived in a commune in Michigan, where he was arrested during a
sit-in. But both sons kept their heritage a secret from their friends
until 1973, when a new book by attorney Louis Nizer, *The Implo-
sion Conspiracy*, declared their parents were absolutely guilty.
That led them to grant interviews, give speeches and write *We
Are Your Sons*.

They also filed under the Freedom of Information Act, which so
far has caused the government to release over 200,000 pages of
documents relating to their parents' case. Not all of the documents
support their claim that their parents were innocent. "It's something I have to live with every day," Robert said in 1983. "I would
rather know the truth. I wish I could get into a time machine and
know it all."

Today, Robert and Michael are both married, have two children
each and live in Springfield, Massachusetts. Michael is a professor
of economics at Western New England College and a member of
the Union for Radical Political Economics. Robert, who has described himself as a "democratic socialist" and used to teach an-
thropology at his brother's school, received his law degree in 1985
and now is a tax attorney. He said in 1988, "I sort of wish I could
talk to my parents. I find myself wanting to show them the world
as it is now, and ask them what do they think of their actions. You

look back at the '50s and at all that has changed—Ronald Reagan kissing babies in Red Square. I hope that they would feel it was worth it."

DAUGHTER of JULIUS ROSENWALD

JULIUS ROSENWALD didn't invent the mail-order business. But it was his ideas, his maniacal efficiencies, that made it work and turned Sears, Roebuck & Co. into a retail giant. Rosenwald was a men's clothing retailer in Chicago when he bought a one-quarter share of Sears for $37,500 in 1895. By 1900, having streamlined the orders department and removed the nonsense "miracle cures" from the popular fat catalogue, Rosenwald was a millionaire, and that was only the bare beginning. As he acquired the rest of Sears and grew much richer, he moved his wife and five children out to a beautiful estate. But he still dressed them in secondhand clothes. On the other hand, Rosenwald gave away more than $65 million in his lifetime, including the money to build more than 5,000 "Rosenwald schools" for black children in the South.

"I think one thing we children each learned from our parents was the importance of the example we set," said Rosenwald's middle daughter, Edith. "And I don't mean a snobbish sort of fashion . . . just the opposite in fact." Edith wasn't the only one who got that message. Her older brother, Lessing, would follow their father as head of Sears (and donate more than two hundred Rembrandts to the National Gallery of Art), and her younger brother, William, would become a founder of the United Jewish Appeal.

But it was Edith, people said, who took after her father the most. Her obsession with efficiency, every bit as impassioned as her father's, earned her the nickname "Effie." Still, being a daughter and therefore, in those days, not in line for a seat in the Sears boardroom, Edith channeled her vigor elsewhere. And the city of New Orleans would never be the same.

Edith arrived there in 1921, after marrying Edgar Bloom Stern, a cotton broker. "Southern women are brought up to be decorative, not forceful, modest not vital," recalled Edith, whose idea of dealing with a problem was to blurt, "Don't be ridiculous!" "I must have seemed a monster to them." Being Jewish, Edith found herself excluded from many social functions, including Mardi Gras. So with her father's money Edith built Longue Vue, a forty-six-room mansion in suburban Metairie, where she hosted so many lavish parties she literally entertained her way into Southern society.

That was only the start. Unhappy with the local schools, Edith built a nursery school—the first of its kind in the South—for her three children and later started an elementary school for them too. In 1945, supporting a reform candidate for mayor, she passed out Sears brooms to hundreds of her society friends and marched on city hall. Her candidate was elected. In the course of that campaign, she discovered cases of fraud on the voter lists. So again she mobilized the society women to sit in the dusty rooms of city hall and cross thousands of fake, mostly dead, voters off the rolls. The Voters Registration Service still oversees the city's elections.

Edith and her husband founded the Stern Fund, which gave millions to liberal causes and helped start Dillard College, a black school in New Orleans. It was, in fact, Edith Rosenwald Stern's outspoken support of civil rights and integration in the 1960s that sorely tested her popularity. Edith, who died in 1980 at eighty-five, once comforted a friend who had received a vicious letter because of her support of civil rights. "My dear," the indomitable philanthropist said, "I get them every day."

CHILDREN of JEAN JACQUES ROUSSEAU

IN 1762, PHILOSOPHER Jean Jacques Rousseau published a book on child-rearing that still today remains on the reading list in some education classes. *Emile* was the story of a tutor who raised a child from birth until he was twenty-five. The tutor advocated that the child should be allowed to learn as he discovered things, not taught by rote, and thus Rousseau is considered by some to be the founder of progressive education. Rousseau also encouraged wealthy French mothers of his day to breast-feed their own babies, instead of employing wet nurses, and to stop swaddling their infants so tightly.

Rousseau offered lots of good advice about raising children in *Emile*, and in fact one of the reasons he wrote it was because several of his women friends had asked him for advice on raising theirs. Rousseau clearly had thought about it a lot. "He who is incapable of fulfilling his obligations as a father has no right to become one," he wrote. "Neither poverty, nor the claims of work, nor the fear of what the public may think can relieve him of the duty of feeding his children and bringing them up himself. Readers, you may believe me when I warn any man of feeling who fails in such sacred duties that he will long shed bitter tears for the omission, and will never be consoled."

That was Rousseau's apology for his own brief—very brief—stint as a father. Rousseau, though he did not admit it publicly until after he was dead and his *Confessions* were published, fathered five illegitimate children and forced his mistress, Thérèse, to give up each one to the foundling hospital. He never saw any of them. He wrote in his *Confessions*, "That was just the expedient I needed. I made up my mind cheerfully and without the least scruple. The only scruples I had to overcome were those of Thérèse; I had all the difficulty in the world in making her adopt this one means of saving her honor. Her mother, who had a different fear—that of another brat to feed—came to my aid and finally Thérèse gave in."

Rousseau, whose own mother died soon after he was born in Geneva and whose father abandoned him when he was ten, had plenty of excuses for abandoning his children. They were born early in his career, the first in 1747. "How could I feed a family?" he wrote. "If I were to resort to the writer's craft, how would I achieve the tranquility of mind necessary for lucrative work, my garret filled with domestic cares and the disturbance of children?" By giving up his children, Rousseau reasoned, he was preventing them from growing up with the stigma of illegitimacy. Also, besides Thérèse, who stayed with him for thirty-three years, Rousseau shared his house with Thérèse's overbearing mother and her unruly brothers and sisters. "I trembled at the thought of entrusting mine to that badly brought up family," he wrote.

"I will content myself," he said in his *Confessions*, "by saying that in handing over my children to be brought up to the public authorities, for lack of means to bring them up myself, and by making it their destiny to become workers or peasants rather than adventurers or fortune-hunters, I believed myself to be acting as a citizen and a father would act, and I looked upon myself as a member of Plato's republic." Plato had suggested that all children be raised by the state.

Rousseau said his children would be better off in the foundling hospital. But in eighteenth-century Paris, where it is estimated that as many as one-third of newborn children were abandoned, merely surviving at the foundling hospital was doubtful. Two-thirds of the babies there died in their first year and as few as five percent reached maturity.

Rousseau, who said he was haunted by his children's fate throughout his life—and also was haunted by what his fate would be should his deeds become known—did once make an effort to track down his offspring. In 1761, the year before *Emile* was published, Rousseau was very sick and believed he was dying. He confessed the story of his children to a woman friend and asked her to try to locate them. She couldn't.

Emile did have immediate consequences for Rousseau. Besides telling women how to raise their children, the book also advocated free-thinking and encouraged revolution. The book was seized and burned in many cities, and Rousseau had to flee from France to escape arrest. He spent years on the run before he returned to Paris, where he grew paranoid and bitter about being ostracized for his writings. In 1776 he was seen trying to hand out copies of his recent tracts to strollers in the Tuileries. He died two years later of uremic poisoning. In his last essay, Rousseau wrote of his children, "I would do it again with fewer doubts, if it had to be done."

CHILDREN of BERTRAND RUSSELL

NOBEL PRIZE–WINNING philosopher and mathematician Bertrand Russell decided in 1890, when he was eighteen, that he was an atheist, and remained vehement on the subject more than thirty years later, when his young son John had to undergo delicate double mastoid surgery. "On Tuesday, the critical day, I had come to London to debate the 'Xtian' religion against Bishop Gore," Russell wrote. "I was told that suffering is sent as a purification from sin. Poor little John never sinned in his life. I wanted to spit in their faces—they were so cold and abstract, with a sadistic pleasure in the tortures their God inflicts."

Russell was nothing if not outspoken. Criticized by both the left and the right, depending upon the issue, the British philosopher wrote prolifically against war and in favor of a looser morality than people were ready to accept. He was jailed for six months for opposing World War I. Even after his Nobel Prize for Literature in 1950 earned him greater respect, Russell's protests against nuclear weapons got him jailed again—for seven days in 1961— when he was eighty-nine.

Russell began his career as a mathematician because, he said, "I discovered what appeared to be definite answers to the problems which had baffled me for years." He searched for the same sort of definition in his philosophy, but he rarely found it in his personal life. He was married four times and had many lovers, including the actress Colette. He married his first wife, an American Quaker, in 1894. And though their childless relationship ended in 1901, they didn't divorce until 1921, when Dora, the woman who would become his second wife was pregnant with their first child.

John was born when Russell was forty-nine. His second child, Katharine, was born two years later. Russell delighted in them both. "In spite of my efforts," he wrote, "John has considerable religious faith; he informed me that in the mornings he informs Apollo and Neptune what he wants them to do that day. But both children prefer magic to religion; they like the witches' cauldron in *Macbeth* Act IV, and know the passage nearly by heart." For John and Kate and other children, Russell and his wife started their controversial Beacon Hill School, which taught free-thinking and was heavily criticized for allowing the children to run naked on hot days. "The children," said Colette, "were the children of one's dreams: happy, fearless, free."

Their happiness largely ended in 1930, when Dora informed Russell that she was pregnant by another man. Both previously had agreed to an open marriage, Russell said, "So I tried to endure the new child and behave towards her as if she were my own. . . . But the resulting strain of daily and hourly insincerity was intolerable, and made family life a torture." They divorced in 1935, by which time Dora had had a second child by the same man. Russell spent thirty years trying to prevent Dora's illegitimate daughter from using his name.

Russell was never again as close to his own two children. Later, his third divorce would cost him his warm relationship with his son by that marriage, Conrad, who became a professor of English history at Yale.

In 1953 Russell once again was surrounded by young children after John and his wife announced they were tired and abruptly

walked out on their three daughters; it was left to Russell and his fourth wife to raise his three grandchildren, especially after John suffered a breakdown.

Russell was perhaps equally distressed by what became of his only daughter. Kate married an American who worked in the State Department. They began attending church and eventually Kate's husband became an Episcopal minister and the couple went to Uganda as missionaries. Russell and his daughter never discussed this great divergence, and later the atheist philosopher said with uncharacteristic brevity, "I myself, naturally, had little sympathy with either of them on this score."

Kate partly credited her father for her religious conversion. "The religion my parents had grown up with was a dry morality without grace, a series of impossible demands that left them defeated and depressed," she wrote in her 1975 memoir, five years after Russell died in Wales at the age of ninety-seven. "And yet they passed on to us the same impossible demands from which they had suffered. . . . Consequently, we in our turn were loaded down with inescapable and, to us, inexplicable guilt."

Kate did not see her father, one of the most famous atheists of his time, as being entirely unreligious. "I believe myself that his whole life was a search for God," she said. "Or, for those who prefer less personal terms, for absolute certainty."

CHILDREN of BABE RUTH

THE NEWSPAPERS, always eager for a story on baseball's greatest hero, got a good one on September 23, 1922. "Babe Ruth and Mrs. Babe All Mixed Up on Baby's Birthday," blared the *New York Daily News*. Reporters had begun their intensive investigation after the previously childless couple were spotted with a baby that was well over a year old. Helen Ruth said the little girl was their daughter Dorothy and that she had been born on June 7, 1921, at St. Vincent's Hospital on 12th Street in Manhattan.

The Bambino, however, when questioned during a game in Cleveland, said "Gee, but she's a great kid! She'll be just two years old come next February 2, and boy! make believe she won't be some baby." Besides adding four months to Dorothy's age, Ruth also said she had been born at Presbyterian Hospital on 168th Street. Ruth said he and his wife had never mentioned the baby before because no one had asked. "It happened that the newspapers didn't get wind of it then and neither Mrs. Ruth nor I made any effort to make it generally known."

Reporters, of course, were not satisfied with either story. A search turned up no record of Dorothy's birth at either hospital. Employees at the Ansonia, where the Ruths lived, said they had seen the baby only recently. Reporters even were so bold as to ask Helen if her daughter was adopted. "Adopted?" she shot back. "I should say not. That baby's mine, mine, *mine!*" Helen revealed that she and her husband, married since 1914, had had three previous children. A girl named Helen had lived just a few days, she said, George Jr. had lived for four months, and Margaret had died when she was one and a half. Helen said Dorothy was born with rickets and had been cared for by a nurse for her first year because the Babe was afraid he'd be ridiculed for having a weak baby. When asked for confirmation, Ruth said simply, "Whatever my wife says goes with me."

The story eventually faded, with the truth about Dorothy's past left unclear. But the incident also left much unsaid about the Ruths' marriage. Though publicly a happy couple, Ruth and his wife had grown apart since 1914, when the young baseball player had married the sixteen-year-old coffee-shop waitress; Ruth had had several affairs, and Helen, introverted and uncomfortable with the Babe's fame, suffered nervous breakdowns.

In 1923, according to the book *My Dad, The Babe*, written by Dorothy in 1988, Ruth began seeing Claire Hodgson, a widow from Atlanta, who had moved to New York with her young daughter, Julia. By 1925, Helen had moved back to Boston. Dorothy was sent to a boarding school, which is where she was in 1929 when Helen died in a fire in her home in Watertown. The press, which didn't even know Babe Ruth and his wife were living apart, provided sensational coverage of the fact that Helen had been living with another man.

Instead of going to live with her father, Dorothy initially was sent to the New York Foundling Hospital, where she was given the name Marie Harrington. Dorothy said she never found out where the name came from, but it was the one used by Helen in her will, in which she left everything "to my beloved ward and charge, Dorothy, the former Marie Harrington."

After a few months Ruth took Dorothy to live with him and his new wife, Claire, and her daughter. "As the months went by, my position in my new mother's heart became clear: I was excess baggage," Dorothy wrote in her book. "Claire's favoritism toward her own daughter, Julia, created a no win situation, one with which I regretfully would have to cope for the next ten years." Dorothy said Claire and Julia would accompany Ruth as he played baseball all over the country, while she was left in New York. Ruth, Dorothy said, was too busy to realize that she felt neglected. Dorothy left home at eighteen and married when she was twenty, in 1940.

Ruth died in 1948, but Dorothy said it wasn't until 1980 that she discovered the truth about her real parents. As a child she had known a woman named Juanita Jennings, who had married her father's accountant. Once widowed, Juanita moved in with Dorothy, who was married to her second husband and raising six children in Connecticut. Two weeks before the eighty-six-year-old woman died in 1980, Dorothy said Juanita told her that she was her real mother. Juanita said she had had an affair with Ruth when he was in California on an exhibition baseball tour in 1920. When she became pregnant, Ruth moved her to New York and supported her. A year after Dorothy was born, Juanita told her, the Ruths adopted her.

Dorothy's book paints a very unflattering picture of her stepmother, Claire, who died in 1976. Julia Ruth Stevens, whom Ruth adopted in 1930 and who now is married to a retired contractor in

New Hampshire, calls the book "a great bunch of lies. My mother was a wonderful person." After Claire died, Dorothy Ruth Pirone carried on the family name, accepting awards honoring her father. Both Dorothy and Julia attended a ceremony at Yankee Stadium in August 1988 honoring the fortieth anniversary of Ruth's death. They sat on opposite sides of the field. In May 1989, Dorothy died at the age of sixty-eight.

Both women—through an agent—sued and won settlements against calendar and baseball-card makers who used Ruth's name and picture without their permission. "I am very proud to be Babe Ruth's only child and believe that he would be equally proud of the work I've done in his name," Dorothy wrote in her book. "In an eerie sort of way, that work has brought me closer to him in death than I was ever able to get in life."

CHILDREN of
U.S. REPRESENTATIVE LEO J. RYAN

ONE OF THE MOST horrifying events in recent years occurred on November 18, 1978, when more than nine hundred followers of Jim Jones's People's Temple committed suicide in Jonestown, Guyana. They drank their poison-laced fruit drink after some cult members had murdered three journalists and U.S. Representative Leo J. Ryan, a California Democrat, who were about to board a plane after visiting the cult.

So it was understandably newsworthy two years later when Ryan's oldest daughter, Shannon Jo, became a follower of the Bhagwan Sheree Rajneesh, an Indian guru who later set up a controversial community in Oregon, Rajneeshpuram. Shannon, who changed her name to Ma Prem Amrita, which she said meant "lover of the eternal," denied the obvious connection. "If I thought there was any chance of this becoming another Jonestown, I'd run away," she told *People* magazine in 1981. "It is impossible that Bhagwan would ever ask people to kill anyone. But if he asked me to do it, I don't know. I love and trust him very much. To me he is God."

Shannon, twenty-eight at the time, had arrived at the cult after following a twisting path. She had graduated from the University of California at Davis with an art degree and later became a cashier in a Lake Tahoe casino. She was making bread-dough Christmas tree ornaments in Burlingame, California, when her father, who had divorced her mother a few years before, was killed. "It was very scary for me to trust anyone," she said. "I was not open to a guru in any form." But then in 1980, while studying "transpersonal counseling," she met someone who had visited the Bhagwan in India. She made her own visit, paying for her ticket with part of the payment she received from her father's life insurance. In 1982, Shannon married another Bhagwan follower from England; they have since divorced. "With Bhagwan, even Kool-Aid becomes champagne," said the woman who performed the marriage.

Meanwhile, Shannon's younger sister, Patricia, reacted in a different way to her father's death. She is an adviser to two anticult organizations, the Cult Awareness Network and the American Family Foundation, and gives speeches on the subject. A former congressional aide, Patricia lobbied for a Congressional Gold Medal to be awarded posthumously to her father. Shortly before President Reagan presented the medal in 1984, Patricia said of her sister's involvement with the Bhagwan, "I'm concerned about it, wary about it. Obviously, she has been subjected to some kind of brainwashing."

After the Bhagwan was forced to leave the United States in 1986 to settle charges of emigration fraud, the Oregon cult broke up. But Patricia says her sister still believes in the Bhagwan, though, she said, "We don't talk about that too much." Shannon now is getting her master's degree in psychology in San Diego, and Patricia is a lobbyist for a health organization in Washington. Their younger sister, Erin, is a lawyer for the State Department; their older brother, Chris, works for the Environmental Protection Agency; and their younger brother, Kevin, lives in California.

S

CHILDREN of BEVERLY SILLS

OFTEN, BEING THE CHILD of someone famous means being constantly reminded of your parent's great talent or achievement. But for the children of Beverly Sills it has been different. Because the son and daughter of the famous opera diva have never heard her sing. Both of Sills's children are deaf. Her son, born in 1961, is also autistic.

As a result of their handicaps Sills's children have had very different childhoods from the one remembered by Sills, who grew up listening to her mother's 78 rpm opera records. "She would play them even before she made coffee in the morning, and they would echo throughout the house all day long," Sills wrote in one of her autobiographies. "Before I was seven, I had memorized all 22 arias on the recordings, and could sing them in phonetic Italian." At the age of four, Sills sang on a New York local radio talent show and at nine won first prize on "Major Bowes' Amateur Hour."

Sills was enjoying a successful though not spectacular opera career when she gave birth to her daughter, Meredith "Muffy" Greenough, in 1959. Muffy was born with a disease that caused her difficulty in breathing and a high fever. But it was not until two years later, just after Peter "Bucky" Greenough was born, that Sills and her husband learned that Muffy was deaf. A few weeks later doctors also told them that Bucky was retarded. Later he was diagnosed as autistic, and only a few years ago, when Bucky was twenty-two, it was also determined that he was deaf.

While Bucky had to be placed in an institution, Muffy was able to follow her mother's rise to international opera fame, which included a stunning debut at the Metropolitan Opera in 1975 and a recently completed tenure as general director of the New York City Opera. Muffy, as a child, would put her fingers on the stereo speakers to feel the sound of her mother's voice. She also traveled all over the world as her mother's career blossomed.

In 1971 Muffy acted as a candle-bearer in the funeral scene of *Lucia*, in which her mother was starring at City Opera. Sills, who was supposed to be dead, whispered to the bass who was singing the role of the chaplain, "Raimondo! Move your ass! I can't see Muffy!"

Sills' daughter learned to speak and lip-read and now is in management with NYNEX in New York.

"In a sympathetic way," Sills wrote in her most recent autobiography, "people have often commented on the irony of an opera singer's having a daughter who can't hear her sing. Believe me, that particular concern didn't enter the picture at all. I was a mother whose gorgeous daughter was deaf."

Some critics also have pointed to Sills's children as the turning point in her singing career. It was after she stopped singing for two years to care for her handicapped infants that Sills returned to become one of the most celebrated opera singers of the century. "My own feelings are that after going through terribly trying times I was released from a lot of fears," Sills said. "I felt that if I could survive this I could survive anything."

Still, she added, "as for my career, I'd trade it all in if someone could guarantee me a healthy child."

CHILDREN of B. F. SKINNER

IN THE FIELD of psychology, few have aroused as much anger and acclaim as Burrhus Frederic Skinner. When most of his colleagues were embracing Freudian psychology in the 1930s, Skinner became a "radical behaviorist," ignoring the deep emotional recesses of the mind and focusing instead on observable behavior. The Harvard professor studied psychology not on the couch but in the lab, starting with his infamous "Skinner box," a simple container where he tested the behavior of animals. Skinner believed behavior could be scientifically measured and, therefore, controlled and modified. It was that theory that made him controversial, and his books, including *Walden Two* in 1948 and *Beyond Freedom and Dignity* in 1971, found critics among conservatives and liberals alike.

But none of Skinner's work inspired as much popular imagination and ire as did a rather simple invention he built for his younger daughter, Deborah, when she was born in 1943. Designed to make it easier for parents to care for an infant, Skinner's "Air-Crib" was a self-contained, climate-controlled, soundproof box that was supposed to be the ideal environment in which to raise a baby. There was a big window so the baby could look out, but she wouldn't be disturbed by loud noises and germs. The warm, moist air meant the baby could wear just a diaper and wouldn't be confined by bulky clothing or blankets. On top of a canvas mattress was a ten-yard-long sheet attached to a roller that could be cranked to place a clean section into the crib.

Skinner's crib received wide attention when he wrote an article about it for the *Ladies' Home Journal* in 1945. Headlined "Baby in a Box," the story led some to confuse the crib with the psychologist's "Skinner box," in which he had tested rats and pigeons. Wrote one angry reader, "The only time human beings are subject to boxes is when they are dead." But for all the criticism, Skinner also received hundreds of letters from parents who wanted instructions to build their own cribs. One company attempted to market the dwelling, calling it an "Heir Conditioner."

Skinner adamantly defended his new box and said his daughter thrived in it. Deborah, Skinner said, never had a cold until she was six. She slept regularly, she rarely cried and she never had diaper rash. "Completely free to move about, she was soon pushing up, rolling over, and crawling," he said. Though he was loath to compare his Air-Crib to his Skinner box, Skinner admitted he did conduct a few experiments, such as teaching Deborah to pull rings and levers that would activate sounds or bright pennants.

But concerned about more than the physical health of the baby, critics claimed Skinner's crib was an emotionally desolate environment for babies because they were rarely cuddled. Years later there were rumors that Skinner's experiment had failed, that his younger daughter had committed suicide, or was psychotic, or was suing her father for her cruel upbringing.

In fact, Deborah is alive and well and living in London. She is a successful artist, married to a political scientist. The first baby raised in an Air-Crib did not, however, do well in school. According to the last of his three memoirs, Skinner once wrote to his daughter, "I'm not embarrassed by any supposed shortcomings of yours or afraid you will prove to the world that I am a bad psychologist. Live your own life, not mine. Be yourself. I like your Self."

Skinner's older daughter, Julie, who was not raised in an Air-Crib but occasionally was subject to her father's experiments, graduated from Radcliffe and later received a doctorate in psychology. Now a professor of educational psychology at Indiana University and married to a sociologist, Julie raised both her daughters in Air-Cribs.

CHILDREN of JOSEPH STALIN

SOMETIMES YOU HEAR about a powerful, fearsome leader who showed his softer side to his children. This is not one of those stories. When Stalin's oldest son, Yakov, tried to kill himself with a gun in 1928 but ended up only wounded, Stalin said, "Ha, he couldn't even shoot straight!" The totalitarian ruler of the Soviet Union, whose purges sent millions to their deaths, showed barely more humanity for his two sons. Only for his daughter did he reserve some parental tenderness, even if it did mean exiling her first boyfriend to northern Russia.

Stalin had little hand in raising any of his children. Yakov, born in 1908 to his first wife, who died two years later, was raised by the wife's parents. His two children by his second wife, Vasily and Svetlana, were raised by nannies and tutors after that wife, depressed over Stalin's massacres, committed suicide in 1932.

When Yakov moved in with his father's second family in their Kremlin apartment so he could continue his education, the youth's very presence seemed to annoy Stalin. He slept on the living-room couch and Stalin beat him and finally banned him from Moscow. Soon after World War II began, Yakov was a senior lieutenant in an artillery division when he was captured by the Germans in July 1941. Stalin had ordered his citizens and soldiers to fight to the death—to surrender was betrayal. So at first Stalin refused to believe that his son had been taken prisoner. Then he declared that Yakov must have been tricked. He arrested his son's wife, whom he disliked because she was Jewish. She was imprisoned until 1943.

Meanwhile, Stalin refused to try to have his son released. "They want me to make a deal with them," Stalin told his daughter in 1944. "I won't do it! War is war!" The Germans publicized their seemingly important prisoner, and even dropped leaflets with Yakov's picture over Moscow. Stalin replied publicly that he had no son named Yakov. Sometime after that, various accounts say Yakov either was shot or threw himself against an electric wire fence surrounding his prison camp.

Stalin ignored his second son, Vasily. Born around 1920, Vasily grew up as his father consolidated his power, and he took advantage of that. Pampered by Stalin's staff, Vasily threw big parties, caroused with a variety of women, and drank heavily. By World War II, though he had been expelled from military school, Vasily had become a fighter pilot. He performed well enough to be promoted to lieutenant general by the age of twenty-four, though he was unpopular among his troops.

After the war he became air commander of the Moscow military district, but Stalin himself dismissed him in 1952 after Vasily allowed a May Day air show to proceed in bad weather, causing several planes to crash. Stalin publicly reprimanded his son, who by then was an alcoholic. After Stalin died, Vasily was expelled from the Air Force and later spent time in prison. He died of a heart ailment linked to his alcoholism in 1962. His son, Alexander, who has changed his last name, is director of the Red Army Theater in Moscow.

Stalin showed affection only for his daughter, Svetlana, who was born in 1926. When she was little he called her "my little sparrow," and "little housekeeper." But as she grew up he grew stricter, once admonishing her for wearing a tight sweater. "Modesty embellishes a Bolshevik," he told her. When she was sixteen, Svetlana fell in love with a middle-aged film producer she had met at one of Vasily's parties. Aleksei Kapler was married and Jewish, and the two carried on an apparently innocent infatuation, mostly going to movies together. Some months later, in March 1943, Stalin lowered the boom, declaring Kapler a British spy and exiling him to northern Russia for five years.

Svetlana married someone else in 1944, but Stalin didn't approve and the marriage broke up in 1947 without her father and her husband ever having met. Svetlana grew more distant from her father and saw him less and less, though after her daughter by her second husband was born in 1950, Stalin wrote, "Take care of yourself. Take care of your daughter, too. The state needs people, even those who are born prematurely. Be patient a little longer—we'll see each other soon. I kiss my Svetochka. Your 'little papa.' "

Svetlana was with her father when he died March 5, 1953, four days after he suffered a cerebral hemorrhage. Vasily also was there, drunk, and accusing the doctors of poisoning Stalin. In 1957 Svetlana officially changed her last name from Stalin to Alliluyeva, which had been her mother's maiden name. "I could no longer tolerate the name of Stalin," she said later. "Its sharp metallic sound lacerated my ears, my eyes, my heart."

On March 6, 1967, while she was in India to deliver the ashes of her common-law Indian husband to his family, Svetlana walked into the American Embassy in New Delhi and defected. She had become a member of the Russian Orthodox Church in 1962 and had fled, she said, "to seek the self-expression that has been denied me for so long in Russia." She carried in her suitcase a manuscript she had written in 1963 to her children, now grown and left behind in the Soviet Union. *20 Letters to a Friend*, published in 1968, presented a fairly loving account of her father, who had been portrayed throughout the world as a tyrant. A year later, after meeting with dissidents and learning what had not been made public in the Soviet Union, Svetlana wrote a second book, *Only One Year*, in which she said, "He gave his name to this bloodbath of absolute dictatorship. He knew what he was doing. He was neither insane nor misled."

Svetlana married an architect in 1970 and the following year, at the age of forty-five, gave birth to a daughter, Olga, in California. She was divorced in 1973 and then was out of the limelight until November 2, 1984, when she returned to the Soviet Union. She had been living in Cambridge, England, for the previous two years under the name Lana Peters while her daughter was in school. She told the press that she had moved back to Russia because she deeply missed her two children in Moscow and had become disillusioned by the West. She said she had been hounded by the press and by lawyers and publishers. Her third book had been rejected.

Just as abruptly, Svetlana left the Soviet Union again in April

1986. She said that after being away for seventeen years she found her native country had changed too much. She had trouble speaking Russian, and relations with her two Soviet children had been tense. Her daughter Olga, an American citizen, also had been unhappy. Svetlana settled in Spring Green, Wisconsin, while her daughter returned to school in England. The latest word came in November 1987, when Svetlana denied a report that she was moving to England, but said she may spend some time there if her daughter chooses to attend a British college.

T

SON of LEO TOLSTOY

"To MARRY A LADY is to tie to oneself all the poisons of civilization," said Leo Tolstoy, and the Russian author of *War and Peace* and *Anna Karenina* had forty-eight years of such a marriage to know from whence he spoke. But before he drifted into his tormented relationship with the properly bred Sonya, whom he married in 1862, Tolstoy was in love with a peasant woman working on his large country estate. "I am afraid when I see how attached to her I am," Tolstoy wrote in his diary of Aksinya Bazykin, whose husband was away in the army. "The feeling is no longer bestial, but that of a husband for a wife." But since Aksinya was not a lady, there could be no marriage.

The affair did result in a baby boy, Timothy, who proved to be the first and one of the most intractable problems in Tolstoy's later marriage to Sonya. "I think that someday I shall kill myself from jealousy," wrote Sonya a few months after they were married, and

Tolstoy had let her read his diary. When she saw Aksinya and her young son who, despite Tolstoy's orders, came to wash the floors of the main house with other peasant women, Sonya, pregnant with her first child, again contemplated suicide. "It is horrible. I looked with such pleasure at his daggers and guns. One thrust—it would be easy. While there is no child."

Sonya went on to have thirteen children, nine of whom survived infancy. And while they, for the most part, grew up spoiled in luxury, Timothy and his mother continued to work on the estate. Tolstoy's legitimate children and his bastard son, in fact, played with each other and knew of their relationship. "According to the custom of the time," wrote Tolstoy biographer Henri Troyat, "the master's real children—those fortunate enough to bear his name— were not at all hostile toward Timothy and treated him as a brother who had lost out in his dealings with the law."

Tolstoy, however, kept his distance from his oldest child, at least until his later years, when he underwent a deep religious conversion and tried—against Sonya's violent opposition—to renounce his wealth and his status. A year before he died he wrote, "They say that Timothy is my son, and I have never even asked his pardon, I have not repented, I am not repenting every hour of the day, and I set myself up to criticize others!"

Instead, Tolstoy was surrounded by his legitimate children. All five of his sons were failures and many of his children were disgusted by his antiaristocratic views. "If I were not his son, I would hang him," said his son Andrei, who joined the Army against his father's wishes. Son Leo, an unsuccessful writer who was bitter at his father's fame, coldly insulted Tolstoy to his face and wrote that he was "a baneful influence largely responsible for the present revolutionary spirit in Russia." Leo and Andrei wanted to have their father committed for senility in 1909, the year before Tolstoy finally fled his family only to fall ill and die in a small train station at Astapovo.

After Tolstoy's death, his children and wife continued to bicker over control of his writings, which he had left to Sasha, the daughter who had helped him flee. Timothy, who was said to look more like Tolstoy than any of his legitimate children, continued to work as a coachman on Tolstoy's estate. His final fate is unknown.

SON of SPENCER TRACY

FOR YEARS the best-kept secret in Hollywood was the relationship between Spencer Tracy and Katharine Hepburn. From the time they met on the set of *Woman of the Year* in 1942 until Tracy died in 1967, Tracy and Hepburn were together, but never in public. Tracy was rarely seen with his wife, Louise, either. They had, in fact, separated long before Tracy met Hepburn. After he died it was widely reported that the reason Tracy hadn't divorced his wife was because he was Catholic.

But that probably was not the only reason. Another was his children, especially his son, John, who was born nine months after Tracy married Louise in a quick ceremony that had taken place in Cincinnati between the matinee and evening performances of a stock theater tour where they had met. Tracy was on the road again when his wife discovered that their nine-month-old son was deaf. Said Tracy's actor friend Pat O'Brien: "What happened next was typical of both Louise and Spence. Louise suffered, and took her boy to doctors to find out what could be done. Spence suffered, and went out and got drunk. It was the first *big* drunk of his life, as far as I know."

But it was not Tracy's last, by far. Throughout much of his career—even after he was a success on Broadway and later a huge star in Hollywood—Tracy would disappear for a week or two at a time on alcoholic binges. Tracy himself said later, "At first I thought it all started with me over my shock and disappointment when my son, John, was born deaf. Now I realize that was all bull—. I was drinking long before that." Still, one friend said that John's deafness "affected Spence's whole career, and had changed him and aged him almost overnight. . . . All due to frustration because he couldn't make Johnny a normal kid."

When asked how to be a good actor, the two-time Oscar winner loved to say simply, "Learn your lines and don't bump into the furniture." But his daughter, Susie, born a year before her parents separated for the first time in 1933 and now a professional photographer, said recently, "You couldn't convey the depth of feeling he did on screen without knowing what pain was personally."

Tracy was often on the road when John was a baby, so it was Louise who taught their son to lip-read and talk. Tracy admitted he didn't have the patience for it, that he "was no damn good at it. I would come in after she had been working with the boy for hours and start undoing the good Louise had done." After he and his wife separated, Tracy saw his children one day a week. "With all the medical problems the kid had when he was young, I saw him develop into quite an athlete," Tracy said. "I took him with me when I played polo, and he got up on a horse and soon he was one of the best polo players at the club. I also watched him develop into a championship swimmer in school. He couldn't hear the starter's gun, but he picked up a sixth sense, maybe from the vibration of the shot, and I never saw him make a false start."

John went to art school and became an artist for Disney Studios. He married and had a son, but the marriage ended two years later and the divorce sent Tracy on one of his worst binges ever. Later, John developed frequent illnesses and had to be cared for by his mother. He suffered a stroke, and now lives in a California nursing home.

But his name remains familiar. In 1942, Louise founded the John Tracy Clinic at the University of Southern California. Financed in its early years by Tracy, it has grown into one of the world's largest educational centers for young deaf children and their parents.

U

SON of KING UMBERTO OF ITALY

THE END of World War II closed the door on a lot of royal families of Europe. And none were snubbed more than King Umberto of Italy and his Royal House of Savoy. Other kings were ousted by coups or treaties—King Umberto was voted out by his own people. His father, King Vittorio Emanuele III, had been blamed for permitting the terror of Mussolini, and the Allies forced him to abdicate in May 1946. Umberto then ascended the throne, but a month later the Italians voted with a 54 percent majority to put an end to the monarchy and form a republic. King Umberto and his family were exiled a week later.

From there, the House of Savoy separated. The king took up residence in Portugal while his wife, Queen Marie-José of Belgium, took their four children to Switzerland. They had only one son, Vittorio Emanuele, and it was to him that a small faction of loyal monarchists looked for the restoration of the Italian crown.

Vittorio Emanuele, nine years old when his family was banished from his homeland, grew up in Swiss boarding schools and was expelled by one. Though his title was meaningless, he moved in high circles and in the late 1950s befriended the Shah of Iran. Living in Geneva, Vittorio became a consultant for an Italian helicopter company and is reported to have made a fortune, with the Shah's help, selling arms to Iran and other Middle Eastern countries. Vittorio's friendship with the Shah led him to have two wedding ceremonies. He first married Marina Doria, an Italian commoner, in Las Vegas in 1970. The next year they exchanged vows again in Tehran as guests of the Shah.

The would-be heir apparent attracted much unwelcome publicity in 1978 over an unfortunate shooting incident. Vittorio had docked his yacht at Cavallo, an island near Corsica, for the summer. One night in August, he got into a harsh exchange of words with a group of Italian playboys at a restaurant. The other men later followed Vittorio back to his yacht and proceeded to steal the prince's dinghy. Vittorio had often played with guns—once firing over the head of his wife—and so he got his M-1 carbine and fired over the heads of the men.

Vittorio missed the troublemakers, but the bullet hit a yacht toward which they were heading. It pierced the side and hit a German teenager aboard in his upper thigh, nearly severing his leg. The boy's leg had to be amputated and four months later he died of complications. Vittorio, meanwhile, was arrested by Corsican officials and spent fifty days in jail before his lawyers arranged to settle the matter out of court. The Italian press said the ex-royal family paid the boy's family millions of dollars.

Since then, Vittorio has made little news except in 1983 when his seventy-eight-year-old father, King Umberto, was dying of bone cancer. Vittorio appealed to Italian officials to rescind his family's exile and allow the deposed king to die in Italy. That also would have allowed Vittorio back into Italy. But the government took no action and Vittorio, himself now the king-in-exile, remains a businessman in Switzerland.

V

CHILDREN of CORNELIUS VANDERBILT

"A MILLION OR TWO is as much as anyone ought to have," said Cornelius Vanderbilt as he considered to whom he would leave his, the nation's biggest, fortune. "But what you have is not worth anything unless you have the power. And if you give away the surplus, you give away the control." You would think that a man with thirteen children would find at least one worthy of his inheritance, which by the 1870s included a two-ocean shipping empire and the country's largest railroad network. Maybe.

First, nine of the Commodore's children were daughters, which as far as he was concerned took them out of the running because they would get married and no longer be Vanderbilts. And of his four sons, one died young, and his favorite, his youngest son, George, died of tuberculosis after fighting in the Civil War. Of the two remaining boys, Cornelius had epilepsy, which Vanderbilt tried to cure by sending him to an insane asylum. Later, after Cornelius went bankrupt from gambling, Vanderbilt cut him off and was barely willing to let this son see him on his deathbed. Vanderbilt, a ruthless robber baron who started out as a tobacco-chewing, swearing sailor from Staten Island, had no patience for any kind of weakness.

That left only his oldest son, William, who in his father's eyes was far from promising. A weak, timid youth, William received a solid education, but since he showed no interest in the shipping business Vanderbilt showed little interest in him. Vanderbilt gave William a job as a ship chandler's clerk only to fire him. William took a job as a bookkeeper in a brokerage house and was living in a furnished room on a salary of nineteen dollars a week when, at the age of nineteen, he married the daughter of a prominent Brooklyn minister. Soon after, William's health failed from a nervous condition that probably was related to the tense relationship with his father.

Vanderbilt, with uncharacteristic, if slight, generosity, gave his son the fresh air he needed to recover by buying him a seventy-acre farm near the family's former homestead on Staten Island. It was a shack of a house, but there William began to show signs of being his father's son. He turned a profit on the small piece of land and eventually expanded his holdings to 350 acres. His father was impressed enough to help him take over the bankrupt Staten Island Railroad in 1857—even before the Commodore got into the business—and William turned the valueless stock into shares that sold for $175.

When Vanderbilt started his own railroad empire in 1864, he summoned forty-three-year-old William back to Manhattan to help run the New York & Harlem Railroad. Within a few years, "the old man," as William called him, had turned over the day to day affairs to "Billy," as Vanderbilt called his son. William played a major role in expanding Vanderbilt's New York Central Railroad to Chicago, but he always deferred to his father.

Believing as he did that his fortune was worth nothing without the controlling interest, Vanderbilt eventually decided to leave the bulk of his estate to William. That understandably upset his many daughters, who even on the Commodore's deathbed were trying to convince him to give them an equal share and let their husbands run the railroads. Vanderbilt wasn't swayed. When he died in 1877 at the age of eighty-two, he left each of his daughters between $250,000 and $500,000. Cornelius received an even more measly $200,000 in trust. Five years later, after he had traveled around the world, Cornelius checked into the Glenham Hotel on Fifth Avenue and shot himself in the head.

To William went the empire. It was estimated that his inheritance was worth $105 million—equal to the cash reserves of the federal government at the time—and William's four sons were given another $11.5 million. William's brother and sisters accused him of plotting to steal their father's fortune, and a court hearing got awfully nasty before the case was settled for an undisclosed sum.

After that, William treated his father's fortune in ways that must have had the old man spinning. He built himself a huge, block-long mansion on Fifth Avenue between 51st and 52nd Streets, employing over 600 workers and stuffing it with his vast, mediocre art collection. When he was shunned by the social elite at the opera, William built his own—the Metropolitan—with Jay Gould. And completely unlike his father, William paid $100,000 to buy and transport an Egyptian obelisk, Cleopatra's Needle, that now stands in Central Park.

But the biggest alteration of the Vanderbilt fortune came in 1879, when William sold off more than half his railroad stock and invested the money conservatively in bonds. With few taxes and good interest rates, William's fortune soared. But the control that was all-important to his father had been permanently destroyed. William allowed representatives of J. P. Morgan and John D. Rockefeller to join the board and from then on the Vanderbilts' grasp of their railroad grew weaker and weaker.

William—to whom the phrase "The public be damned" is attributed—didn't seem to care. He had learned well from his father how to run the railroads. But having grown up practically in exile until he was forty-three, William never inherited his father's empire-building spirit. "I am the richest man in the world," he said when he retired in 1883. "I am worth $194 million. I would not walk across the street to make a million dollars."

When William died of a stroke two years later at the age of sixty-four, he left a fortune almost double that of his father's. But he further diluted the old man's empire by splitting most of his estate between his two oldest sons—giving each some $65 million. His son William devoted his time to his yacht, and Cornelius garnered recognition by building the opulent Breakers mansion in Newport, Rhode Island. One of Cornelius's sons was the lush Reginald, father of little Gloria.

Taxes and the end of the railroad era took their toll, so that Cornelius Vanderbilt's fortune—the nation's biggest in the 1870s—

became just some scattered few millions three generations later. The Commodore had been able to pass on the reins intact, but he couldn't bequeath his talent for handling them.

CHILDREN of QUEEN VICTORIA

IT REALLY IS not much of a stretch to say that England's Queen Victoria caused the Russian Revolution. Though the woman who reigned over the British Empire for more than sixty-three years died in 1901, sixteen years before the tsar fell, it was her blood that altered the course of Russian history. Queen Victoria gave birth to nine children who married so well that at one time some of them or her thirty-four grandchildren sat on seven continental thrones, bestowing upon Victoria the title "Grandmama of Europe." But besides her regal alliances, Queen Victoria also passed on hemophilia.

Queen Victoria was unaware that she carried the bleeding disease until it developed in her youngest son, Leopold, born in 1853. Even then the queen insisted "this disease is not in our family," meaning her royal Hanover line. In fact, doctors believe Victoria probably did carry the disease—which largely affects males but is transmitted by females.

So little was known about hemophilia at the time that the queen and her children didn't realize the danger as her family married into most of Europe's other royal lines. Her oldest daughter, Victoria, is believed to have passed the disease into the German Habsburgs, though not to her most famous son, Kaiser Wilhelm II. Princess Beatrice passed it on to her daughter, Ena, whose marriage to the King of Spain, Alfonso XIII, was destroyed when two of her sons developed hemophilia. In all, at least sixteen descendants of Queen Victoria in the next three generations suffered from hemophilia.

The most significant legacy of the disease passed through another of Queen Victoria's five daughters, Princess Alice. She married German royalty, but after she died in 1878, her five children were raised under the close supervision of Queen Victoria. That was especially true of Alice's youngest daughter, Alix, who was only six when her mother died. The pale, pretty girl, who was modest and reserved in proper British fashion, once said to her royal grandmother, "Have you not been as a mother to me since beloved Mama died?"

Alix disappointed her grandmother when she rejected the proposal of one of her cousins. But she already had fallen in love with someone else, Tsarevich Nicholas, heir to the throne of Russia. Much sooner than she expected Alix became Tsaritsa Alexandra after Tsar Alexander III died suddenly in 1894 and twenty-six-year-old Nicholas was crowned.

Alexandra never grew comfortable with the painfully formal Russian court, and because of her stiffness neither was she well liked. Still she dutifully became pregnant soon after she was married; the child turned out to be a girl and therefore not an heir to the throne. She gave birth to three more daughters before finally producing the much-hoped-for son, Alexis, in 1904. By that time Russia was in turmoil, stuck in a war with Japan and facing a domestic crisis after the "Bloody Sunday" massacre.

To make matters worse, Nicholas and Alexandra discovered within a few months that Alexis was a hemophiliac. Alexandra realized that she had passed on the mysterious disease, and the tsaritsa was overwhelmed as she watched her son cry out in pain with dark bruises and swellings under his skin. She became overprotective and was always distracted by the thought that her son might fall and again be near death. Her own health grew worse and she frequently retired to bed or a wheelchair. Nicholas and Alexandra never told the Russian people that their son had hemophilia, for fear that the country would lose confidence in the heir. But their attempts to protect Alexis from harm also made the tsar's family seem more aloof. Alexandra rarely was seen in public and she shut herself off even from her court to pray at length.

She believed her prayers were answered when she met Grigory

Rasputin, the ragged mystic with a reputation as a miracle healer. And in fact, Rasputin did seem to relieve Alexis's pain, though medically it is not clear how. Even if Rasputin was not in St. Petersburg, he would send a telegram saying he was praying and Alexis would feel better.

After Rasputin alleviated one particularly bad bleeding episode in 1912, Alexandra put her complete faith in the Siberian monk—not just to heal her son, but also to guide the riled nation. It was "Our Friend," as she called him, who counseled that Tsar Nicholas should take command of the Russian Army in World War I, leaving Rasputin and Alexandra to misgovern the country.

The rest, as they say, is history. By the time Tsar Nicholas abdicated in 1917—two months after Rasputin was savagely murdered—Alexandra, the prim, proper granddaughter of Queen Victoria, was considered a bloody tyrant, called by the people in the street, "the German whore." A year later the entire family was murdered.

Obviously, a lot of storms gathered together to blow away the Russian aristocracy. But what if Queen Victoria hadn't carried hemophilia? And what if it hadn't infected Alexandra's son? What if Rasputin hadn't taken advantage of the illness to gain power? What if . . . ?

W

GRANDSON of RICHARD WAGNER

THE SPECTACULAR, heavy-handed operas of Richard Wagner have ridden a tumultuous course in the century since the German Romantic composer died. Favored by "Crazy" Ludwig II, king of Bavaria, for their lush sets and music, Wagner's operas later were embraced by Adolf Hitler as expressions of Aryan supremacy. That Wagner had written anti-Semitic essays further blackened the reputation of his music after Hitler got hold of it. But today Wagner's operas, including *The Flying Dutchman, Parsifal,* and the Ring cycle, are widely performed, which is due to the almost single-handed efforts of his grandson Wieland.

After Wagner died, his works were left to Siegfried, his only son and third illegitimate child by Cosima Liszt. Cosima was the daughter of composer Franz Liszt, and Wagner married her after Siegfried was born. From 1906–1930, Siegfried directed his father's operas at the Bayreuth Festival, a prominent annual musical event north of Nuremberg, headquartered in a vast theater that Wagner had built specifically to feature his operas. The festival gained peculiar prominence in the 1930s as Hitler came to power and attended some of the performances.

Siegfried Wagner and his wife, Winifred, had become friends with Hitler in the early 1920s when the Nazi leader was still a struggling politician. Hitler often visited the Wagners in Bayreuth, and Siegfried's four children grew up calling him "Onkel Wolf." As a child, Wieland was once reported to have embraced Hitler and said, "You should be our daddy, and daddy should be our uncle." Hitler gave Wieland a Mercedes when he was seventeen, and later kept the young Wagner out of the fighting in World War II so he could carry on the legacy of his grandfather's operas. "In order to understand National Socialist Germany," said Hitler, "one must know Wagner."

Under the guidance of his mother, who took over the Bayreuth Festival after Siegfried died in 1930, Wieland began designing sets for Wagner productions and produced his first Wagner opera in 1943. It was performed in the very traditional manner that Wagner had specified and that Hitler liked. A year later the festival was shut down as Germany neared the end of the war. Wieland saw Hitler one last time, in December 1944, to ask him to return several of Wagner's original manuscripts that Wagner had given to King Ludwig and that had been passed on to Hitler. The dictator refused, and the works probably were destroyed in the final battle of Berlin.

After the war, Wieland's mother stated publicly that she still believed in Hitler and thought he had been betrayed by his associates. Winifred Wagner was found guilty of collaborating with Hitler and she was banned from reopening the Bayreuth Festival. Wieland would say little except, "After Auschwitz there can be no more discussion about Hitler."

In 1951, Wieland and his younger brother, Wolfgang, reopened the Bayreuth Festival. But the new productions were like no Wagnerian opera ever seen before, and drastically different from what had pleased Hitler. Far from the lavish, Romantic sets, Wieland restaged his grandfather's operas on an almost empty, cavernous stage, darkly shadowed and starkly modern. The result was controversial, and some audiences booed, but critics focused on Wagner's music, not his politics.

Wieland later said he had dramatically restaged Wagner's operas because the fall of Hitler had dramatically changed his thinking. "I was brought up in a mausoleum," he said. "Dangerous" books by Freud, Kafka, and many others had been banned. Once he read some of those books, Wieland said he found universal meanings in Wagner's operas far beyond their German tradition. "Hitler liked Wagner for all the wrong reasons," Wieland said. "If he had understood what 'The Ring of the Nibelungs' is really about, he would have forbidden it."

Wieland broke off relations with his mother. Later, so did Wolfgang, who forbade her to attend the Bayreuth Festival. Winifred Wagner died in 1980 at the age of eighty-two. She had outlived Wieland, who had died of lung cancer fourteen years earlier. But by that time, it was Wieland's vision of his grandfather's operas that had made him one of the most influential opera directors in the world and had restored Wagner to the highest ranks. "My generation was taught not to take youthful impressions on trust, but to regard them with a certain degree of skepticism," Wieland said. "We have seen and experienced things that our fathers and grandfathers were powerless to prevent; acts of destruction which go far beyond human imagining."

SON of H. G. WELLS
and REBECCA WEST

IT MIGHT HAVE BEEN the British literary match of the century. Instead, it produced one of the greatest family feuds.

Rebecca West, whom Harry Truman would later call "the world's best reporter," was only twenty when she reviewed a book by H. G. Wells—who at forty-six was well established as the father of science fiction, the author of such classics as *The Time Machine* and *The War of the Worlds*—and called him "the Old Maid of novelists." Wells, though married, was intrigued enough to want to meet her, and they soon began a ten-year affair that grew stormy in a much shorter time, as West went on to become this century's grand dame of English letters, a novelist, essayist and reporter.

The only lasting legacy of the relationship between Wells and West was their son, Anthony. He was born soon after their affair began, and undoubtedly kept them together far longer than at least Wells, who had many affairs, would have liked. Anthony, in fact, wrote later that he thought his father would have preferred that West have an abortion. Lacking that, Wells wanted to protect his reputation, so he sent West to an obscure seaside resort to have the baby. He rarely visited—he also had abandoned his wife during both her pregnancies—and kept his distance even after he moved West and their son to a town near his home in London. "Panther," wrote Wells, using his pet name for West, and the middle name of their son, "I love being with you always. I also love being with my work with everything handy. I *hate* being encumbered with a little boy and a nurse, and being helpful. I hate waiting about."

Neither was West thrilled with motherhood. "I *hate domesticity*," she wrote. "I can't imagine any circumstances in which it would be amusing to order two ounces of Lady Betty wool for socks for Anthony. . . . I want to live an unfettered and adventurous life like a Bashebazouk." Wells insisted that Anthony not be told that he was the boy's father. So Anthony grew up calling his mother Aunty Panther and his father Mr. Wells, or Wellsie. "As far as I was concerned," Anthony later wrote, "[Wells] was the usually genial and friendly man who came by in a motorcar from time to time to carry my Aunty Panther off or to bring her back."

Anthony didn't find out the truth until he was seven, "a classic set-up," he later wrote, "for inducing emotional malnutrition, and all the distortions and hallucinations that go with it." Growing up in and out of boarding schools, he lived with a mother who indulged or ignored him depending on her mood, and he worshiped a father he rarely saw. His mother's marriage to a Scottish banker in 1930 only made things worse. Anthony was a poor student, and his failure to be admitted to Oxford caused him to suffer a nervous breakdown at eighteen that put him in analysis with a colleague of Freud's.

Under the glare of his mother's spectacular and long success— she was the first woman to cover the House of Lords, and her reportage on Yugoslavia in 1941, *Black Lamb and Grey Falcon*, became a classic—Anthony tried to strike out on his own. He married at twenty-one, studied painting, and later took money from the trust fund Wells had set aside for him to start a cattle-breeding farm.

Then, Anthony tried his hand at writing, and at last he had found a career, one that also provided a battlefield on which his troubled relationship with his mother would explode. Relations between the two, already tense after West tried to prevent Anthony from divorcing his first wife, worsened while Anthony was writing his first novel. West didn't want him to publicize the fact that he was the son of Wells, who had died in 1946. Anthony wrote back, "If I do not say with pride who my father was my silence says our relationship was disgraceful. I will not do it."

The feud exploded publicly in 1955, when Anthony's novel, *Heritage*, was published. The tale of an illegitimate son whose famous mother neglects him unsurprisingly enraged West. In one of her characteristic long letters to her son, she wrote, "I am sure I loved you and have always loved you. But I cannot interpret these things as anything but evidence that you hate me and have always hated me. . . . You are a gift to me—but in your book you did everything you could to withdraw that gift." West threatened to sue any publisher who sold *Heritage* in England and none did until 1984, the year after she died at the age of ninety. Anthony did not attend the funeral, and West left her estate and letters to her nephew.

West and her son had kept in touch over the years, but their feud never ended. Anthony had a distinguished career as a writer for *The New Yorker*—a magazine to which West frequently contributed her writings—but West frequently interpreted his work as an attack on her. In a new foreword to the 1984 edition of *Heritage*, Anthony wrote that his mother "was determined to do what hurt she could, and that she remained set in that determination as long as there was breath in her body to sustain her malice."

Anthony got in further shots in another book also published in 1984, *H. G. Wells: Aspects of a Life*, which told a lot about Wells but also, said the *New York Times* critic, keeps coming "back to the subject of Rebecca West, who, when all is written, is the ultimate target. . . . Judging from this brilliantly written book, for Mr. West the agony has never abated."

Anthony died of a stroke at the age of seventy-three in 1987. Wrote a critic for the *Los Angeles Times*, "Anthony West never has got over his parents. The pain and allure of their relationship to each other—and their lack of a relationship to him—have overshadowed his life despite his considerable talent and success as a writer and critic."

CHILDREN of OSCAR WILDE

CHARGES THAT famed author Oscar Wilde slept with another man produced the trial of the decade in London in the 1890s. The sensational case left Wilde a broken man when he was released from prison in 1897, and he died three years later at the age of forty-six. But often forgotten in this tragedy are Wilde's two sons, Vyvyan and Cyril, who were eight and nine when their father was arrested, and whose lives were also violently disrupted.

The two boys had spent their happy childhood unaware of their father's double life. Vyvyan, the younger son, remembered Wilde as "a smiling giant, always exquisitely dressed, who crawled about the nursery floor with us and lived in an aura of cigar smoke and eau de cologne." Wilde sang to his sons and read them stories in their comfortable London home.

But after Wilde was arrested in 1895, his sons never saw him again. Their toys were sold to help settle his bankruptcy. And faced with a barrage of scandalous publicity, their mother, Constance, took them to Switzerland after Wilde was convicted. When they were asked to leave their first hotel, Constance changed their last name to "Holland." Wilde tried to write to Cyril and Vyvyan after he was released and settled in France, but he was told his letters would be destroyed. Constance also refused to let Wilde see his sons. "She says *she* will see me twice a year, but I want my boys," Wilde wrote. "It is a terrible punishment, and oh! how well I deserve it. But it makes me feel disgraced and evil, and I don't want to feel that."

Cyril and Vyvyan were sent to separate boarding schools in Germany and Monaco; then, after Constance died in 1898, they were sent back to England to their mother's aunt, who also put them in separate boarding schools. Two years later fourteen-year-old Vyvyan was told that Wilde had died. That surprised him, he remembered, because he had assumed his father was already dead.

Vyvyan had been too young to know what his father had done to get into trouble, but he remembered living in fear that his real identity would be discovered. "We had known what it was to have our father feted and admired, and now to have to deny him and to lock up all knowledge of him in our hearts was a terrible burden for children to bear." When he was told the truth when he was eighteen, Vyvyan replied, "Is that all? I thought he had embezzled money."

His older brother, Cyril, who apparently had known of the scandal from the beginning by reading newsstand placards, was much more haunted by their father's past. He wrote to Vyvyan in 1914, "All these years my great incentive has been to wipe that stain away; to retrieve, if may be, by some action of mine, a name no longer honoured in the land. The more I thought of this, the more convinced I became that, first and foremost, I must be a *man*. There was to be no cry of decadent artist, of effeminate aesthete, of weak-kneed degenerate. . . . I ask nothing better than to end in honourable battle for my King and Country."

Cyril got his wish. An officer in the British Army in India when World War I broke out, Cyril pushed for and was granted a transfer to the battlefields of France. On May 9, 1915 Wilde's twenty-nine-year-old son was killed by a German sniper.

Vyvyan, however, lived to see his father feted again. Though the boys' first guardian prevented them from receiving royalties from Wilde's works—because he said the money would hurt their reputation—that guardian died in 1904. The payments were restored by Robert Ross, Wilde's literary executor and probably also his first male lover. Ross introduced Vyvyan to Wilde's old friends in London society and for a time he was celebrated, somewhat discreetly, as a famous son. As his father's reputation was restored, Vyvyan said he received royalties averaging £10,000 per year.

Vyvyan's parentage was made public in 1914 when his marriage announcement was published. Ross was his best man. His wife was killed four years later when her dress caught fire, and Vyvyan didn't marry again until 1943. Two years later he had a son, Merlin, when he was fifty-nine. Vyvyan, like his father, ended up a writer. He translated books from several foreign languages and translated reports for the BBC during World War II. Besides three memoirs of his father, Vyvyan Holland also wrote several books on good food and wine. His last, published the year he died, 1967, was called *Drink and Be Merry*. His father would have approved.

GRANDSON of KAISER WILHELM II

"IF GERMANY had remained a monarchy, there would have been no Hitler, and no Holocaust." Some historians would agree, but Louis Ferdinand has a proprietary interest in saying it. If Germany had remained a monarchy, Louis Ferdinand would now be king.

A grandson of Kaiser Wilhelm II—the man blamed for World War I and therefore Hitler's rise—Louis Ferdinand was just eleven years old when the Kaiser abdicated his throne in 1918. At the time there was talk that Kaiser Wilhelm could have preserved the power of the Hohenzollern family dynasty if he had passed the crown to one of his sons or grandsons, whom the Allies didn't hate so much. But instead the Kaiser retired in exile to the Netherlands. His oldest son and heir, Crown Prince Friedrich Wilhelm, also kept a low profile, giving up his royal prerogatives in favor of more mundane activities on a Dutch island that earned him the title "Blacksmith of Wierengen."

As Friedrich Wilhelm's second son, Louis didn't have the responsibilities of an heir apparent, albeit to a nonexistent throne. He received a doctorate in philosophy from the University of Berlin in 1929, and soon afterward he sailed for the United States. A few years later several of Louis's uncles and brothers would join the Nazis, but Louis was not around to be swept up by the terrible movement. He was in the United States chasing French film star Lili Damita, who was trying to make it in Hollywood. The press had a field day with their romance and Louis was sufficiently carried away to make marriage plans.

Fearing that his father might cut him off, Louis decided to find a job to support himself. He had met Henry Ford during his train trip across the country to Hollywood and Ford had told him he could always have a job with his car company. So when Louis called, Ford offered the German ex-prince a job on the assembly line at a Ford plant in Los Angeles. Louis worked the 6:30 A.M. shift, but he wasn't exactly one of the guys. Ford provided his royal employee with a coupé.

But Louis had not gotten far enough away from his father. When he told Friedrich Wilhelm that he planned to marry Lili, his father ordered him to leave America. Just then, and not coincidentally, Henry Ford sent Louis a telegram offering him a job in Buenos Aires. Louis headed south for another car-assembly job and another coupé. He later returned to Detroit for manager training when Henry Ford started planning to build a factory in Germany.

Louis did return to Germany in 1933 but not to run a car factory. After his older brother married a commoner, Louis became next in line for the nonexistent throne. In 1937 he married Grand Duchess Kyra Kyrilovna, the sister of a claimant to the Russian throne. Louis joined the German Air Force at the start of the war, but Hitler retired him after his older brother was killed in action in 1940. In his 1952 memoirs, *Rebel Prince*, Louis said he attended meetings of Hitler's opponents in which they discussed using him as the rallying point to overthrow the Führer. But Louis said he deferred to his father, the legitimate heir, who refused to join the plot.

Since the war, Louis has stayed out of German politics and manages the ex-royal family's remaining holdings. His three sons and three daughters (one son died in 1977 of injuries suffered in a military accident) are regularly covered by the German popular press. Now over eighty and living in West Berlin, Louis Ferdinand holds no illusions about his chances for ever becoming a king. "We are," he says, "completely harmless."

Y

CHILDREN of BRIGHAM YOUNG

BRIGHAM YOUNG was a man whose family tree was a forest in his lifetime. The Mormon leader believed in polygamy and practiced what he preached; he had fifty-seven children by sixteen wives, which doesn't count his nine childless marriages. He was a proud father for the first time in 1834, and his pride continued until 1870 when he was sixty-nine.

Young's reasoning was simple: If a man's wife dies and he remarries, eventually he could wind up in heaven rejoined with both women, or more if he remarried more than once. "And if it's right for a man to have several wives and children in heaven at the same time," Young said, "is it not a consistent doctrine that a man should have several wives and children by those wives at the same time here in this life?"

Young was not a great religious leader, but as an administrator he was supreme. The son of a New England soldier of the American Revolution, Young was a handyman when he joined Joseph Smith's Church of Jesus Christ of Latter-day Saints in 1832 and rose to take it over after Smith was murdered by a mob in 1844. To escape persecution, Young led his followers to Utah, where he directed one of the most successful pioneering settlements in the history of the country.

He was just as organized at home. As the church prospered in Salt Lake City, so did Young and his fast-growing family. He built two large mansions, Beehive House and Lion House, and several other homes for most of his wives. The main houses were always full. Of Young's fifty-seven children, forty-six grew to maturity, and of his twenty-five wives, sixteen survived him. Among his wives were five older women whom he had taken in "caretaker" marriages to give them a home. Beehive House had its own store, where each wife had her own charge account. There was a school, a laundry, organized games, and, of course, a huge kitchen. On average, about fifty Youngs would gather for meals.

Since Young was busy with church matters and was rarely present at home, except for meals and prayers, his wives, one of whom bore ten children, had almost complete responsibility for raising and disciplining of the children. One of his last wives, Amelia, remembered that when she moved into Lion House in 1863, "there were 75 of us in the family, including the hired help. We were all members of the same family, and treated each other as such. I can't say he had any favorites. He was equally kind to all in his lifetime and left each surviving wife an equal legacy."

For a man who may have had trouble keeping the names of all of his children straight, Young did surprisingly well. One daughter, Clarissa, remembered her childhood as "one long round of happiness." In later years Young wrote his children long and frequent letters, advising them on their individual lives and urging them to follow the Mormon way. Said Young, "I endeavor to govern my family by kindness. I tell them what is right and I get them to obey me without whipping them. If I cannot get my family to do as I wish them without quarreling with them, I will not say a word about it."

Some of that family harmony did not survive Young when he died at the age of seventy-six in 1877. While it was thought that Young would leave an estate of more than $2 million, it turned out that much of the property belonged to the church and had been put in Young's name to protect it from federal authorities. When his will was read, the seventeen wives, sixteen sons, and twenty-eight daughters who were present learned that they would have to share only a little more than $200,000. Seven heirs, including four sons and daughters, sued for more money. The executors, after being jailed for three and a half weeks by a judge anxious to resolve the matter, settled with the disgruntled children and wives for $75,000.

One of the estate's executors who went to jail was Young's second-oldest son, Brigham Young, Jr., who spent much of the rest of his life trying to stay out of jail for a different reason. Taking after his father, Brigham Jr. had six wives and thirty-one children. But because of his father, there were now federal laws prohibiting more than one wife. Brigham Jr. spent years hiding out from federal authorities before he finally went to Europe. He was allowed to return in 1900 and died three years later at the age of sixty-six.

Most of the rest of Young's children led more normal lives, though generalizations about fifty-seven children certainly are hard to draw. Several of his sons, of course, were missionaries for the Mormon church. Among those who settled in Utah were a blacksmith, a farmer, a teacher, and a salesman. Willard Young graduated fourth in his class at West Point, and later, in the Army Corps of Engineers, he supervised improvements on the Missouri and Mississippi rivers. At the other end of the spectrum, Willard's older half-brother, John, suffered a series of business failures and ended up as an elevator operator in New York City, where he died in 1924 at the age of eighty. Some daughters married outside the church and it was said that "the Lord owed Young a grudge for something and paid him off in sons-in-law."

Young's last surviving child, Mrs. Mabel Young Sanborn, died in 1950 at the age of eighty. She was, most likely, the only person who died that year whose grandfather had fought in the American Revolution 174 years before.

Z

SON of DARRYL ZANUCK

UNLIKE MANY of his Hollywood stars, movie mogul Darryl Zanuck
didn't ignore his children. At least not his only son, Richard, who
from an early age clearly was groomed to follow in his father's
very large footsteps. Zanuck, after producing *The Jazz Singer* and
other hits at Warner Brothers, had created Twentieth Century–
Fox, where he oversaw classics such as *The Grapes of Wrath, Gentleman's Agreement*, and *All About Eve*. Richard grew up on his
father's bustling film lot where he sold the *Saturday Evening Post*
to Zanuck's employees. While his two sisters grew up playing with
Elizabeth Taylor and dating Richard Burton, Richard spent many
nights sitting beside his father as they watched rough cuts of new
movies. The gruff, bossy studio chief known for saying, "Don't
say yes until I finish talking," actually seemed to pay attention
to Richard's opinion. So attentive, in his way, was Zanuck about
his son's upbringing that he provided the girl with whom Richard
was to lose his virginity.

Zanuck, who left Fox in 1956 and started his own independent
production company, brought his son into the business as soon as
Richard graduated from Stanford. In 1962, when Zanuck muscled
his way back into the near-bankrupt Fox, he made twenty-seven-
year-old Richard his vice president in charge of production. Father
and son solved Fox's financial troubles with *The Sound of Music*.
Then as Zanuck spent more time in Europe with his various girl-
friends, he left much of the studio's business to his son. "My father
was demanding," Richard says. "But he also filled me with a sense
of heritage, of knowing who I was. He made me feel special, that
I had a special opportunity to take advantage of."

Trouble was, Richard took advantage too soon. By the late 1960s, Fox was ailing again after a string of major flops like *Dr. Doolittle* and *Star!*. Richard's idea—which Zanuck at first approved—was that Richard should become president and Zanuck be "promoted" to chairman of the board. But the more Zanuck thought about it, the more he felt he had been pushed upstairs and out. The board initially supported Richard, who proceeded to cancel the acting contract of his father's latest girlfriend. Richard denies that he was trying to oust his father, but that was the way Zanuck saw it. "He took it as a direct challenge to the throne," Richard says. "And when there's a direct challenge to the throne, it has to be dealt with. Even if it's by one's only son."

Charging that his son was trying to pull "the con job of the century," the sixty-eight-year-old Zanuck returned from Europe for the first time in years. On December 29, 1970, he presided over a board meeting at which the Fox directors obediently requested Richard's resignation. "Jesus Christ, it was brutal," Richard says. "And my father talking, just sitting there, he showed absolutely not any sign of compassion for me. And that hurt me." Richard returned to his office to find his parking space being repainted.

But Zanuck's victory proved to be temporary. Five months later, he himself was forced to resign as Fox's condition worsened. After he suffered a stroke that summer, Zanuck—who apparently hadn't taken his boardroom battle with his son personally—and Richard reconciled. Zanuck lived in ailing retirement until he died in 1979. His son has gone on to build quite a nice career of his own, producing several movies with David Brown. The last one Zanuck saw was *The Sting*, which won eight Oscars and still ranks as one of the biggest moneymakers of all time. Richard's next film was an even bigger blockbuster—*Jaws*. It has been estimated that Richard (who has continued his success with *The Verdict* and *Cocoon*) made more money on those two films than his father had in his entire career.

SON of KING ZOG OF ALBANIA

LITTERED THROUGHOUT EUROPE—and this book—there are kings and sons of kings who have lost their crowns and, reconciled to that, are living fairly comfortably and quietly in exile. Leka I is the exception. Heir to the youngest dynasty in Europe, one that ruled the poorest nation on the continent and one that was toppled three days after he was born, Leka is the only deposed European monarch who is fighting—literally—to get back his crown.

His father was Ahmed Zogolli, a tribal chief who, after Albania was carved out of the Ottoman Empire before World War I, managed to survive several turbulent and violent political struggles finally to be crowned King Zog in 1928. He tried to improve his country's desperate economic state—at the time it didn't have a railroad—but King Zog was no match for Mussolini's invading troops on April 7, 1939. Three days later the king followed his wife—an eighth cousin once removed of Richard Nixon's—and newborn son into exile, something for which his nation never forgave him, especially after the new leaders claimed King Zog had made off with bags of gold and a bucket of jewels.

King Zog never tried to regain his throne—his nation has been ruled by Communists since World War II—and he died in Paris in 1961 at the age of sixty-five. Soon after, twenty-two-year-old Leka gathered a group of expatriate Albanians in a Paris hotel and had himself declared king. Educated in Egypt, at Phillips Academy in Massachusetts, and at the Sorbonne, Leka did not leave it at that. He began traveling the world visiting Albanian émigrés and raising money. He made many political friends; he gave a baby elephant to then Governor Ronald Reagan after visiting him in California.

Meanwhile, he made money selling weapons to Middle Eastern guerrilla groups. Then in 1975 Leka, who stands six feet eight inches tall, wears fatigues, and carries a bayonet, began developing his own army. He said his soldiers penetrated Albania that year. "Since then," he said in 1978, "we have been sending in leaflets fairly constantly; we drop them from balloons and float them down rivers in plastic bags. We also plant mines, organize sabotage. Nasty little things." In 1977 Leka was arrested in Bangkok with a roomful of weapons, including machine guns and rocket launchers. In 1979 he was forced to leave Spain because government officials didn't like the arsenal at his compound outside Madrid.

Leka, who married the daughter of an Australian sheep farmer, has since settled in Johannesburg. He is still active in Albanian émigré groups around the world, but if he has made any recent efforts to overthrow the government of Albania, he has been very quiet about it. Critics, in fact, have said that Leka isn't really committed to regaining his father's crown, that such talk merely is a cover for his arms deals. Leka insists that is not so. "It would be a very expensive dream if it were a dream," he told Reuters in 1985. "It would be expensive in lives and money. And I'm not prone to suicide."

Index